GRAVES of our FOUNDERS

Volume II

Their Lives, Contributions, and Burial Sites

JOE FARRELL • LAWRENCE KNORR • JOE FARLEY

Mechanicsburg, PA USA

Published by Sunbury Press, Inc.
Mechanicsburg, Pennsylvania

www.sunburypress.com

Copyright © 2021 by Joe Farrell, Joe Farley, and Lawrence Knorr.
Cover Copyright © 2021 by Sunbury Press, Inc.

Sunbury Press supports copyright. Copyright fuels creativity, encourages diverse voices, promotes free speech, and creates a vibrant culture. Thank you for buying an authorized edition of this book and for complying with copyright laws by not reproducing, scanning, or distributing any part of it in any form without permission. You are supporting writers and allowing Sunbury Press to continue to publish books for every reader. For information contact Sunbury Press, Inc., Subsidiary Rights Dept., PO Box 548, Boiling Springs, PA 17007 USA or legal@sunburypress.com.

For information about special discounts for bulk purchases, please contact Sunbury Press Orders Dept. at (855) 338-8359 or orders@sunburypress.com.

To request one of our authors for speaking engagements or book signings, please contact Sunbury Press Publicity Dept. at publicity@sunburypress.com.

FIRST SUNBURY PRESS EDITION: June 2021

Set in Adobe Garamond | Interior design by Crystal Devine | Cover by Lawrence Knorr | Edited by the authors.

Publisher's Cataloging-in-Publication Data
Names: Farrell, Joe, author | Farley, Joe, author | Knorr, Lawrence, author.
Title: Graves of our Founders : Volume 2 : Their Lives, Contributions, and Burial Sites / Joe Farrell Lawrence Knorr Joe Farley.
Description: First trade paperback edition. | Mechanicsburg, PA : Sunbury Press, 2021.
Summary: Joe Farrell, Joe Farley, and Lawrence Knorr have traveled across the eastern USA to the graves of over 200 founding fathers (and mothers) responsible for the birth of the United States of America. Included in this first volume are biographies and grave information for 53 of these luminaries who made significant contributions to the Revolutionary cause.
Identifiers: ISBN 978-1-62006-290-6 (softcover).
Subjects: HISTORY / United States / Revolutionary Period (1775-1800) | BIOGRAPHY & AUTOBIOGRAPHY / Political.

Product of the United States of America
0 1 1 2 3 5 8 13 21 34 55

Continue the Enlightenment!

Contents

Introduction.. 1

Benjamin Franklin The First American 5
Thomas Adams Delegate from Virginia 17
John Alsop Merchant House of Alsop 20
Gunning Bedford Jr. Constitution Signer from Delaware ... 26
Daniel Boone Western Pioneer 30
Jacob Broom Surveyor from Delaware 40
Abraham Clark House burned, sons tortured 44
Thomas Cushing, III Protégé of John Hancock 49
John Dickinson Penman of the Revolution 55
James Duane Conservative Founder 60
Thomas Fitzsimons The Irish Founder 66
Nathaniel Folsom Merchant Militiaman 71
Nathaniel Gorham President of Congress 75
Cyrus Griffin The Last President of Congress 79
John Hancock The Signature 85
Benjamin Harrison V Father and Great-Grandfather of Presidents 91
William Hooper A Tory in the Continental Congress 100
Francis Hopkinson The Patriot Renaissance Man 105
Titus Hosmer Connecticut Lawyer 109
Samuel Huntington First President of the United States? . 114
Richard Hutson First Mayor of Charleston 119
John Jay The First Chief Justice 124
Thomas Johnson One of the Original Supremes 135
William Samuel Johnson The Great Conciliator 140
John Paul Jones "I have not yet begun to fight!" 145
Rufus King The Last Federalist Candidate for President .. 153
John Langdon Senator from New Hampshire 159
Edward Langworthy An Orphaned Founder 164

Robert Livingston The Chancellor 167
Thomas Lynch Jr. Youngest Signer of the Declaration to Die 172
William Maclay The First Democrat........................ 176
Henry Marchant Liberty Lawyer 181
Francis Marion Swamp Fox............................. 186
Hugh Mercer The Hero of Princeton 195
Daniel Morgan Victor at Cowpens 202
Gouveneur Morris The Penman of the Constitution 209
Thomas Nelson Jr. The Governor Who Was All-In 215
Robert Treat Paine The Objection Maker 221
Edmund Pendleton "Here Comes the Judge!" 226
Israel Putnam Old Put................................. 232
Edmund Randolph Jefferson's Chameleon..................... 240
Philip John Schuyler Father-in-Law of Hamilton............... 246
Charles Scott Head of Intelligence......................... 252
Arthur St. Clair First Governor of the Northwest Territory........... 261
Baron Friedrich Wilhelm von Steuben The Prussian General 268
Thomas Sumter Carolina Gamecock........................ 276
Charles Thomson Secretary of the Continental Congress............ 283
Matthew Tilghman Father of the Revolution in Maryland........... 288
John Walton The Other Walton 292
Mercy Otis Warren The Muse of the Revolution................ 295
William Williams Puritan Patriot 301
James Wilson A Legal Theorist........................... 307
John Witherspoon President of Princeton 312

Sources... 318
Index 323

Introduction

Welcome to *Graves of Our Founders Volume Two*. This work aims to examine the lives and contributions of the amazing men and women who using their courage and talents, established the country those of us who live here, and many who do not have come to love. Our original plan called for a four-volume series, with each covering approximately fifty founders, and that goal remains. However, based on our research, we have found that adding volumes that examine specific geographical regions is beneficial. As a result, we published a volume titled *Pennsylvania Patriots* in 2019, and similar works will likely follow.

Over the past decade, we have made trips to numerous cemeteries to produce twelve volumes of the popular Keystone Tombstones and two titled Gotham Graves. This series covering the founders follows the same format of those works and involved more effort in both time and research. Our travels to visit the graves of those we have identified as founders have taken us to more than the thirteen original states. Accessing information about some of the lesser-known individuals who made contributions to the creation of the United States at times has been challenging. We hope that our efforts in meeting those challenges will please our readers.

The first question we had to answer regarding this series was who to include. In other words, who qualifies to be considered a founder? The standard we settled on resulted in the inclusion of signers of either the Continental Association, the Declaration of Independence, the Articles of Confederation, or the Constitution. In addition, we have also identified non-signers of the above-referenced documents who made significant contributions to the creation of the United States of America.

Francis Marion, perhaps better known as the "Swamp Fox," whose story is told in this volume, is an example of the latter group.

We all agree that our visits to the gravesites and the research on the founders have been rewarding and educational. However, in some cases, the visits have been sobering, shocking, and shameful. The well-known founders such as Washington, Jefferson, Hamilton, and Madison have been laid to rest in well-maintained graves accessible to the public. Unfortunately, this is not the rule. Too many of our nation's founders are buried in neglected places and have been left unattended and thus are subject to decay. Some are inaccessible, and others cannot be located at all due to the development of the land and poor record keeping. One of our goals in doing this series and including photographs of the graves is to bring this problem to light and hopefully spurn action to address this issue before it is simply too late.

Considering the condition of many of these graves, we have established a website, www.adoptapatriot.com, where one can find information on all the people we have identified as founders. We continue to update this site as we come across new information. In addition, the website includes a Wall of Shame where we highlight those gravesites that we have concluded are in the worst shape due to neglect or are in remote difficult to reach locations or where the founder is under memorialized given their contributions to the nation. It is our sincere hope that many of these graves will be restored, renewed, or relocated.

One thing we have learned about the founders in writing this series, and we are confident that most of them would agree with us, is that they were products of their times and not perfect nor infallible. They disagreed on many of the issues they faced, and none may have been as hotly debated as slavery. As a matter of fact, on our many trips, we have had some heated debates as to how the various founders dealt with slavery on both public and personal levels. It is difficult to reconcile men who undertook a war against the most powerful army in the world, proclaiming that all men are created equal while, at the same time, many of these same men held other men, women, and children in bondage. The contradiction is obvious and quite difficult to excuse. Nevertheless, we have attempted to tell each founder's story truthfully and deal with the

INTRODUCTION

slavery issue on a case-by-case basis. There are several chapters in this Volume, including those on John Witherspoon and John Jay, where we hope our readers will find that we have met that standard.

As the country nears the upcoming 250th anniversary of the Declaration of Independence, we view these volumes as timely reminders of the founders' sacrifices and contributions to create this nation. We should never forget those who put their lives and fortunes on the line and succeeded in establishing the greatest country the world has ever known. We are inspired by the words of Marcus Cicero:

POOR IS THE NATION HAVING NO HEROES
SHAMEFUL THE ONE THAT HAVING THEM FORGETS

Benjamin Franklin
(1706–1790)

The First American

Buried at Christ Church Burial Grounds,
Philadelphia, Pennsylvania.

Declaration of Independence • U.S. Constitution • Diplomat

Referred to as "The First American" by historian H. W. Brands and others, it is not exaggerating to say that no Pennsylvanian is as well known or as well respected as Benjamin Franklin. He excelled at so many things. He was an author, a political theorist, a scientist, an inventor, a diplomat and politician (though he might disagree), and a revolutionary. He was well into middle age when he began to agitate for the colonies and became the senior statesman throughout the American Revolution, involved in the formulation of the new nation's key documents and treaties.

Benjamin's father, Josiah Franklin, was born in the village of Ecton, Northamptonshire, England where he married his first wife, Anne Child, in 1677. The couple arrived in America in 1683. By that time, they had three children, and after arriving in America, they had four more. Josiah made a living as a printer and candle-maker. After his first wife died, he married Abiah Folger, the daughter of a miller, and had ten more children. Benjamin Franklin was born in Boston, Massachusetts on January 17, 1706. He was Josiah's 15th child and his last son.

Franklin's parents wanted a career in the church for him. He was sent to the Boston Latin School, but after two years, his parents could

Benjamin Franklin

no longer make the payments to allow him to continue. Franklin never graduated, but through his reading, he continued what would be called a self-education. At the age of twelve, he went to work for his brother James, a printer, who taught him the trade. James founded *The New England Courant*, the first independent newspaper in the colonies. Franklin began to write letters to the paper under the name of Mrs. Silence Dogood. The views expressed became the subject of conversation around Boston. When James discovered that Franklin was the famous author, he punished him. In addition to verbal abuse, his brother was known to beat Franklin. Having had enough, Franklin fled his apprenticeship at age seventeen, and according to the laws of the time, became a fugitive.

Franklin arrived in Philadelphia in 1723, seeking a fresh start. With his experience, he was able to find work in printing shops. Pennsylvania's

Royal Governor William Keith convinced Franklin to return to England to find the equipment needed to start a new newspaper in Philadelphia. When the governor failed to provide the backing for the enterprise, Franklin found work in a printer's shop in London. He returned to Philadelphia in 1726 and went to work for a merchant as a clerk, shopkeeper, and a bookkeeper.

The first stamp of the United States featured Ben

Franklin organized a group of men known as the Junto in 1727. The goal of the group was to engage in activities that would improve the members as individuals and at the same time, benefit the community. The group created a library. Franklin came up with the idea to form a subscription library to increase the number of books available. The members combined their funds to buy additional books that would be available for all to read. Franklin hired the first librarian in 1732.

In 1728, Franklin's employer passed away, and Franklin returned to the printing business. The next year, he became the publisher of a newspaper called *The Pennsylvania Gazette*. The newspaper provided Franklin with a mechanism to make known his views on the important issues of the time. His observations were well received, and his stature continued to grow. Wrote Franklin in his autobiography, "I took care not only to be in reality industrious and frugal but to avoid all appearance to the contrary. I dressed plainly; I was seen at no place of idle diversions. I never went out fishing or shooting . . ."

In 1730, Franklin entered into what would be called a common-law marriage with Deborah Reed. He could not marry Reed because she already had a husband, though he had abandoned her. One of the reasons that may have led Franklin to make this decision was the fact that he had recently acknowledged that he was the father of an illegitimate son named William, and he wanted to provide his son a family life. William's mother remains unknown. Benjamin and Deborah had two other children. The first was a son named Francis, who was born in 1732 and died in 1736. The second child, a daughter named Sarah, was born in 1743.

During this period, Franklin also began a career as an author. In 1733, he began to publish *Poor Richard's Almanac*. Franklin seldom published under his name, and in this instance, the author was identified as Richard Saunders. Some of his witty adages such as "Fish and visitors stink in three days" are still quoted today. Though published under the name Saunders, it was common knowledge that Franklin was the author. His reputation continued to grow. The almanac itself was a tremendous success, selling about 10,000 copies per year. In today's world, that would translate to nearly three million copies.

Franklin founded the American Philosophical Society in 1743. The purpose of this organization was to provide a forum where scientific men, like himself, could discuss their projects and discoveries. It was around this time that Franklin began studying electricity. That study would remain a part of his life until the day he died. The story of the kite, the string, and the key is probably a false one. The television show *MythBusters* simulated the supposed experiment and concluded that if Franklin had proceeded as described, it would have killed him.

In addition to his scientific studies, Franklin was also an inventor. Among his more noted inventions are the Franklin stove, the lightning rod, and bifocal lenses. Franklin viewed his devices as yet another way he could help improve society.

In 1747, Franklin decided to get out of the printing business. He formed a partnership whereby David Hall would run the company, and the two would share the profits. This provided Franklin with a steady income and also gave him the time to pursue his studies and other interests. His writings, inventions, and discoveries had by now made him well known throughout the colonies and in Europe.

As he grew older, Franklin became more and more interested in public affairs. He was drawn into Philadelphia politics and was soon elected to the post of councilman. In 1749 he became a Justice of the Peace, and two years later, he was elected to the Pennsylvania Assembly.

In 1753, he was appointed to the post of joint deputy postmaster general of North America. In this role, he worked to reform the postal

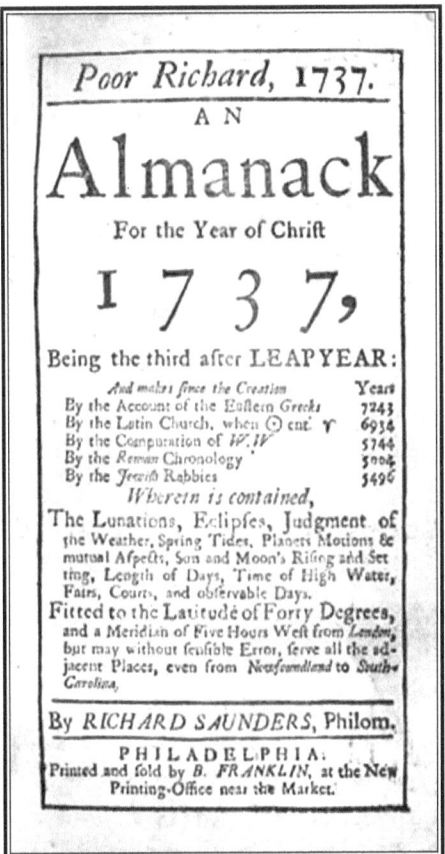

Poor Richard's Almanac

system. Among his accomplishments was the adoption of the practice to deliver mail weekly. During this time, Franklin founded the first hospital in the colonies. Honors continued to come his way. Both Harvard and Yale awarded him honorary degrees.

In September 1753, Franklin was one of the emissaries from Pennsylvania accompanying Conrad Weiser, the Indian agent and interpreter, to Carlisle to negotiate a peace treaty with the Six Nations. Franklin wrote about the influence of rum on the proceedings:

"We strictly forbade the selling any liquor to them; and, when they complained of this restriction, we told them, that, if they could continue sober during the treaty, we would give them plenty of rum when the business was over. They claimed and received the rum. In the evening, hearing a great noise among them, the commissioners walked to see what was the matter. We found they had made a great bonfire in the middle of the square; they were all drunk, men and women, quarreling and fighting. Their dark-colored bodies, half-naked, seen only by the gloomy light of the bonfire, running after and beating one another with firebrands, accompanied by their horrid yellings, formed a scene the most resembling our ideas of hell that could well be imagined; there was no appeasing the tumult, and we retired to our lodging. At midnight a number of them came thundering at our door, demanding more rum, of which we took no notice. The next day, sensible that they had misbehaved in giving us that disturbance, they sent three of their old counselors to make their apology. The orator acknowledged the fault, but laid it upon the rum; and then endeavored to excuse the rum by saying, 'The Great Spirit, who made all things, made everything for some use, and whatever use he designed anything for, that use it should be always be put to'; now, when he made rum, he said, 'Let this be for the Indians to get drunk with; and it must be so.' And indeed, if it be the design of Providence to extirpate these savages, in order to make room for the cultivators of the earth, it seems not impossible that rum may be the appointed means. It has already annihilated all the tribes who formerly inhabited the seacoast."

The following May, Franklin was with Weiser again at the Albany Conference to once again treat with the Native Americans. This led to the Albany Purchase of more land in Pennsylvania for the colony, taking most of the Juniata Valley.

As the French and Indian War broke out, Franklin was involved as a representative from Pennsylvania. He visited with General Braddock before his ill-fated 1755 expedition into western Pennsylvania, offering the British general much-needed provisions.

In 1756, the Pennsylvania Assembly allotted funds to Franklin and Weiser to construct forts on the Pennsylvania frontier, essentially

Benjamin Franklin (1706–1790)

Plaque at Christ Church Burial Ground
near the grave of Franklin

along the Blue Mountain. Franklin handled the forts for Berks County and east. Weiser managed the fortifications from Berks County to the Susquehanna River.

In 1757, the Pennsylvania Assembly selected Franklin to go to England to oppose the political favoritism that was being shown to the Penn family who were descended from Pennsylvania's founder William Penn. The family was exempt from paying any land taxes and retained the right to veto legislation passed by the Pennsylvania Assembly. Franklin worked on this mission for five years, but it failed as the Royal government refused to turn their backs on the Penns.

During his stay in England, more honors came his way. In 1759, the University of Saint Andrews awarded him an honorary degree. Three years later, Oxford followed suit by awarding Franklin an honorary doctorate for his scientific achievements. It was as a result of this award that he became known as Doctor Franklin. To top it off, he also secured an appointment for his illegitimate son William. The younger Franklin was named Colonial Governor of New Jersey.

When Franklin returned to America, the feud between the Penns and the Assembly was ongoing. Franklin became the leader of the anti-Penn party known as the Anti-proprietary Party. In 1764 he was elected Speaker of the Pennsylvania House. As the speaker, Franklin attempted to change Pennsylvania from proprietary to royal government. The move was not popular with the voting populous who feared that such a change would infringe on their freedoms. As a result, Franklin was defeated in the elections held in October of 1764. After his defeat, the Anti-propriety Party sent him back to England to try yet again to fight the influence of the Penn family.

While in London, Franklin spoke out in opposition to the Stamp Act of 1765, but the measure passed over his objections. This did not deter him, and he continued to fight the Act. His efforts contributed to its eventual repeal. As a result, he became the leading representative of American interests in England.

During his time in Europe, Franklin decided to tour Ireland. This visit would have a profound effect on him. When he witnessed the poverty in Ireland, he became convinced that it was a result of regulations and laws similar to those through which England was governing America. He concluded that America would suffer a fate similar to Ireland's if England's colonial exploitation continued.

Franklin's common-law wife never accompanied him overseas because of her fear of the ocean. While he was on this trip, she implored him to return to America. She claimed she was ill and blamed her condition on his absence. Franklin stayed in England, and Deborah Reed died as a result of a stroke in 1774.

Franklin returned to America in May of 1775. By this time, the American Revolution had already begun with the Battles of Lexington and Concord. Pennsylvania selected him as one of their delegates to the Second Continental Congress.

In July of 1775, the Continental Congress appointed Franklin to the post of United States Postmaster General. He was the country's first postmaster. The appointment made sense based on Franklin's previous postal experience. The postal system that was established then evolved into the United States Postal Service that is still operational today.

While serving in Congress, he was appointed to the Committee of Five chosen to draft the Declaration of Independence. Thomas Jefferson did the bulk of the work on the Declaration, though Franklin did make several minor changes to the draft Jefferson provided to the other members of the committee. As the Declaration was signed, the President of Congress, John Hancock, remarked: "We must all hang together." Franklin replied, "Yes, we must indeed all hang together, or most assuredly, we shall all hang separately." At seventy, Franklin was the oldest to sign the document.

Later in 1776, Franklin was sent to France to represent American interests. He was already well known in that country due to his writings, inventions, and scientific discoveries. Wrote John Adams about Franklin in France, "His reputation was more universal than that of Leibnitz or Newton, Frederick or Voltaire, and his character more beloved and esteemed than any or all of them . . . His name was familiar to government and people . . . to such a degree that there was scarcely a peasant not familiar with it, and who did not consider him as a friend to humankind. When they spoke of him, they seemed to think he was to restore the Golden Age."

His appointment bore fruit. Franklin succeeded in securing a military alliance between the United States and France in 1778. This alliance was of critical importance to the Americans in their struggle against England. Most historians doubt that the American Revolution would have succeeded without the help of France. Franklin also played a crucial role in negotiating the Treaty of Paris in 1783. This treaty ended the American Revolution and established the United States as an independent country.

Franklin returned to the United States in 1785. Only George Washington exceeded his stature as a champion of American independence. That same year, he was elected President of Pennsylvania, a post

Ben and Deborah Franklin's grave

that would be similar to the governor today. Franklin served in this position for just over three years.

In 1787 he was selected to serve as a Pennsylvania delegate at the Constitutional Convention in Philadelphia. For four months, the delegates met and argued over whether the country should establish a strong federal government. On the day the voting on the proposed constitution was to take place, many of the delegates believed it would be voted down. Before the voting, Franklin advised the Convention that he had a few comments to make. At the time he was too frail to deliver the

Detail of Franklin's grave

speech himself, so he had fellow Pennsylvania delegate James Wilson read it for him. In the speech, Franklin spoke of his misgivings about the Constitution. However, in the end, he said, "Thus I consent, sir, to this Constitution. The opinions I have of its errors, I sacrifice to the public good." He went on to say, "On the whole, sir, I cannot help expressing a wish that every member of the convention who may still have objections to it would, with me, on this occasion doubt a little of his own infallibility and make manifest our unanimity." When the vote was taken, it was close to unanimous. Only three of the forty-one delegates refused to sign the document, and all thirteen states eventually ratified it.

His public life at an end, Franklin wrote about his pending mortality, "Death is as necessary to the constitution as sleep; we shall rise refreshed in the morning. The course of nature must soon put a period to my present mode of existence. This I shall submit to with less regret, as having seen, during a long life, a good deal of this world, I feel a growing curiosity to become acquainted with some other; and can cheerfully, with filial confidence, resign my spirit to the conduct of that great and good Parent of mankind, who created it, and who has so graciously protected and preserved me from my birth to the present hour."

Franklin died in his Philadelphia home on April 17, 1790. He was 84 years old. He is the only founding father who signed all four of the documents central to the establishment of the United States: the Declaration of Independence, the Treaty of Paris, the Treaty of Alliance with France, and the United States Constitution. Over 20,000 people attended his funeral. He was laid to rest in the Christ Church Burial Ground in Philadelphia. Across the young nation, the front pages of newspapers were bordered in black. Reporting on the funeral, Philadelphia newspapers wrote, "Near the place of internment in Arch Street, 85 minute guns were discharged in the most regular manner by Captain Sommer's company of the militia regiment of artillery, and the vessels in the port of the various foreign nations, as well as our own, hoisted their colors, in the usual order, on the mournful occasion. In short, every possible mark of respect was paid to the manes of this venerable and illustrious citizen and philosopher." The U.S. House of Representatives declared a month of mourning.

Benjamin Franklin is remembered in too many ways to provide a complete list, but here are a few:

He is the face on the $100 bill, affectionately referred to as a "Benjamin." He has also been on numerous postage stamps.

The following places were named in Franklin's honor:
- The unofficial short-lived State of Franklin. It later became eastern Tennessee.
- Counties in at least sixteen states.
- The Franklin Institute in Philadelphia.
- Franklin and Marshall College in Lancaster.
- Franklin Field in Philadelphia.
- The Benjamin Franklin Bridge across the Delaware River between Philadelphia and Camden, New Jersey.
- Several U.S. Navy ships.

Thomas Adams
(1730–1788)

Delegate from Virginia

Body lost or destroyed / burial site unknown

Articles of Confederation

Some of the founders of our country are well known to almost all Americans. Others we become aware of through American History courses. Still, others are known to only serious students of United States history. There are a few founders whose memory has been lost to all but those who have examined the revolutionary period under a microscope. This founder falls into the latter category. When one sees or hears the name Adams associated with the founding of the United States, thoughts immediately are drawn to the state of Massachusetts and Samuel, John, and Abigail. This founder was not even a relative of that trio, and he hailed from Virginia. His name was Thomas Adams, and he served in the Continental Congress during the American Revolution, where he added his signature to the Articles of Confederation.

Adams was born sometime in 1730 in New Kent County, Virginia. His grandfather was a tailor and has been described as one of London's leading merchants. He was educated at what was known as the common school, which was a reference to nonurban institutions of learning. It is unknown if he attended any institutions of higher learning, but whatever education he did receive qualified him to work as the clerk of Henrico County, Virginia.

Thomas Adams

According to his Congressional biography, from 1762 until 1774, Adams lived in England, where he had extensive business interests. When he returned to America, tensions between the mother country and the colonies were high. He sided with his fellow colonists in opposing the harsh economic policies adopted by the English Parliament. Shortly after returning to the country of his birth, he was elected to the Virginia House of Burgesses. He was among the delegates who signed the Articles of Association. This document strongly criticized the British government and its "ruinous system of colony administration." The Articles, in Virginia, were the result of the action taken by the colonial governor, John Murray, when he dissolved the House of Burgesses. It was at this time that Adams became chairman of the New Kent County Committee of Safety.

In 1778 Adams was elected to represent Virginia in the Continental Congress. He would serve in the Congress for two years, and it was in this capacity that he affixed his signature to the Articles of Confederation.

In 1780 Adams left the Congress and moved to Augusta County, Virginia. He was elected to the Virginia State Senate, where he served from 1783 until 1786. After retiring from public service, he lived the remainder of his days on his estate known as the "Cowpasture." It was here he passed away on July 8, 1788. Very little detail exists relative to this Founder's life. Almost none of his letters have survived. The College of William and Mary has nine letters that involve Adams though most deal with his family's burial ground. The location of his burial site is unknown.

Even with so little information left behind, it is possible to surmise the qualities that Adams possessed. His business success suggests that he was intelligent and industrious. The faith his fellow citizens had in him is attested to by the many positions he held as an elected representative. His courage is evident because he supported the revolution against England even though he had significant business interests in the mother country. In short, his character was in keeping with the many well and better-known founders who were his contemporaries.

John Alsop
(1724–1794)

Merchant House of Alsop

Buried in the Trinity Church Cemetery,
New York, New York.

Continental Association

John Alsop was a successful merchant from New York City who was involved in local politics and was elected to the Continental Congress. There, he signed the Continental Association and was active in promoting boycotts against England. However, when it came time to sign the Declaration of Independence, he hesitated, citing confusion about his authority to do so. Though hopeful of reconciliation with England, Alsop continued to support the Revolutionary cause from a financial perspective. He is probably best known as the father-in-law of Rufus King and the progenitor of numerous noteworthy descendants.

John Alsop was born in 1724, in New Windsor, Orange County, New York, the eldest son of John Alsop Sr., an attorney, and his wife, Abigail (née Sackett) Alsop. The elder Alsops were both descended from sea captains, and John was also a descendant of Richard Alsop, the Lord Mayor of London, in 1597. When Alsop was a boy, his father moved the family to New York City, where he continued his law practice and became a substantial landowner.

John Alsop (1724–1794)

John Alsop

Besides a note about "preparatory studies," Alsop's education is lost to history. He and his brother Richard learned the merchant trade and established a business in New York City importing and selling dry goods and cloth. They prospered and soon became one of the great merchant houses in the city. On June 6, 1766, Alsop married Mary Frogat. On October 17, 1769, their only child, Mary Alsop, was born.

As success took root, Alsop used his leisure time for political and civic pursuits, and brother Richard retired to Middletown, Connecticut. John Alsop was elected to the New York Assembly representing New York County. He was also one of the New York Hospital Association's incorporators, serving as its first governor from 1770 to 1784.

While attending the New York Assembly, Alsop called for a meeting of delegates from all the colonies to counter the Intolerable Acts. He suggested articles be drafted and sent to King George III. The assembly could not agree which delegates should attend the newly formed Continental Congress, confused by the counties sending their own slates. In 1774, John Jay, Philip Livingston (who was Richard Alsop's business partner), James Duane, Isaac Low, and John Alsop were elected in various ways to go to Philadelphia. Alsop was elected by New York City, New York County, and several other counties. John Jay presented Alsop's credentials, along with the others, to vouch for them. Alsop began serving in September 1774 and was one of the signers of the Continental Association, despite its negative impact on his business. He was reelected in 1775 and served through early July 1776.

During his service in Congress, Alsop served on the Secret Committee involved in the procurement of military supplies and the assignment of Benjamin Franklin, Silas Deane, and Arthur Lee as American Commissioners in Paris. Alsop was one of the merchants involved in procuring and supplying gunpowder to the Continental Army.

While serving in the Continental Congress, Alsop continued to serve in the provincial assembly and on the Committee of Sixty, which functioned as the provisional government of New York City. These bodies were involved in boycotting British goods and funding the army.

Early in 1776, New York City became the British focus, and tensions increased among the inhabitants. In June, Alsop traveled with George Washington from Philadelphia to New York and assisted in housing and supplies for the 8000 soldiers in the army. When the British invaded in July, Alsop was faced with voting for the Declaration of Independence in Philadelphia. He refused to do so, citing the ambiguity of his authority. Many of his constituents were Loyalists or neutral, and he was unsure what his constituents wanted. He felt he did not have their consent to take such a bold step. Rather than signing the document, Alsop resigned from the Continental Congress on July 16, 1776.

In August, after the British took New York City, Alsop's home was captured by the British in Newtown, New York, on the east side of Long

John Alsop (1724–1794)

The grave of John Alsop.

Island. Alsop kept working in Manhattan, but after the British took that, too, he escaped to Middletown, Connecticut, for the rest of the war.

After the war, Alsop continued his involvement with the New York Hospital and served as a vestryman at Trinity Church in Manhattan. He worked to rebuild his business in New York and was the president of New York City's Chamber of Commerce from 1784 to 1785. On March 30, 1786, his daughter Mary married Rufus King, who later signed the U.S. Constitution, was a U.S. Senator, and served as the U.S. minister to the Court of St. James, effectively the U.S. ambassador to the United Kingdom.

John Alsop died at home in Newtown, New York, on November 22, 1794, at 70. He was buried at Trinity Church in Manhattan. Daughter Mary and son-in-law Rufus King were the inheritors of his vast fortune.

Nephew Richard Alsop was a member of The Hartford Wits, a group of writers associated with Yale University. He wrote the *National and Civil History of Chili*. His son, also Richard, was a partner in Alsop & Co. in Chile and Peru.

Nephew Joseph Alsop's daughter Lucy married Henry Chauncey of the New York City firm Alsop & Chauncey. He founded the Pacific Mail Steamship Company in 1848. A descendant of Joseph's married a niece of Theodore Roosevelt.

Also descended from John Alsop:
- Dr. C. Loring Brace IV, noted biological anthropologist.
- Gerald Warner Brace, writer, educator, sailor, and boat builder.
- Charles Loring Brace, philanthropist most renowned for founding the Children's Aid Society.
- David Crosby, guitarist, singer, songwriter, and founding member of three bands: The Byrds, Crosby, Stills & Nash, and CPR.
- Floyd Crosby, award-winning American cinematographer.
- Wolcott Gibbs, editor, humorist, theater critic, playwright, and author of short stories.
- Archibald Gracie III, West Point graduate who was a Confederate brigadier general during the Civil War who died during the Siege of Petersburg.
- Archibald Gracie IV, writer, amateur historian, real estate investor, and survivor of the sinking of the RMS *Titanic*.
- Isabella Beecher Hooker, a leader in the women's suffrage movement and an author.
- Charles King, academic, politician, newspaper editor, and the ninth president of Columbia University.
- Charles King, soldier and distinguished writer.
- James G. King, businessman and Whig Party politician who represented New Jersey's 5th congressional district in the United States House of Representatives. His daughter, Frederika Gore King, married Bancroft Davis.
- John Alsop King, governor of New York from 1857 to 1859.
- Rufus King, newspaper editor, educator, U.S. diplomat, and a Union brigadier general in the Civil War.

- Rufus King, Jr., an artillery officer in the Union Army during the Civil War who received the Medal of Honor.
- Ellin Travers Mackay, 2nd wife of composer and lyricist Irving Berlin.
- Alice Duer Miller, writer and poet.
- Halsey Minor, technology entrepreneur who founded CNET in 1993.
- Mary Alsop King Waddington, author.
- Jane Wyatt, actress who played the housewife and mother on the television series *Father Knows Best* and the human mother of Spock on the science fiction television show *Star Trek*.

Gunning Bedford Jr.
(1747–1812)

Constitution Signer from Delaware

Buried at Wilmington – Brandywine Cemetery,
Wilmington Delaware.

Continental Congress • U.S. Constitution

Gunning Bedford Jr. was an American lawyer and politician from Wilmington, Delaware, who served in the state legislature and the Continental Army before being elected to the Continental Congress. He was a delegate to the U.S. Constitutional Convention and signed the famous document at its conclusion. He was a delegate to the Delaware Ratification Convention, where he urged ratification. Delaware was the first to do so.

Gunning Bedford was born in Philadelphia on April 13, 1747. He was the fifth of seven children and one of nine Gunning Bedfords in the family. They numbered his grandfather, father, son, three cousins, two second cousins, and a third cousin. He always used Jr. to distinguish himself among them. He left there at age 20 to attend the College of New Jersey, which is now Princeton University and where he was a classmate of James Madison. He graduated with honors in 1771. He married Jane Ballareau Parker, and sources differ on how many children they had.

He studied law with Joseph Read in New York and eventually gained admission to the bar and set up practice in Dover and Wilmington, Delaware. He served in the Continental Army during these years and, in July 1775, was elected to serve as Deputy Muster General for New York. In June 1776, he was promoted to Muster Master General for

Gunning Bedford Jr. (1747–1812)

Gunning Bedford Jr.

New York. Other than that, little is known about his Revolutionary War activities.

He began his career in elective politics in 1783 when he was elected to the Delaware House of Representatives for the first of four terms and then one three-year term (1788–1791) in the State Senate. In 1784 he was appointed Delaware's first Attorney General. He held that position for five years.

Bedford also served in the Continental Congress from 1783–1785. In 1786 he was selected to represent his state at the Annapolis Convention but did not attend the sessions. Attendance was very low at Annapolis, and it failed to achieve its goals, but it led to a call for what became the Constitutional Convention.

The government that had been established under the Articles of Confederation was floundering by 1786. Bedford and George Read, Jacob Broom, John Dickinson, and Richard Bassett were appointed a commissioner to meet in Philadelphia for what was to become one of the most important events in our nation's history—the United States Constitutional Convention.

Bedford arrived on May 28, 1787, and regularly attended its sessions. He was a large and forceful man and spoke often. He was concerned primarily with the fate of the small states in a federal union potentially dominated by powerful populous neighbors. He warned the delegates in Philadelphia in a speech on June 30 that the small states might have to seek foreign alliances for their protection. The idea was shouted down as treasonous and threw the convention into turmoil. At first, he joined with those who sought to merely amend the Articles of Confederation, but when the idea of drafting a new Constitution was accepted, he became more flexible and supported what was known as the New Jersey Plan. This plan provided equal representation for the states in the national legislature, a point on which the Delaware legislature had instructed its delegates not to compromise.

In early July, a compromise committee was formed by Benjamin Franklin, and Bedford was appointed a member. This committee recommended that in the second branch of congress, each state should have an equal vote. On July 16, when a vote was taken, the great compromise was adopted by a 5-4 vote.

Bedford returned to Delaware and was a delegate to Delaware's Ratification Convention in 1787. He used his experience and eloquence to encourage early ratification. He and Richard Bassett signed both the Constitution and Delaware's ratification document. Delaware became the first state to approve the Constitution.

In 1789 and again in 1793, Bedford served as a presidential elector and cast his vote both times for George Washington. On September 24, 1789, he was nominated by President George Washington to be the first judge for the United States District Court for the District of Delaware. He was confirmed by the Senate on September 26 and received his commission the same day. He resigned as Delaware's Attorney General and held the District Judge position until his death.

Gunning Bedford Jr. (1747–1812)

The grave of Gunning Bedford Jr.

Bedford never lost interest in his local community, and he worked for the improvement of education in Wilmington. He served as president of the Board of Trustees of Wilmington Academy, and when that institution became Wilmington College, he became its first president.

On March 30, 1812, he died at Wilmington at the age of 65 and was buried first in the Presbyterian cemetery there. Later, when the cemetery was abandoned, his body was transferred to the Masonic Home Cemetery in Christiana, Delaware. In 2013, after the sale of the Masonic Home, his monument, Bedford, and the remains of his family were relocated to the historic Wilmington-Brandywine Cemetery in Wilmington. His grave is marked with a large beautiful, bullet-shaped monument. The monument lists his major accomplishments and then reads, "He so behaved in these high offices as to deserve and receive the approbation of his fellow citizens. His form was goodly, his temper amiable, his manner winning, and his discharge of private duties exemplary. Reader, may his example stimulate you to improve the talents—be they five or two, or one—with which God has entrusted you."

Daniel Boone
(1734–1820)

Western Pioneer

Original burial site: Daniel Boone Burial Site and Monument,
Marthasville, Missouri.
Reinterred at Frankfort Cemetery,
Frankfort, Kentucky.

Military • Westward Expansion

Daniel Boone was best known for blazing the path through the Cumberland Gap into Virginia's western claims that became Kentucky. As an explorer and frontiersman, he was a catalyst for westward expansion, becoming one of the country's first legendary folk heroes. He founded Boonesborough, one of the first English-speaking settlements west of the Appalachian Mountains. Over 200,000 settlers followed his Wilderness Road into Kentucky by the end of the 1700s. During the American Revolution, Boone was an officer in the militia, leading the settlers against the British-allied natives. After the Revolution, he worked as a surveyor and merchant and speculated in land, ultimately moving to Missouri, west of the Mississippi River.

Daniel Boone was born on October 22, 1734, in a one-room log cabin in the Oley Valley of what is now Berks County, Pennsylvania, to Squire Boone, a weaver and blacksmith, and his wife, Sarah Morgan Boone. Both of Boone's parents were Quakers. Squire Boone emigrated from England in 1713. He married Sarah Morgan, whose parents were Welsh emigrants, in 1720. Daniel was the sixth of eleven children.

Daniel Boone (1734–1820)

Daniel Boone

Young Daniel roamed the wilderness of what was then Lancaster County, about fifty miles west of Philadelphia. He developed a reputation as a superb hunter. One of the tales from these days, likely a folktale, described Boone calmly shooting a mountain lion through the heart with his flintlock musket as the animal was leaping on him.

In 1742, sister Sarah Boone caused a controversy among the Quakers by marrying outside the denomination. Squire and Sarah apologized for this and the fact their daughter was already pregnant. Five years later, when brother Israel also married a non-Quaker, Squire stood by his son, and the two were expelled from the congregation. Sarah continued to attend the meeting house with her children.

Circa 1750, likely fed up with the falling out with the Quakers, Squire Boone sold his land and moved the family to North Carolina, settling on the Yadkin River, west of Mocksville, in what is now Davie County. Daniel Boone did not attend church again for the rest of his life, though he considered himself a Christian and later had his children baptized. He also received little formal education, though family members tutored him. According to family lore, when a schoolteacher asked about Daniel, Squire said, Let the girls do the spelling, and Dan will do the shooting." However, the image of Boone being semiliterate is incorrect. He was known to take the Bible and novels with him while traveling and was often the only literate person in the groups with which he traveled.

Barely twenty when the French and Indian War began, Boone joined the North Carolina militia as a teamster and blacksmith, accompanying General Edward Braddock on his ill-fated mission. It is interesting to note that George Washington, Daniel Boone, Charles Scott, and Horatio Gates were all part of this expedition and survived. Fortunately, Boone was in the rear with his wagon when the devastating attack occurred.

Upon his return to North Carolina, Boone married Rebecca Bryan on August 14, 1756. They lived in a cabin on Squire Boone's farm and eventually had ten children and raised eight more from deceased relatives. War then came to their valley when the Cherokees raided during the Cherokee Uprising in 1758. Boone returned to duty in the militia until 1760. The family, meanwhile, moved north to Culpepper, Virginia.

Following his military service, Boone made a living as a hunter and trapper, harvesting pelts for the fur trade. He and his companions would comb the wilderness for weeks at a time. Often, he would travel alone. One likely apocryphal tale mentioned Boone returning home to find his wife had given birth to a daughter fathered by his brother. They had feared Boone was dead because he did not return when expected. Boone then raised the daughter as his own and forgave his wife. Early biographers omitted this story, but there are conflicting accounts regarding which daughter and which brother.

As the game population decreased in the mid-1760s, Boone found it harder to make a living and was in debt. He attempted a move to Florida, but Rebecca refused to go. Instead, the family moved west of the Blue Ridge Mountains, where the fur trade was still sustainable.

Boone and his brother Squire first set foot in Kentucky in 1767 but failed to find the hunting grounds they were seeking. In 1769, Boone and five companions went on a two-year expedition to explore Kentucky. All did not go well. In late December, Boone and one of his fellow hunters were captured by the Shawnees and robbed of their furs. They were told to never return to what they perceived as their hunting grounds. Upon release, Boone continued his expedition and shot an Indian to escape capture. He returned home in 1771 but was back in Kentucky in 1772.

In 1773, Boone, his brother Squire, and fifty others, attempted to create the first English settlement in Kentucky. William Russell, the brother-in-law of Patrick Henry, was in the group. While foraging, Boone's son, James, and Russell's son, Henry, were tortured and killed by Indians. Boone's party abandoned the expedition and returned home. These events were part of Dunmore's War between Virginia and the natives. Boone assisted as a member of the militia and was promoted to captain. The war ended in October 1774 at the Battle of Point Pleasant. Kentucky was no longer beholden to the Shawnees.

Boone was next hired by a North Carolina judge named Richard Henderson to help establish a colony in this region. He traveled to Cherokee towns to gather a meeting at Sycamore Shoals in March 1775. There, Henderson purchased the Cherokee's claim to Kentucky. Boone then blazed the trail through the Cumberland Gap into central Kentucky called Boone's Trace, later the Wilderness Road. Boone founded Boonesborough in Kentucky, along the Kentucky River. Boone's family joined him on September 8, 1775. This was the first permanent settlement west of the thirteen colonies. Rebecca Boone was the first white woman in the west who was not a captive of the Indians. Kentucky did not immediately become the fourteenth colony. Rather, the settlement was in a western county of Virginia. Boone described a happy life as "a good gun, a good horse, and a good wife."

At the outset of the American Revolution, the natives seized the chance to drive the settlers out of the region. Many left, and only two hundred remained in Kentucky, primarily at the stockaded settlements at Boonesborough, Harrodsburg, and Logan's Station. On July 14, 1776, Boone's daughter and two other girls were captured by the Indians and taken north into the Ohio country. Boone and his men went in pursuit and ambushed the natives, rescuing the girls. This was perhaps the most famous event in Boone's life, fictionalized by James Fenimore Cooper in *The Last of the Mohicans*, published in 1826.

In 1777, the British encouraged native war parties to raid in Kentucky. Early in 1778, Boone and his companions were captured by warriors of Chief Blackfish. Boone then bluffed for time to vacate Boonesborough in the spring since the women and children were unlikely to survive winter in the wilderness. Some of his men did not realize his ruse and thought he had switched sides. This later led to a court-martial of Boone.

Boone and his men were then taken captive to Blackfish's town of Chillicothe. As was their custom, the Shawnees adopted the captives as replacements for fallen warriors. Boone was given the name Sheltowee (Big Turtle) and likely adopted by Blackfish. He accompanied Blackfish to Detroit to meet with British Governor Hamilton, who attempted to sway Boone to switch sides. Boone insisted he would abandon Boonesborough. After returning to Chillicothe on June 16, 1778, Boone learned Blackfish intended to move on Boonesborough. He took off on horseback and then on foot to reach Boonesborough 160 miles away, covering the distance through the wilderness in five days. There he warned the settlers of the pending attack.

Boone led a preemptive attack on the Shawnees to remove any doubt of his loyalty and then successfully defended Boonesborough during Blackfish's siege, which began on September 7, 1778. Following the ten-day siege, Boone was court-martialed but acquitted based on his testimony. He then returned to North Carolina to rejoin his family.

In late 1779, Boone and a large party headed back into Kentucky to find a new settlement called Boone's Station. Among the pioneers was the family of Captain Abraham Lincoln, the grandfather of the future president. Lincoln had also been born in Berks County, a few miles from Boone. When the settlers needed to file land claims in Williamsburg, Virginia, Boone collected over $20,000 from them and returned to Williamsburg to handle the matters on their behalf. While sleeping in a tavern, the cash was stolen. While some settlers forgave Boone for the loss, he worked many years to repay the others.

By the end of the Revolution, Boone was less of a woodsman and more a leading citizen. Boone joined General George Rogers Clark in his invasion of the Ohio country. Following the Battle of Piqua on August 7, 1780, Boone was hunting on his way home with his brother Ned. Shawnees ambushed them, and Ned was killed. The natives believed Ned was Daniel because he resembled him. They removed his head and returned to declare Daniel Boone dead. Meanwhile, Boone returned home and was promoted to lieutenant colonel in November.

The following spring, Boone was elected as the representative to the Virginia Assembly in Richmond. While on the way to take his seat, British dragoons under Banastre Tarleton captured him and several other legislators. The captives were released on parole several days later. The British surrendered at Yorktown in October 1781, but the fighting continued in Kentucky. At the Battle of Blue Licks, in August 1782, Boone's son Israel was killed, and the Kentuckians were defeated. Boone then joined Clark's expedition into Ohio, marking the end of the war. He was then elected sheriff of Fayette County in 1782.

Boone next moved to Limestone (later Maysville), Kentucky, where he kept a tavern and traded horses, speculated in land, and surveyed. In 1784, John Filson's book *The Discovery, Settlement and Present State of Kentucke* was published, which included an account of Boone, making him a celebrity.

The war with the natives heated up again in September 1786. Boone participated in the expedition led by Benjamin Logan. Boone was able to help negotiate a truce and prisoner exchange. However, the hostilities continued until the Battle of Fallen Timbers eight years later.

Over the next decade, Boone attempted numerous business pursuits and moved to several times, including Point Pleasant, now in West Virginia. Unfortunately, he could not maintain his prosperity and was always going into debt. When times were tough, he would give up the trades and go back into the woods to hunt and trap. In the mid-1790s, Boone moved back to Kentucky. In 1798, Boone County was erected and named after him.

In 1799, Boone sought new opportunities outside the United States, traveling to Spanish Louisiana, to what is now St. Charles County, Missouri. There, the Spanish governor appointed Boone judge and military leader in exchange for encouraging settlement. Boone served in this capacity until the Louisiana Purchase was implemented in 1804. Once again, Boone met with financial trouble as his Spanish land grants were now invalid. These claims were not restored until 1814. It is rumored after his lands were restored, Boone made one last trip to Kentucky to pay off his debts, but this is likely a legend.

During his final years in Missouri, despite being in his 70s, Boone accompanied expeditions up the Missouri River as far the Yellowstone River, a round trip of over 2000 miles. In 1816, after reaching Fort Osage on another expedition, an officer wrote of Boone, "We have been honored by a visit from Col. Boone . . . He has taken part in all the wars of America, from Braddock's war to the present hour," but "he prefers the woods, where you see him in the dress of the roughest, poorest hunter."

On September 26, 1820, Daniel Boone died at his son's home on Femme Osage Creek, near Marthasville, Missouri. He was buried next to Rebecca, who had died seven years earlier. The graves were unmarked until the 1830s. In 1845, Boone's remains were disinterred and reburied at the cemetery in Frankfort, Kentucky, by Boone relatives. However, it has been claimed by resentful Missourians that the wrong bodies were dug up and moved because the grave markers were in the wrong place. An examination of a plaster cast of Boone's skull made during the reburial was examined by a forensic anthropologist in 1983 and determined to likely be of an African, most likely a slave buried in the same cemetery. To this day, both locations claim to have the remains of Daniel Boone.

Daniel Boone was a legend in his own time, though many of the stories about him were exaggerations or outright fabrications. Said Boone, "Many heroic actions and chivalrous adventures are related of me which

Daniel Boone (1734–1820)

Daniel Boone's memorial in Frankfurt, Kentucky.

exist only in the regions of fancy. With me, the world has taken great liberties, and yet I have been but a common man."

As mentioned previously, Filson's book of 1784 laid the groundwork for Boone's legend. Most of the accounts in this book are true and were

Daniel Boone's original grave in Marthasville, Missouri.

meant to attract settlers to Kentucky. This book was translated into German and French and reprinted numerous times.

In 1822, Lord Byron mentioned Boone in his epic poem, *Don Juan*, likening him to someone who always sought to escape civilization as it began in encroach.

The Biographical Memoir of Daniel Boone, the First Settler of Kentucky, was based on an interview of Boone by Timothy Flint. This book was published in 1833 and became one of the best-selling biographies of the century. Like Parson Weems's treatment of George Washington, Flint embellished Boone's adventures, including fighting with bears and swinging from vines. The family was embarrassed by these exaggerations, but they were popular with boys and were often the subject of dime novels.

Daniel Boone (1734–1820)

Over the years, Boone's legend grew. In 1852, Henry Tuckerman dubbed him "the Columbus of the woods." Later, historian Michael Lofaro called Boone "the founding father of westward expansion." During the latter part of the 1800s, Boone was portrayed as an Indian hunter. There were false claims that he had killed dozens of natives. He may have only killed one in self-defense. Said Boone of the Indians, "they have been kinder to me than the whites."

Boone has since been honored on a postage stamp and with a commemorative half dollar. He has had numerous places named after him. He has also been the inspiration or subject of numerous novels and comic strips. A movie was made about him in 1936, and a popular television series in the 1960s, where Fess Parker played him. It must be noted, Daniel Boone was not a big man, as the show's theme song claimed. And he never wore a coonskin cap.

Jacob Broom
(1752–1810)

Surveyor from Delaware

Buried at Christ Episcopal Churchyard,
Philadelphia, Pennsylvania.

U.S. Constitution

Jacob Broom, from Wilmington, Delaware, was the son of a farmer and blacksmith who assisted the military during the Revolution as a surveyor and became involved in Delaware politics afterward. He was selected to attend the Constitutional Convention and signed the U.S. Constitution.

Broom was born October 17, 1752, the son of James Broom and Esther Willis Broom from Wilmington, Delaware. The mother was a Quaker, but the younger Broom was later affiliated with the Episcopal Church. James Broom prospered at farming and was also a blacksmith. Young Jacob was likely educated at home and probably at the Old Academy in Wilmington. Broom initially followed his father into farming but also studied surveying and got involved in the mercantile trade and real estate in partnership with his father. On December 14, 1773, he married Rachel Pierce, the daughter of Robert and Elizabeth Pierce, with whom he had eight children.

As a young man of 24, in 1776, Jacob became the assistant burgess (vice mayor) of Wilmington. Over the years, he held numerous local offices including chief burgess four times, borough assessor, and president

Jacob Broom (1752–1810)

Jacob Broom

of the city "street regulators." They oversaw the streets and sewers, laying logs across the roads to assist with drainage. It is said Broom never lost an election in which he campaigned.

Given his mother's pacifist Quaker influence, Jacob did not take up arms directly against England when the Revolutionary War began. Instead, he utilized his surveying skills to assist in the making of maps for the army. There is a record of him doing so for George Washington before the Battle of Brandywine, which occurred about fifteen miles from the Broom homestead on September 11, 1777. The map hung for many years at the Historical Library of Philadelphia at Thirteenth and Locust Streets. It is not known how many other surveys Jacob made for the army.

At the end of the Revolution in 1783, George Washington, having resigned his post as commander of the army, passed through Wilmington on his way to Mount Vernon. Broom spoke in honor of the future president urging him to "contribute your advice and influence to promote that harmony and union of our infant governments which are so essential to the permanent establishment of our freedom, happiness, and prosperity." Washington then followed with a speech of his own in response.

Broom was elected to the Delaware state legislature for the years 1784 to 1786 and 1788. He became involved in national politics when he was selected to attend the Annapolis Convention to discuss trade between the states. This meeting was a precursor to the Constitutional Convention and was poorly attended. Broom did not go either.

In 1786, the president of the Delaware Assembly, Nickolas Van Dyke, appointed Broom justice of the peace for New Castle County. The next year, Broom was asked to be one of the Delaware representatives at the Constitutional Convention in Philadelphia along with George Read, John Dickinson, Gunning Bedford, and Richard Bassett. Broom attended all the sessions and consistently voted for measures related to a stable central government, aligned with the Federalists. Regarding Senators, he favored a single nine-year term with equal representation from the states. He wanted the states to pay their representatives in Congress and would give those representatives the power to veto state laws. He viewed the office of President as an appointment for life and wanted the state legislatures to select the presidential electors. While Broom held strong opinions, he rarely spoke, permitting other more influential and experienced delegates to make his points. Georgia delegate William Pierce described Broom as "a plain good Man, with some abilities, but nothing to render him conspicuous. He is silent in public, but cheerful and conversable in private." Broom signed the U.S. Constitution on behalf of Delaware, which was the first state to ratify it on December 7, 1787.

Back home in Wilmington under the new republic, Broom became the first postmaster general for Wilmington, holding the post from 1790 to 1792.

He erected a new home and cotton mill in 1795 on the Brandywine Creek, on the outskirts of Wilmington near the village of Montchanin. This house, called "Hagley," still stands and is a historic landmark known as the Jacob Broom House. In 1802, after a fire took the mill, he sold the property mill to Éleuthère Irénée du Pont, a French immigrant. Du Pont built his gunpowder mill on the property and used the house as

The grave of Jacob Broom.

his residence and business headquarters. The property was subsequently incorporated into the Hagley Museum and Library.

Broom chaired the board of directors for Wilmington's Delaware Bank. He was also involved in other pursuits such as a machine shop that repaired mill machinery, a failed scheme to mine bog iron ore, and improvements to toll roads, canals, and bridges.

Broom was deeply religious and was a leader at the Old Swedes Church in Wilmington. He was also involved in the reorganization of the Old Academy into the College of Wilmington. He served on the first board of trustees. This institution later became incorporated into the University of Delaware.

Broom died in 1810 at the age of 57 while on a business trip to nearby Philadelphia. He was buried at the Christ Episcopal Churchyard. The exact location of his grave is unknown.

In 1987, the Delaware State Society of the Daughters of the American Revolution placed a cenotaph there in his honor.

Broom Street in Madison, Wisconsin is named after Jacob Broom.

Abraham Clark
(1726–1794)

House burned, sons tortured

Buried at Rahway Cemetery,
Rahway, New Jersey.

**Continental Congress • Declaration of Independence
United States House of Representatives**

Abraham Clark suffered much for the independence of the United States. He served in the Continental Congress as a representative from New Jersey, voted for independence, and signed the Declaration of Independence. This, of course, was an act of treason and all the signers risked their lives and welfare. Many lost their homes and land, and property and many families were split up during the war.

Abraham Clark was born in Elizabethtown (now Elizabeth), New Jersey, on February 15, 1726, the only child of Thomas Clark and Hannah Winans. At a young age, he established himself as a math prodigy. He was tutored in surveying, which gave him a steady income that allowed him to pursue an education in law. He was admitted to the state bar and quickly gained the reputation as a man for the little man as he would represent many who could not afford a lawyer. He became known as the "Poor Man's Counselor," was known for his integrity and generosity, and was very popular, particularly among the middle class.

Clark met Sarah Hatfield at the age of 22, and the couple was soon married. They had ten children, eight of whom survived to adulthood. He entered politics in 1752 when he served as clerk of the New Jersey

Abraham Clark (1726–1794)

Abraham Clark

colonial legislature. He later became Sheriff of Essex County and, in 1775, was elected to the Provincial Congress. The Provincial Congress was a transitional governing body of the province of New Jersey with representatives from all New Jersey's then thirteen counties to supersede the Royal Governor.

As the issue of independence heated up, Clark was highly vocal in favor of independence. Early in 1776, the New Jersey delegation to the Continental Congress was opposed to independence. On June 21, 1776, the state replaced all five delegates with delegates favoring separation, including Clark, John Hart, Francis Hopkinson, Richard Stockton, and John Witherspoon. They arrived in Philadelphia on June 28, 1776 and voted for the Declaration of Independence. On August 2, he signed the famous document. Few of the signers suffered as much as he did. The British invaded and burned his home and captured and tortured his sons.

Clark had two sons who were officers in the Continental Army. Aaron and Thomas were both officers in the New Jersey state artillery in Henry Knox's Regiment. Both were captured by the British and incarcerated on the prison ship *Jersey*, notorious for its brutality. Records said when the British discovered who they were, they were tortured and beaten. Thomas, for some reason, was put in the dungeon where he lay in his own urine, feces, and blood, and the only food he received was that pressed through a keyhole by fellow prisoners. Thomas most likely crossed the Delaware with George Washington, but in any event, he fought at the Battles of Trenton and Princeton and later at Brandywine, Germantown, and Monmouth. Abraham Clark never spoke of his sons' service and plight. He did not want them targeted by the enemy, nor did he seek special treatment for his sons. Now that Clark became aware of his sons' situation, he broke down and raised the issue in Congress. The British offered Abraham Clark the lives of his sons if he would recant the signing and support of the Declaration of Independence. He refused. When other members of Congress heard of the plight of Abraham's son, they were outraged. They ordered George Washington to take a British officer as a prisoner and starve him to death in a dark hole. The communication of that congressional order to General Howe was enough to end the persecution of Thomas, and he survived his imprisonment. He survived, but this cruel treatment permanently ruined his health, and he died at the age of thirty-five on May 13, 1789.

Clark knew what the signers were getting themselves into, and soon after the signing wrote to his friend, Colonel Elias Drayton: "as to my title, I know not yet whether it will be honorable or dishonorable; the issue of the war must settle it. Perhaps our Congress will be exalted on a high gallows . . . I assure you, Sir, I see, I feel, the danger we are in."

Clark remained in the Continental Congress until April 1778, when he was elected to the New Jersey Legislative Council. He was subsequently re-elected to Congress in 1780 until 1783, and then again from 1786 to 1788. He was one of New Jersey's representatives at the Annapolis Convention of 1786, at which representatives of five of the thirteen states gathered to address grievances that had arisen over the cumbersome

Abraham Clark (1726–1794)

Abraham Clark memorial.

Articles of Confederation. Among those attending were Alexander Hamilton, John Dickinson, Edmund Randolph, and James Madison.

Clark was elected to the Constitutional Convention of 1787 but was too ill to attend. The Constitution established a U.S. House of Representatives and a U.S. Senate and a plan for national elections. In 1790, Clark was elected to a seat in the House, serving in the Second (1791–93) and Third (1793–95) Congresses. He remained in Congress until his death. On September 15, 1794, Clark watched some men build a bridge on his land in what is now Roselle, New Jersey when he suddenly felt ill. Believing that he had suffered a bout of severe sunstroke, he staggered to his carriage and got himself home. There he was put to bed and died hours later. He was sixty-eight. He was buried in Rahway

Cemetery next to his father. His wife survived him by a decade, and when she died, she was laid to rest with her husband. These words are inscribed on his tombstone: "he loved his country and adhered to her cause, in the darkest hours of her struggles against oppression."

On July 4, 1848, the citizens of Rahway erected a ten-foot obelisk monument in Clark's honor near his burial site. In 1924 the stone slabs marking both Abraham and Sarah's burial site were encased in a concrete monument. In 1941 a replica of Clark's original house was built about a block away from his original house. The original was destroyed in a fire in 1900. The replica is located at 101 West Ninth Avenue, Roselle, New Jersey. Visitation is by appointment. Abraham Clark High school stands just a few blocks from the home.

Clark is also memorialized in Washington, DC, in a large mural in the rotunda of the National Archives and John Trumbull's famous painting in the U.S. Capitol building.

The graves of Abraham Clark and his wife.

Thomas Cushing, III
(1725–1788)

Protégé of John Hancock

*Buried at Granary Burial Ground,
Boston, Massachusetts.*

Continental Association

Thomas Cushing III was a prominent lawyer, merchant, and politician in Boston, Massachusetts. He was elected to the First and Second Continental Congresses and signed the Continental Association. However, he was a voice for reconciliation with England and did not agree with the Declaration of Independence. Regardless, as a protégé of John Hancock, he continued in service of the revolutionary cause.

Thomas Cushing III was born March 24, 1725, in Boston, Massachusetts, to Thomas Cushing II, a wealthy merchant, and his wife, Mary (née Bromfield). The elder Cushing was active in town politics and as a member of the Old South Church. He also served in the Massachusetts colonial assembly from 1731 to 1747, rising to speaker after 1742. Young Thomas was the second of at least seven children.

Cushing first attended the Boston Latin School before attending Harvard, where he graduated in 1744. He then continued to study law and achieved a master's degree by 1747. Cushing was admitted to the bar and entered the family's merchant business of importing wool products to the colonies. On October 1, 1747, he married Deborah Fletcher, of whom little is known. The number of children from this union is in doubt, with estimates ranging from two to seven.

Thomas Cushing

Following in his father's footsteps, Cushing entered local politics in 1753, winning election as a selectman in Boston, an office which he held for ten years. In 1761, he was elected a member of the Massachusetts General Court, where he served for fourteen years. While frequenting political discussions at Boston taverns, he developed relationships with Samuel Adams and John Hancock. With the latter, a lifelong friendship blossomed, Cushing always supporting the charismatic leader financially and otherwise. While Cushing worked in the background in support of

Hancock, he always let his friend take the credit. This led many to see Cushing as little more than a henchman of Hancock.

Following the French and Indian War, when the British were seeking recompense via taxes and duties on the colonies, Cushing, as a merchant, was a loud voice against them, noting the potential negative economic impacts on both sides of the Atlantic. Wrote John Adams of Cushing at the time, "[He] is steady and constant and busy in the interest of liberty and the opposition and is famed for secrecy and his talent for procuring intelligence."

On March 19, 1764, the *Boston Evening Post* reported the election of Thomas Cushing, Samuel Hewes, and Ezekiel Lewis as selectmen for the city of Boston, serving in the Massachusetts Assembly. Cushing, who held the position for ten years, soon rose to Speaker of the Assembly, becoming the most powerful elected politician in the colony, second only to the royal governor. One historian noted Cushing's "charm and wit" led to his annual re-election until the colonial assembly was swept away by the Revolution.

As speaker during the rising tensions in Massachusetts, Cushing played a key role as a frequent correspondent with the royal governor and the assembly's agent in London, Benjamin Franklin. Both agreed to try to moderate the situation at that time, following the Boston Massacre. In 1772, Cushing and Hancock declined to serve on the Boston Committees of Correspondence, maintaining their moderation. At that time, Franklin tried to deflect the blame for the tensions from the British government to Royal Governor Thomas Hutchinson, who was suggesting colonial rights be abridged. Franklin sent letters from royal appointees to that effect to Cushing. He was to show them only to a select few people, but when the radical Samuel Adams got wind of them, he published them in 1773. This caused an uproar, increasing tensions on both sides and calling for Franklin to resign as a colonial agent. Following this public lambasting, Franklin switched firmly to the pro-independence cause. The Boston Tea Party then ensued.

Cushing now reluctantly joined the Committee of Correspondence and denounced the Coercive Acts. When the governor dissolved the assembly, a Provincial Congress was called, and Cushing was a delegate. On June 17, 1774, Cushing, John Adams, Samuel Adams, and James Bowdoin were elected as delegates from Massachusetts to the First Continental Congress in Philadelphia.

In October 1774, General Thomas Gage arrived in Massachusetts and succeeded Hutchinson, establishing military rule over the rebellious colony. Meanwhile, Congress passed the Continental Association, collectively stating their grievances to the King. Cushing penned his name to this document. Cushing was included on the list of radical leaders sent to General Gage because, as speaker, his signature was affixed to all petitions. Gage never detained Cushing. Wrote Cushing to his wife at the time:

> I wish I could write you any politics, but as I am enjoined to secrecy, must refrain. It is currently reported in the city that the Congress have voted that no goods shall be imported from Great Britain and Ireland after the first day of December next, and that none imported after that day shall be used or consumed, and that the Congress have also voted that no goods or merchandise shall, after the 10th day of September next, be exported from the Colonies to Great Britain, Ireland, or the West Indies, unless our grievances shall be redressed before that time, and I do not deny or contradict these reports.

Cushing was reelected to this seat on December 5, 1774; February 6, 1775; and November 1775. He attended the session from September 5 to October 26, 1774; from May 10 to August 2, 1775; and from September 11, 1775, to about January 2, 1776. Cushing continued to urge moderation and was against declaring independence. He continued to believe economic pressure would force England's hand without further conflict and believed the preferred path forward was a colonial union under Great Britain. Other Massachusetts delegates began to distrust him. This cost him his seat in Congress. Elbridge Gerry, who was pro-independence, narrowly defeated him, ending his term on January 31, 1776. This gave the pro-independence camp in Massachusetts a majority. When Cushing returned to Massachusetts from Philadelphia,

Thomas Cushing, III (1725–1788)

Thomas Cushing's grave.

he continued to work against independence, orchestrating delays in the polling process by which the state would vote for independence.

John Hancock, who was then president of the Continental Congress, then stepped in for Cushing. He made him commissioner of marine affairs, overseeing the procurement of ships for the Continental Navy. For several years he was also the chief commissary responsible for supplying Massachusetts troops.

In 1778, Cushing was involved in an unsuccessful attempt to create a new constitution for Massachusetts, which the voters rejected. Perhaps frustrated, in 1779, he declined to be run for the Continental Congress. In 1780, Cushing was not involved in drafting the new state constitution that was adopted that year. That year, Cushing was appointed as one of the chief commissaries responsible for supplying the French troops at Newport, Rhode Island, a position that permitted him to enrich himself through favorably priced contracts.

Cushing ran for the state senate in 1780 and won. The newly elected senators then selected Cushing as the President of the Senate. However, when Hancock ran for governor of Massachusetts in 1780, Cushing ran with him as lieutenant governor. Both won and Cushing promptly resigned from the senate after only a few weeks. Cushing served as lieutenant governor until 1788, and in 1785, when Hancock had resigned, Cushing was the acting governor until the new governor, James Bowdoin, could take office. Cushing had run for the position himself but lost.

During Bowdoin's second term as governor, Shay's Rebellion broke out in response to his harsh economic policies. Hancock ran against Bowdoin in 1787 and won. Once again, he served with Cushing. In 1788, Cushing was a delegate to the state ratifying convention of the new U.S. Constitution. He also became one of the founders of the American Academy of Arts and Sciences.

Thomas Cushing died suddenly in Boston on February 28, 1788. He was buried in the Granary Burying Ground in Boston. Cushing, Maine, is named after him.

John Dickinson
(1732–1808)

Penman of the Revolution

Buried at Friends Meeting House Burial Grounds,
Wilmington, Delaware.

**Thought Leader • Military • Articles of Confederation
U.S. Constitution**

This founder favored reconciliation with the mother country as opposed to declaring American Independence. As a delegate from Pennsylvania to the Continental Congress, he abstained on the vote for independence. He also declined to sign the document that declared it. After his fellow delegates passed that motion, he left Congress and joined the Continental Army and fought in the Revolution. Despite not favoring independence he had worked with Thomas Jefferson on a document titled *A Declaration of the Causes and Necessity of Taking Up Arms*. He also authored *Letters from a Farmer in Pennsylvania* in which he argued that the English Parliament did not have the authority to tax the colonies. These writings earned him the title "Penman of the Revolution." Thus his writings were seen to have ignited the fires for a cause that he refused to endorse. During his life, he served as the president of two states Pennsylvania and Delaware, and he represented the latter at the 1787 Constitutional Convention. His signature is also affixed to the document produced by that gathering. Thomas Jefferson called him a true patriot, and he was undoubtedly a man known to stand by his principles regardless of the cost. His name was John Dickinson.

Dickinson was born on or around November 8, 1732, on his family's tobacco plantation, which was located in Maryland. His father had inherited the estate of 2,500 acres which he expanded to 9,000 acres. He also purchased land in Delaware where he started another plantation and christened it Poplar Hall. These were profitable ventures that were worked using slave labor until 1777 when the subject of this chapter freed the slaves of Poplar Hall.

In his youth, Dickinson was educated at his home by tutors. The most important of these was William Killen, who became the lifelong friend of his student. Killen himself would become Delaware's first Chief Justice and Chancellor. At the age of 18, Dickinson began the study of law under John Milan in Philadelphia. He also spent three years in England to continue those studies before being admitted to the Pennsylvania Bar in 1757.

By 1770 Dickinson was a successful lawyer and one of the wealthiest men in the colonies. That year he married Mary "Polly" Norris whose father was the Speaker of the Pennsylvania General Assembly. Dickinson's wife would inherit 500 acres in Carlisle, Pennsylvania that the couple would donate to John and Mary's College in 1784. The College was renamed Dickinson College. Thus he was bestowed the honor of having an institution of higher learning named in his honor while he still walked the earth.

The Norris family were Quakers as the Dickinson's had been until a dispute with the sect over a family marriage led to a break with the Quaker society. Though Dickinson himself never became an active Quaker, he believed in many Quaker principles though not pacifism since he did not object to a defensive war. It was this belief that allowed him to join the Continental Army and fight in defense of the newly formed United States.

After his wedding, Dickinson's political career blossomed. It was during this period that he enhanced his reputation throughout the colonies through his writings, as mentioned earlier, that were critical of the English Parliament's imposition of the Townshend Acts. Dickinson wrote that while the English government could regulate commerce, they had no authority to tax. He warned his fellow citizens that accepting the

John Dickinson (1732–1808)

John Dickinson

Townshend Acts would result in other taxes being levied on the colonies in the future.

In 1774 Dickinson was selected to represent Pennsylvania in the Continental Congress. It was here that he urged his fellow delegates to pursue a peaceful solution with England. It was his view that independence was not in the best interests of the colonies. His arguments failed to convince Congress, and when the vote was conducted on July 2, 1776, to declare independence, he abstained. He felt that standing by his convictions would be detrimental to his political future. He said, "My conduct this day, I expect will give the finishing blow to my once too great and, my integrity considered, now too diminished popularity."

Though he refused to sign the declaration, during his lifetime, Dickinson was recognized as a significant influence on the subject based on his previous writings. As a matter of fact, in 1787, Thomas Jefferson read an article in the *Journal de Paris* that put forth the position that it was the influence of Dickinson that resulted in the adoption of American independence. Jefferson wrote a long letter to the editor in which he insisted that Dickinson was on the other side of the question and would point out the error in the article himself if given a chance. The author of the declaration never mailed the letter which was discovered among his papers after his death. Some have theorized that Jefferson didn't have the letter delivered because it would appear as self-serving even though he makes clear that its purpose was to correct the historical record.

Leaving Congress, Dickinson accepted a position as a Brigadier General in the Pennsylvania militia. In this position, he commanded 10,000 troops which were dispatched to Elizabeth, New Jersey in anticipation of a British attack. After being passed over by promotions that went to two junior officers, Dickinson resigned his commission and returned to Poplar Hall in Delaware. It was here that he learned that his home in Philadelphia had been confiscated by the British and turned into a hospital. Some believe that Dickinson's failure to support independence resulted in the decision on promotions that prompted his resignation.

It appears that Dickinson's fears that refusing to sign the Declaration would result in a significant loss of public support were unfounded. In 1777 the Delaware General Assembly tried to send him back to the Continental Congress, but he refused to serve. Instead, he served as a private in the Kent County Militia under Caesar Rodney. When his friend Thomas McKean tried to promote him to the post of Brigadier General of the Delaware Militia he again declined to serve in that capacity. It was during this period that Dickinson freed the 37 slaves who worked at Poplar Hall.

In 1779 Dickinson agreed to represent Delaware in the Continental Congress. As a member of this group, he signed the Articles of Confederation which was a document he had worked on as a Pennsylvania delegate in 1776. He left Congress in 1781 after learning that a loyalist raid had severely damaged Poplar Hall. Back in Kent County, he was elected to represent that area in the State Senate. Shortly after taking his seat the General Assembly elected him to the office of President of Delaware. Less than a year later he was also elected to the Supreme Executive Council of Pennsylvania. When the Pennsylvania General Assembly elected him president of the council, he became the State President of both Delaware and Pennsylvania simultaneously.

John Dickinson (1732–1808)

The modest grave of John Dickinson

In 1787 Dickinson was among Delaware's representatives at the Constitutional Convention. He played an essential role there. Dickinson aided in the development of the Great Compromise which resulted in seats in the House of Representatives being based on population while each state received two seats in the United States Senate. Sick and ailing as the Convention reached its end he returned to Delaware but directed George Read to affix his name to the Constitution. Though he had opportunities to serve in the government established by the Constitution, Dickinson declined. Some believe he made this decision because he had experienced enough of the strains of public life in the years between the Stamp Act Congress and the Constitutional Convention. He left the world of politics entirely in 1793 after serving a final term in the Delaware Senate.

Dickinson lived until 1808. He spent the final 15 years of his life working on the abolition of slavery while making significant donations to organizations working in Dickinson's words to the "relief of the unhappy." He passed away at the age of 75 and was laid to rest in the Friends Meeting House Burial Ground located in Wilmington, Delaware. Responding to Dickinson's passing, Thomas Jefferson wrote, "A more estimable man, or a truer patriot, could not have left us. Among the first of the advocates for the rights of his country when assailed by Great Britain, he continued to the last the orthodox advocate of the true principles of our new government and his name will be consecrated in history as one of the worthies of the Revolution."

James Duane
(1733–1797)

Conservative Founder

Buried beneath the Christ Episcopal Church,
Duanesburg, New York.

Continental Congress • Continental Association
Articles of Confederation

This founder's biography, written by the historian Edward Alexander, was titled *A Revolutionary Conservative*. It is true that this patriot sincerely wished for the colonies to find a way to reconcile with England without having to resort to an armed rebellion. However, once that Revolution began, he became a leader of the war effort. He would serve in multiple posts during his lifetime. He represented New York in the Continental Congress, was a New York state senator, the first post-colonial mayor of New York City, and a United States district judge. His name was James Duane.

Duane was born on February 6, 1773, in New York City. His father, Anthony Duane, was an Irish Protestant from County Galway who came to the New World as an officer in the Royal Navy. He left the navy and married Eva Benson, who was the daughter of a local merchant. The couple had two sons Abraham and Cornelius. Anthony Duane grew wealthy through the purchase of land used for rental and development. His wife died, and Duane remarried Althea Ketaltas, who

James Duane

gave birth to the future founder. Ketaltas was the daughter of a wealthy Dutch merchant, and by the time their son was born, his parents were very well-to-do colonial settlers.

Duane's mother passed away in 1736, and his father died in 1747. The fourteen-year-old Duane became the ward of Robert Livingston. He received his early education at Livingston Manor. By 1754 he demonstrated a thorough command of the law, and he was admitted to the bar. From that year until 1762, he operated a private law practice in the city of his birth. He closed that practice when he became a clerk of the Chancery Court of New York.

Duane married Mary Livingston in 1759. She was the eldest living daughter of his former guardian. The couple had six children. Duane's wife influenced his political thinking. He had been a member of James Delancey's conservative political faction, which opposed British policies and at the same time opposed the use of any violence to protest these measures. Livingston did not share those views, and Duane evolved to the point of becoming a leader among New York's patriots.

In 1767 Duane became the Attorney General for the province of New York. He served as a boundary commissioner within a year, a position he would assume again in 1784. In 1774 he returned to the private practice of law. By this time, his practice was earning him 1,400 pounds a year. He owned a house in Manhattan and an estate close to Schenectady, New York, of 36,000 acres and housed more than 200 tenants. Among his clients was the Trinity Church, who he represented in legal action that resulted when heirs of Anneke Jan's claimed that they were the rightful owners of a majority of lower Manhattan, a tract of land awarded to the church by the British crown.

In 1774, Duane was among New York's representatives to the First Continental Congress meeting in Philadelphia in response to the British blockading Boston Harbor and Parliament's passage of the Intolerable Acts. The American Congress message to England was the Continental Association which Duane supported and signed. The Association took effect on December 1, 1774. It called for a trade boycott with the mother country. Congress hoped that economic sanctions would pressure the English Parliament to repeal the Intolerable Acts. Duane was one of several members of Congress who still hoped for reconciliation with England. He supported the Galloway Plan of Union, which was presented to Congress by Pennsylvania delegate Joseph Galloway. The plan called for creating an American Parliament that would act together with the Parliament of Great Britain. Congress did not accept it though its defeat was a narrow one, losing six to five on October 22, 1774.

After Duane returned to New York, he was named to the Committee of Sixty in 1775. The Committee was responsible for enforcing the boycott brought about by the Continental Association. In April of that year, he was again elected to represent his state in the Second Continental Congress. He would serve in this Congress until 1781. On May 15, 1776, Congress published a resolution saying the colonies needed to form new governments. John Adams believed this was "the most important resolution that was ever taken in America" because by forming their own governments, the colonies were in effect declaring their independence. Duane opposed the resolution and wrote to his fellow New Yorker, John Jay, that there was "no reason that our colony should be too precipitate in changing the present form of government." Despite these reservations relative to breaking with the mother country, he supported the Declaration of Independence, but due to his service with the Provincial Congress of New York, he was not present in Philadelphia to sign that document.

In July of 1776, Duane attended the New York Constitutional Convention. Apparently, by this time, he had changed his views on changing the present form of government since the purpose of the gathering was to draft a constitution to replace the colonial charter.

Duane was present in Philadelphia in 1777 when the Articles of Confederation was written. In July of 1778, he was among the signers of the document that initially united the colonies. The Articles were ratified in 1781, and Duane remained a member of the Confederation Congress until 1783.

Duane remained an active public servant after the war ended. He served as the first post-colonial Mayor of New York from 1784 until 1789. During these years, he successfully revived the city after the damage done during the war and by the British occupation. He was unsuccessful in his attempt to keep the capital of the United States in New York.

In the post-war years, Duane also served two terms in the New York State Senate. He was also one of the prominent New Yorkers who met to create the New York Manumission Society to pressure the state to abolish slavery. In 1789, President Washington nominated Duane to a seat on the United States District Court for New York City. He was confirmed by the United States Senate and served until 1794, when he retired due to health problems. On February 1, 1797, he passed away and was laid to rest beneath Christ Church in Duanesburg, New York.

As recently as 1999, there was a debate in the *New York Daily News* relative to Duane's place as a founder. The debate was prompted by

GRAVES of our FOUNDERS

Grave of James Duane inside the chapel at Duanesburg.

then-Mayor Rudy Giuliani's decision to hang Duane's portrait in City Hall's ceremonial Blue Room. Timothy L. Collins writing in opposition to this decision, stated that Duane "was widely accused of loyalist sympathies before and during the Revolution. He was instrumental in appeasing the crown and impeding the cause of American independence." This view was answered in print by a descendant of the founder, John F. Duane, who acknowledged that while his ancestor was a "conciliator who worked to settle the differences between England and the Colonies before the Revolutionary War, he was no loyalist. Once blood was shed at Lexington on April 19, 1775, Duane became a leader in the war effort. As a member of the Committee of One Hundred, the de facto city government at the outbreak of the Revolutionary War, Duane successfully proposed that all inhabitants arm themselves." Duane's descendant went on to point out that he was instrumental in financing the Colonial Army. He was so successful that he became a trusted confidant of General George Washington. In the authors' view, John Duane presented a convincing case that James Duane be remembered as an "honorable and dedicated patriot who truly was one of the Founding Fathers of our great nation."

Thomas Fitzsimons
(1741–1811)

The Irish Founder

Buried at St. Mary's Catholic Church Cemetery,
Philadelphia, Pennsylvania.

**Continental Congress • U.S. Constitution
U.S. House of Representatives**

Thomas Fitzsimons is one of the most obscure founders. Very few people recognize his name. He never sought the limelight but was willing to play a subordinate role to other key figures. He came to America from Ireland to escape horrible conditions and once here faced personal tragedy but rose above it and achieved great success and wealth as a merchant in Philadelphia. His support for independence from Britain took many forms and led him to be a delegate to the Constitutional Convention, a signer of the Constitution and a member of the U.S. House of Representatives for its first three sessions.

Thomas Fitzsimons was born in Ballykilty in County Cork, Ireland in 1741. It was probably the worst time in Ireland's history to be born there. The 1740–1741 period is known as the Year of Slaughter. The famine is estimated to have killed about 20% of the total population of 2.4 million. This was proportionally greater than during the Great Famine of 1845–1852. Thomas's father is said to have seen fifty babies get buried in the local cemetery outside St. Catherine's Church as starvation took hold.

Thomas Fitzsimons (1741–1811)

Thomas Fitzsimons

It took until 1760 for Thomas and his six siblings and father to arrange for passage to America. Tragically once they did arrive in Philadelphia, Thomas's father died. He was said to be sick and weakened because he gave most of his food ration to his children to ensure their survival.

Thomas was smart and hardworking and started working for merchants in Philadelphia. He married Catherine Meade on November 23, 1761, and formed a business partnership with her brother George. The firm of George Meade and Company soon became one of the leading commercial houses in the city and would successfully operate for over 41 years.

Young Thomas Fitzsimons was thrust into politics when in 1771 he was elected first vice-president of the Friendly Sons of St. Patrick, a politically powerful fraternal association. When Parliament reacted to the 1773 Boston Tea Party with punitive measures, which Americans called the Coercive Acts, Philadelphia merchants were infuriated. They felt that if the British could close the port of Boston, no city in America was safe. In 1774 he was elected to a steering committee organized to direct the protest over the Coercive Acts and to the city's Committee of Correspondence, the patriots' shadow government. In choosing him for these positions, the voters ignored a law that barred Catholics from elective office.

When Pennsylvania began mobilizing and organizing a militia to fight the British, Fitzsimons like many immigrants demonstrated his devotion to his adopted land by springing to its defense. He served as a captain of a company he raised in Colonel John Cadwalader's 3rd Battalion. During the summer of 1776, Fitzsimons' company served in the cordon of outposts that under Colonel John Dickinson guarded the New Jersey shoreline. In November, the British invaded New Jersey, and Washington began a slow withdrawal to the Pennsylvania side of the Delaware River. On December 5, Fitzsimons's company went on duty to cover the Continentals retreat by guarding the river's Pennsylvania shore. This company was supposed to be an essential part of Washington's surprise attack on Trenton on Christmas night, but because of deteriorating weather, they were unable to cross the river. They joined Washington several days later in time to deal with a British counterattack. Later in the war, Fitzsimons served on the Pennsylvania Council of Safety and headed a board to oversee the newly formed Pennsylvania Navy.

This experience in the Revolutionary War convinced Fitzsimons of the need for central control of the nation's military forces. His wartime association with Robert Morris convinced him that a reliable and effective national government was essential for the prosperity of the country. His reputation as a caring officer as well as his work for the poor on numerous relief committees made him very popular. He was elected to the Continental Congress in 1782. There he concentrated on financial and commercial matters working closely with Morris and aligned with Alexander Hamilton and James Madison. Frustrated by the constant conflict and criticism, he resigned in 1783.

In 1786 he began the first of three terms in the state House of Representatives. In 1787 the state selected Fitzsimons to represent it at the constitutional convention along with Thomas Mifflin, Robert

The grave of Thomas Fitzsimons.

Morris, George Clymer, Jared Ingersoll, James Wilson, Gouverneur Morris, and Ben Franklin. Prior to the convention he often spoke on issues relating to commerce and finance, arguing that the central government should have the right to tax both exports and imports to raise revenue and regulate commerce—a position that he had advocated with little success in the Continental Congress. Although not a leading member at that convention, he supported a strong national government, the end of slavery, and granting the House equal powers with the Senate in making treaties. He was not a supporter of universal suffrage. He was one of only two Catholic signers of the United States Constitution, the other being Daniel Carroll of Maryland.

After the Convention Fitzsimons resumed his serving in the Pennsylvania legislature. There he led the fight for a special convention to ratify the Constitution, arguing that since the document derived its power from the people, the people must approve it through representatives elected solely for that purpose.

After the Constitution was established, he served in the first three sessions of the House of Representatives as a Federalist. He was Chairman of the Ways and Means Committee. He co-sponsored the law that authorized the original six frigates of the United States Navy. He failed to win re-election in 1794. He devoted the rest of his life to business and charitable affairs. He served as President of Philadelphia's Chamber of Commerce and as a trustee of the University of Pennsylvania.

Fitzsimons died on August 26, 1811, at the age of 70. His tomb is in the graveyard at St. Mary's Roman Catholic Church which is in present Independence National Historical Park.

Nathaniel Folsom
(1726–1790)

Merchant Militiaman

Buried at Winter Street Cemetery,
Exeter, New Hampshire.

Continental Association

Nathaniel Folsom was a delegate to the Continental Congress from New Hampshire and the Major General of the New Hampshire Militia. He was also a merchant and holder of several state offices. Folsom signed the Continental Association as a member of the First Continental Congress in 1774.

Nathaniel Folsom was born in Exeter, Rockingham County, New Hampshire, on September 18, 1726, the son of Jonathan Folsom and his wife, Ann (née Ladd) Folsom. Nathaniel was the eighth of twelve children, including siblings Anna, Sarah, Lydia, Elizabeth, Abigail, John, Mary, Jonathan, Samuel, Josiah, and Trueworthy. His ancestors were early settlers in Massachusetts and were related to the Gilmans.

Young Nathaniel attended public schools. When his father died in 1740, when he was thirteen, he took employment with a merchant. As a young man, he invested in timber and opened a sawmill. He married first Dorothy Smith (1726–1776), with whom he had seven children: Nathaniel, Dorothy, Jonathan, Anna, Arthur, Mary, and Deborah. Both Deborah and Mary later married John Taylor Gilman, the Governor of New Hampshire. Nathaniel married second Mary Sprague, with whom he had a daughter Ruth.

An imagined Nathaniel Folsom.

With the outbreak of the French and Indian War in 1754, Folsom joined the militia. The next year, he was a captain in Colonel Joseph Blanchard's New Hampshire Provincial Regiment under Sir William Johnson during the Crown Point expedition. At the Battle of Lake George, his company captured the French commander-in-chief, Major General Jean-Armand Baron de Dieskau, the baggage train, and critical supplies. Only six men were lost in his company. Over the rest of the war, Folsom was promoted to major, lieutenant colonel, and then colonel of the Fourth Regiment of the New Hampshire militia.

In 1761, Folsom partnered with his cousins, Joseph and Josiah Gilman, to form the merchant company Folsom, Gilman & Gilman. They operated a general store, a shipbuilding operation, and imported and exported goods. Folsom split from his cousins in 1768 but continued in the timber, lumber, and trade industries. He also became involved in local politics in Exeter, moderating town meetings.

Nathaniel Folsom (1726–1790)

Folsom was a delegate in July 1774, when the revolutionary assembly was convened. They sent him as a delegate to the First Continental Congress in Philadelphia. He attended sessions from September 5, 1774, the Continental Congress's first day, through October 26, 1774. The Continental Association, limiting imports and exports to and from England, was adopted on October 20. Folsom was a signatory.

With the increase in hostilities, Governor Wentworth revoked Folsom's commission as colonel of the militia. This did not deter Folsom from leading his troops to aid in protecting Boston during the British siege. His men safely escorted captured cannons from Portsmouth to Durham. Folsom was given the rank of major general of the New Hampshire militia, numbering about 2000 men. He sent some of his men to aid Fort Ticonderoga.

On April 1, 1777, Folsom was again elected to the Continental Congress. He arrived in Philadelphia on July 20 and began serving the

Nathaniel Folsom's grave marker.

following day. On September 18, word came of the pending invasion of Philadelphia by the British. Whether in haste or as his custom, Folsom hopped on a horse without a saddle and headed out to York. There, he participated in the debates concerning the Articles of Confederation and was against taxation methods being proposed. He felt it unfair to tax property but to exclude slaves in the calculations, as the southern delegates argued. Folsom voted against the Articles of Confederation.

He wrote,

> Inclosed, I send you a copy of the Articles of confederation [sic] as far as agreed to by Congress. The 9th article is, 'That the proportion of public expense incurred by the United States for their common defense and general welfare, to be paid by each State into the Treasury, be ascertained by the value of all lands within each state granted to or surveyed for any person, as such land and the buildings and improvements thereon, shall be estimated according to such mode as Congress shall from time to time direct.' This article was opposed by all the New England Delegates and we are yet in hopes of having it re-considered.

Folsom was a member of a delegation of congressmen who visited Valley Forge during the winter of 1777/78. He and the others reported on the terrible conditions to Congress. After his term ended, he returned to New Hampshire, where he was elected Executive Councilor in 1778. This role was essentially the co-governor of New Hampshire.

In 1783, Folsom was a delegate to New Hampshire's constitutional convention, serving as its president. He was then the chief justice on the Court of Common Pleas in Exeter. Folsom died at Exeter on May 26, 1790, and was buried at the Winter Street Cemetery.

Nathaniel Gorham
(1738–1796)

President of Congress

Buried at Phipps Street Cemetery,
Charlestown, Massachusetts.

Continental Congress • United States Constitution

Nathaniel Gorham was born in Charlestown, Boston, Massachusetts, on May 27, 1738. He was the son of Captain Nathaniel Gorham, a packet boat operator (a packet boat was a regularly scheduled service carrying freight and passengers), and his wife Mary Soley. His third great grandfather, John Howland, came to America on the Mayflower and signed the Mayflower Compact.

He received little formal education but was apprenticed at 15 to Nathaniel Coffin, a merchant in New London, Connecticut. He left Coffin's employ in 1759 and returned to Charlestown and established his own small business there, which quickly succeeded. Four years later, in 1763, he married Rebecca Call, and they had nine children together.

Gorham began his political career as a public notary but was soon elected to the colonial legislature (1771 to 1775), where he emerged as a staunch Patriot. During the revolution, he displayed an exceptional talent for administrating that proved crucial to his state's wartime government. He was selected to serve on the Massachusetts Board of War, which organized Massachusetts' military logistics and manpower (1778–17810). In 1779 he was a delegate to Massachusetts' first constitutional convention. He represented his community in both the upper and lower houses of the new state legislature, serving several times as the lower house speaker.

Nathaniel Gorham

Gorham served as a delegate to the Continental Congress from 1782-83 and 1785-87 and served as its president after the resignation of John Hancock in June 1786. He served as president until November of that year.

In 1786, Gorham was involved in a very controversial matter that became known as the Prussian Scheme. Shay's Rebellion in western Massachusetts convinced many Americans that a stronger, centralized national government was necessary. The shortcomings of the Articles of Confederation were fanning the fears of anarchy. When Massachusetts debtors took up arms, refused to pay their debts, and closed the courts, Gorham predicted worse would follow.

These types of disturbances fueled the movement for convening a convention to modify the Articles of Confederation. Getting consensus to modify the Articles took some time. When the delegates convened in Philadelphia in May 1787, there were widely circulated rumors that the meeting was to offer to enthrone Prince Frederick of Prussia as king of the United States. So intense were the rumors that the convention issued a public denial that any proposal for reestablishing monarchy was being considered. The reason for these rumors was that Gorham, while President of the Continental Congress, wrote to Prince Henry, the younger brother of the Prussian King Frederick the Great, offering to make him king of the United States. Henry's response, found more than a century later, proved what many had assumed was a legend was to decline. He reportedly believed that the American public would not be likely to submit to a king. A letter addressed to Baron von Steuben, dated a few months before the Constitutional Convention, was discovered in the Prussian archives in the early 1900s. It refers to the offer and his refusal. Von Steuben, who was living in New York, was involved in the proposal. Some have attributed the natural-born citizen clause in the US Constitution as an attempt by the Philadelphia Convention to end the persistence of rumors of European royalty being invited to assume a hypothetical US throne.

Gorham was elected as a Massachusetts delegate to the Constitutional Convention in 1787. He played an influential part, frequently speaking, sitting on the Committee of Detail, and serving as chairman of the Committee of the Whole. He pushed for a central government strong enough to protect interstate commerce, promote international trade, and regulate the use of paper money. He favored long presidential and senatorial terms and the appointment of federal judges by the executive. He also wanted a consolidation of military authority through control of the militia by the central government.

To gain support for these things, he was willing to accept southern demands about slavery. Gorham was pessimistic about the future of his state and country. He believed, in the aftermath of Shay's Rebellion, that Massachusetts would divide between east and west over the constitution question and that the country would divide into several independent nations within 150 years.

He signed the Constitution and was a crucial participant in Massachusetts' struggle for ratification. Ratification was won only when Gorham and other Federalists proposed possible amendments to the constitution to attract moderates. The final vote was 187 to 168.

Gorham did not serve in the new government he had helped create. In 1788 he and a friend Oliver Phelps bought 2,600,000 acres in western New York. The deal was a disaster and ruined him financially. By 1790 the two men were bankrupt, which led to a fall from the heights of Boston society and political esteem.

Gorham died in Charlestown, Massachusetts, on January 11, 1796, at the age of 58. He is buried in the Phipps Street Cemetery in Charlestown. Gorham Street in Madison, Wisconsin, and Gorham, New York are named in his honor.

The overgrown grave of Nathaniel Gorham.

Cyrus Griffin
(1748–1810)

The Last President of Congress

Buried at Bruton Parish Churchyard,
Williamsburg, Virginia.

President of Congress

Cyrus Griffin was an attorney from Farnham, Virginia, who served as a member of the Virginia House of Delegates, the Second Continental Congress, and the Ninth Congress of the Confederation. During the final year of the Continental Congress, Griffin was the last President of Congress, overseeing the transition from the Articles of Confederation to the U.S. Constitution. He was then appointed a federal district judge during the Washington administration and served in that capacity for the rest of his life.

Cyrus Griffin was born on July 16, 1748, in Farnham Parish, along the Rappahannock River, in Virginia, the fourth son of Leroy Griffin, a tobacco farmer, and his wife, Mary Ann (née Bertrand) Griffin, of Huguenot heritage. The Griffin family is believed to be an old Welsh family, possibly descended from the last king of Wales, Llewellyn Griffin, who fell in battle against Edward I of England, in 1282, after a reign of 28 years. The Griffins were early settlers in Virginia, along the tidewater area, in the mid-1600s. Thomas Griffin and his brother Samuel emigrated from Wales and settled along the Rappahannock River. When

Cyrus Griffin

Samuel returned to Wales to inherit their late brother's estate, Thomas remained.

Leroy Griffin died while Cyrus was a child, leaving a portion of his estate to him. These funds were utilized to educate Cyrus in Great Britain. He studied law in Scotland at the University of Edinburgh and met Lady Christina Stuart, the eldest daughter of Charles Stuart, the Sixth Earl of Traquair, circa 1770. When Charles, the patriarch of one of Scotland's noble families, learned of the relationship, he was furious. Griffin was the son of a "lowly" planter from Virginia and an Episcopalian. The Stuarts were devout Roman Catholics. Consumed by passion, the young couple eloped to London, where Griffin continued his legal studies at the Middle Temple.

Cyrus Griffin (1748–1810)

John Griffin, their first child, was born in 1771 while the couple was still in England. In 1774, Griffin, who had graduated from law school, returned to Virginia to start his practice. He left Christina and young John behind. He returned the following year as the hostilities of the American Revolution commenced. He sought a dowry from his father-in-law but was unsuccessful. While in England, he worked privately to find a way to reconcile the differences between England and her American colonies. He proposed the following ideas in a letter to his friend Lord Dartmouth in London:

- That the Commissioners be instructed to meet either the whole or any number of those men who compose the Congress at any particular place except Philadelphia.
- That when so met and Ceremonies adjusted, they shall begin from the year 1763 and discuss each separate grievance complained of by America.
- That when any point is fully debated the Meeting shall adjourn to the next day; in the meantime, the Commissioners are to determine with themselves how far or whether they shall totally admit the hardship under consideration; such determination to be sent in writing upon the next morning, and by a special Officer, to the aforesaid delegates sitting to receive the same; the delegates to vote by a majority whether the determination of the Commissioners will be satisfactory.
- That if there should be any points upon which The Commissioners and Delegates cannot perfectly agree those points may be referred to the wisdom of the next parliament, and the Colonies to be heard by Counsel in the said parliament.
- That when all matters are finished at this united convention, the Members of the Congress shall return to Philadelphia, and the said Congress shall instantly dissolve themselves.

Frustrated on both fronts, Griffin took his wife and son with him and returned to Virginia in 1775. The Griffins would later have five additional children, totaling four sons and two daughters.

The young attorney soon became involved in state politics. In 1777, he was elected to the Virginia House of Delegates. Then, on May 29, 1778, he was elected to the Continental Congress. He attended sessions from August 19 to October 21 and about December 23 to December 31, 1778. During this time, he observed the machinations and posturing of members of Congress, writing to Thomas Jefferson about his worries and the perceived lack of honor and patriotism.

Griffin was re-elected to the Continental Congress on June 18, 1779, and served through the year's end. He was corresponding with Benjamin Franklin, who was in France, regarding his dowry's settlement. Franklin had taken up representing Griffin to Charles Stuart. Franklin and Stuart were likely acquainted when Franklin visited Scotland in 1771 with Henry Marchant. Thanks to Franklin, Charles Stuart and his daughter reconciled before his death in 1779. In letters to Franklin, Griffin thanked him for his assistance and worried about the Continental Congress's precarious financial position. He also complained that he is often Virginia's lone representative. Griffin held on, serving through June 1780, when he finally resigned. One of his final letters was to Thomas Jefferson regarding the need to increase the military presence in Virginia as it was invaded by the British.

During his final days in Congress, Griffin was appointed a judge of the Court of Appeals in Cases of Capture, which handled cases involving ships and cargo seized during the war. Griffin served on this court longer than anyone else in its short history, remaining until the Continental Congress ended its jurisdiction in 1787. In 1782, he was one of the committee members appointed by Congress to oversee a settlement of the boundary dispute between Pennsylvania and Connecticut regarding the Wyoming Valley.

Griffin's attempts to return to Congress failed in 1783, 1784, and 1786, when he lost elections. He also failed to gain a seat on the Virginia Executive Council in 1786. However, he did win a seat in the Virginia House of Delegates, which he held until January 1787. Then, on October 23, 1787, Griffin was elected to Congress after the U.S. Constitution had been signed while the state ratification process was underway. Sadly, during this time, his son Cyrus Jr. died.

Cyrus Griffin (1748–1810)

The decrepit stone marking Cyrus Griffin in Williamsburg.

On January 22, 1788, Griffin was elected the fifteenth and final President of Congress, succeeding Arthur St. Clair. He then presided over the Continental Congress's final year as it transitioned to the new constitutional government. His term ended on November 16, 1788.

Griffin lost the election to be a member of the First Congress in the House of Representatives. However, he was elected to the Virginia Executive Council. Before he could take his seat in August 1789, President Washington appointed Griffin to a three-man commission established to negotiate with the Creek Indians. He served on this commission with David Humphreys and Benjamin Lincoln.

Next, Griffin expressed his desire to Washington to become the next U.S. ambassador to France, succeeding Thomas Jefferson. However, Washington had other ideas. During a Senate recess, he appointed Griffin to be a judge on the newly created United States District Court for the District of Virginia. Washington nominated him again on February 8, 1790, and Griffin was approved by the Senate two days later. He served in this capacity for the remainder of his life. In 1807, Griffin may have attended or presided over the treason trial of Vice President Aaron Burr. He also officiated the libel trial of newspaper editor James T. Callendar, embroiled in controversies against Thomas Jefferson.

Cyrus Griffin died at Yorktown, Virginia, on December 14, 1810, at 62. An article in the Baltimore newspaper *The Federal Republican* stated, "He was a gentleman highly respected for his eminent virtues, his integrity, and independence. He has filled many public appointments, and always with honor to himself, and with advantage to the country."

Griffin was laid to rest next to his wife, who had predeceased him in 1807, in the Bruton Churchyard in Williamsburg, Virginia. Both lie in a nondescript, unmarked tomb.

John Hancock
(1737–1793)

The Signature

Buried at Granary Burial Ground,
Boston, Massachusetts.

Articles of Confederation • Declaration of Independence

John Hancock must have been an unusual and remarkable person. He inherited enormous wealth, was educated, nice looking, popular, living a wonderful life, and yet he was willing to risk it all in the cause of the American Revolution. He contributed immensely to our nation's founding in many ways, including serving in the Continental Congress, twice as President of Congress, and as a signer of the Declaration of Independence. His signature on that document was so bold that when people sign their names, they are said to have written their "John Hancock."

John Hancock was born on his family's farm in Braintree, now Quincy, Massachusetts, on January 23, 1737. His father, John, was a minister and died when young John was seven. He was adopted by his uncle Thomas Hancock, one of Boston's wealthiest merchants, and his aunt Lydia (Henchman) Hancock. Young John lived in an elegant mansion on Beacon Hill called Hancock Manor and was sent to the elite Boston Latin School. He graduated in 1750 and enrolled in Harvard. He received his bachelor's degree from Harvard in 1754 at the age of 17. He then entered his uncle's shipping business. In 1760 he moved to England while building relationships with customers and suppliers. He returned in 1761 and soon became a partner in the company, House of Hancock. When Thomas

John Hancock

Hancock died of a stroke in August 1764, John inherited the business, Hancock Manor, two or three slaves, and thousands of acres of land, becoming one of the colonies' wealthiest men. The slaves were eventually freed through the terms of Thomas's will. John developed a reputation for generosity, but his lavish lifestyle had its critics, including Sam Adams.

In 1765 the British Parliament enacted the Stamp Act tax on the colonies, and it was a catalyst for John Hancock. He became involved in politics protesting regulations like the Stamp Act and Townshend Act. He commandeered public acts of protest and joined in support of a boycott of British goods. To avoid British taxes, Hancock allegedly began smuggling goods aboard his vessels. This made him very popular among the locals, and in 1766 he was elected to the Massachusetts House of Representatives.

Hancock came into direct conflict with the British in 1760, when one of his merchant ships, the *Liberty*, was seized in Boston Harbor by

John Hancock (1737–1793)

British customs officials who claimed Hancock had illegally unloaded cargo without paying the required taxes. Being a popular figure, the seizure of his ship led to angry protests by residents. He was taken to court and given a huge fine. It was not the first time Hancock had friction with the Customs Board. Many thought they harassed Hancock because of his politics. He hired John Adams to defend him, and eventually, the charges were dropped without explanation. His guilt or innocence is still debated. Hancock became a local hero for standing up to the British authorities. One result of all this was Hancock and Sam Adams emerged as political partners. Adams was a rabble-rousing firebrand who was hated by the British. He and Hancock, along with James Otis, Paul Revere, and others, formed a grassroots group named the Sons of Liberty. Thus, Hancock became increasingly involved in the movement for American independence, and Massachusetts was at the center of the movement. Boston was dubbed the "Cradle of Liberty."

A result of all the unrest in Boston was a show of military might. Four regiments of the British army were sent to Boston to support the royal officials. The tension between the soldiers and civilians led to what became known as the Boston Massacre in March 1770, in which five civilians were killed and six wounded by British troops. Hancock headed a committee that met with Governor Thomas Hutchinson and demanded the removal of British troops from Boston. He claimed that there were 10,000 armed colonists ready to retaliate if the troops did not leave. The troops being in a precarious position were moved to Castle William, and Hancock was celebrated as a hero reflected in his near-unanimous reelection to the House of Representatives.

Boston became a volatile site once again with the passage of the Tea Act of 1773. Although Hancock did not participate in the Boston Tea Party, he was present at the December 16, 1773, meeting preceding the dumping of the tea and approved of the action. On March 5, 1774, Hancock delivered an important speech on the Boston Massacre's fourth anniversary, denouncing British troops' presence in Boston and questioning Britain's authority over the colonists' lives. The speech was published and widely distributed, enhancing Hancock's stature as a leading Patriot.

In May of 1774, Governor Hutchinson was replaced by Thomas Gage. Whereas Hutchinson tried to win over Hancock, believing that he was too influenced by Sam Adams, Gage took a hard line against both men. In December 1774, Hancock was elected president of the Massachusetts Provincial Congress, which declared itself an autonomous government. Later that month, he was chosen as a delegate to the Second Continental Congress, which served as the colonies' governing body.

Hancock was in the middle of several of the most important events of early American history. He was in Lexington, Massachusetts, on April 18, 1775, when Paul Revere rode his horse to warn fellow colonists that the British were on the move toward Boston. Hancock was with Sam Adams when they heard the alarm. Both men were targeted for arrest by the British. The advance warning allowed them to flee and ultimately escape and make their way to Philadelphia to attend the Continental Congress that convened on May 10. On May 24, Hancock was elected as the third President of the Continental Congress.

When the congress adjourned in August, Hancock made his way to Fairfield, Connecticut, where he wed his fiancée, Dorothy (Dolly) Quincy, on August 28. John and Dolly would have two children, Lydia, who died at ten months, and John George Washington Hancock, who died at nine from a head injury while ice skating.

Hancock was President of Congress when the Declaration of Independence was adopted and signed. He was the first person to sign the historical document and did so with a large, flamboyant signature. According to legend, he signed largely and clearly so that King George could read it without his spectacles.

In October 1777, Hancock told the Continental Congress that he would be resigning the presidency and returning to Massachusetts for health reasons. He had fallen out of favor with both Adamses, who disapproved of Hancock's vanity and extravagance. Many doubted he resigned for health reasons. He rejoined Congress in June 1778, and on July 9, joined representatives from seven other states in signing the Articles of Confederation and then returned to Boston.

Hancock had his chance for military glory shortly after when he led nearly six thousand soldiers to recapture Newport, Rhode Island, from the British. It was a complete failure. He suffered some criticism for the failed attempt but emerged with his popularity intact.

After returning to Massachusetts, Hancock desired to stay in the public eye. As the state needed funds to pay soldiers and purchase weaponry, he used his personal funds to assist in these areas. He also handed out food and firewood to the poor at his own expense. According to biographer William Fowler, "John Hancock was a generous man and the people loved him for it. He was their idol."

The new Massachusetts constitution, which Hancock helped frame, went into effect in October 1780. He was the first democratically elected Governor of Massachusetts in a landslide, garnering over ninety percent of the vote. He remained governor until his surprise resignation in 1785. He again cited health reasons, but some critics claim he wanted to avoid a difficult situation. Historian James Truslow Adams wrote that Hancock's "two chief resources were his money and his gout, the first always used to gain popularity and the second to prevent his losing it." The turmoil Hancock avoided was Shay's Rebellion, which his successor, James Bowdoin, had to deal with. In 1786, after nearly two years out of office, Hancock ran again and defeated Bowdoin and pardoned all the rebels. Hancock was reelected to annual terms as governor for the remainder of his life.

He did not attend the 1787 Constitutional Convention but did preside over Massachusetts's 1788 convention to ratify the constitution and gave a speech in favor of it. Even with the support of Hancock and Sam Adams, the convention narrowly ratified it by a vote of 187 to 168.

In his ninth term as governor, he reconciled with his old friend Sam Adams and in his final election as governor, Adams served as his running mate and as lieutenant governor.

In 1789 Hancock was a candidate in the first U.S. Presidential election. He received four electoral votes out of a total of 138 cast. Following a lengthy illness, John Hancock died at his home with his wife at his side on October 8, 1793, at 56 years of age. After a lavish funeral, he was laid to rest in the Old Granary Burying Ground in Boston, where the Boston Massacre victims are also buried. A large obelisk-shaped stone marks his grave.

The monument to John Hancock.

Benjamin Harrison V
(1726–1791)

Father and Great-Grandfather of Presidents

Buried at Berkeley Plantation,
Charles City, Virginia.

Continental Association • Declaration of Independence

Benjamin Harrison V was a wealthy planter and merchant who served in the colonial Virginia legislature, followed by the Continental Congress, where he signed the Continental Association, Olive Branch Petition, and the Declaration of Independence. He was then governor of Virginia. Harrison's son, William Henry Harrison, became the 9th President of the United States. His great-grandson and namesake became the 23rd President of the United States.

Benjamin Harrison V was born April 5, 1726, in Charles City County, Virginia, to Benjamin Harrison IV and his wife, Anne (née Carter), the oldest of ten children. The family lived on the Berkeley Plantation, built by the elder Harrison. He was a member of the Virginia House of Burgesses, as had been the prior three generations of Benjamin Harrisons going back to the colonist in 1630, only 25 years after Jamestown. The elder Harrison was also a major in the Charles City County militia and the local sheriff. Benjamin's mother was the daughter of Robert "King" Carter, the president and treasurer of the Virginia colonial council, who served as the acting governor of the colony and the rector of the College of William and Mary.

Benjamin Harrison

On July 12, 1745, the elder Harrison and daughter Hannah were killed at Berkeley Manor by a lightning strike as they shut an upstairs window during a storm. Now the patriarch of the family at only 19, Benjamin inherited Berkeley and several other plantations in the area in addition to thousands of acres, a fishery, and a grist mill. His siblings split six other plantations.

In 1748, Harrison married Elizabeth Bassett, the daughter of Colonel William Bassett and Elizabeth (Churchill) Bassett. Together they had eight children. The eldest daughter, Lucy Bassett Harrison, married Peyton Randolph. Daughter Anne Bassett Harrison married David Coupland. Benjamin Harrison VI was a successful merchant and member

Benjamin Harrison V (1726–1791)

of the Virginia House of Delegates. Carter Bassett Harrison served in the Virginia House of Delegates and the US House of Representatives. Their youngest child, William Henry Harrison, became a popular general known as the Hero of Tippecanoe. He was then a congressional delegate for the Northwest Territory, the Governor of the Indiana Territory, and a US senator. In the 1840 United States presidential election, running under the slogan "Tippecanoe and Tyler Too," William Henry Harrison, the first candidate of the Whig party, defeated Martin Van Buren. He fell ill after his inauguration and died just one month into his presidency.

Benjamin Harrison had attended the College of William and Mary at Williamsburg. He did not graduate. Instead, pursuing a life in politics. His brothers also served their communities. Carter Henry Harrison became a leader in Cumberland County, west of Richmond. Nathaniel Harrison was elected to the House of Burgesses and then the Virginia Senate. Henry Harrison fought in the French and Indian War. Charles became a brigadier general during the American Revolution.

In 1749, Harrison was elected to the Virginia House of Burgesses, serving for over a quarter-century representing Surry and Charles City Counties. In 1768, Harrison was appointed to a committee to draft Virginia's response to the Townsend Acts, protesting the tax on tea and other imports as payment for the French and Indian War. In 1770, he was a signer of the association boycotting British imports. He also sponsored a bill declaring Parliament's laws illegal if they were passed without the consent of the colonial legislature. In 1772, Harrison served as a justice and was one of several gentlemen who purchased a building for the city of Williamsburg to use as its courthouse. Also that year, he and Thomas Jefferson were among a group of six Virginia delegates who prepared and delivered an address to King George calling for an end to the importation of sales from Africa. The King rejected this, and both Harrison and Jefferson continued to own slaves.

On March 12, 1773, Richard Henry Lee, the recipient of a report from Samuel Adams in Massachusetts, offered resolutions to establish a Committee of Correspondence to cooperate with that colony and others. Upon the adoption of Lee's resolutions, the Virginia Assembly appointed the following members to act as a Committee of Correspondence: Peyton

Randolph, Robert Carter Nicholas, Richard Bland, Richard Henry Lee, Benjamin Harrison, Edmond Pendleton, Patrick Henry, Dudley Digges, Dabney Carr, Archibald Cary, and Thomas Jefferson.

In December 1773, the colonists of Boston protested the tax on British tea by destroying cargos in the harbor. Harrison initially thought the colonists should reimburse the East India Company for the damages caused by the Boston Tea Party, but the subsequent Intolerable Acts hardened his position against the King and Parliament. On May 24, 1774, he and 88 other Virginia delegates signed an association condemning Parliament and invited other colonies to convene a Continental Congress. Harrison was selected to be one of Virginia's delegates to this new body August 5, 1774, to travel to Philadelphia. Said Edmund Randolph of him, "A favorite of the day was Benjamin Harrison. With strong sense and a temper not disposed to compromise with ministerial power, he scruples not to utter any untruth. During a long service in the House of Burgesses, his frankness, though sometimes tinctured with bitterness, has been the source of considerable attachment."

Harrison arrived in Philadelphia on September 2, 1774, for the First Continental Congress. John Adams, in his diary of the first days of the Congress, wrote that day of his first meeting with the Virginian:

> 2 [Sept]. Friday. Dined at Mr. Thomas Mifflin's, with Mr. Lynch, Mr. Middleton, and the two Rutledges [Edward and John, both of South Carolina] with their ladies. The two Rutledges are good lawyers. Governor [Stephen] Hopkins and Governor [Samuel] Ward [both of Rhode Island] were in company. Mr. [Thomas] Lynch [of South Carolina] gave us a sentiment: "The brave Dantzickers, who declare they will be free in the face of the greatest monarch in Europe." We were very sociable and happy. After coffee, we went to the tavern, where we were introduced to Peyton Randolph, Esquire, Speaker of Virginia, Colonel Harrison, Richard Henry Lee, Esquire, and Colonel Bland. Randolph is a large, well-looking man; Lee is a tall, spare man; Bland is a learned, bookish man. These gentlemen from Virginia appear to be the most spirited and consistent of any. Harrison said he would have come on foot rather

than not come. Bland said he would have gone, upon this occasion, if it had been to Jericho.

On September 6, 1774, recording his observations of some of the early debates in Congress regarding proportional representation, delegate James Duane of New York wrote:

> Col. Harrison from Virginia insisted strongly on the injustice that Virginia should have no greater Weight in the determination than one of the smallest Colonies. That he should be censured by his constituents and unable to excuse his want of attention to their Interest. And that he was very apprehensive that if such a disrespect should be put upon his Country—men we shoud [sic] never see them at another Convention.

Around that time, Silas Deane of Connecticut wrote to his wife about the delegates:

> I gave you the character of the South Carolina delegates, or rather a sketch. I will now pursue the plan I designed. Mr. Randolph, our worthy President, may be rising of sixty, of noble appearance, and presides with dignity. Col. Harrison may be fifty; an uncommonly large man and appears rather rough in his address and speech.

Harrison aligned with John Hancock, while Richard Henry Lee aligned with John Adams. Adams later described Harrison in his diary variously as "another Sir John Falstaff," "obscene," "profane," and "impious." The next month, Harrison was one of the delegates to sign the Continental Association, implementing a trade boycott with Britain.

The following May, when Harrison arrived for the Second Continental Congress, he roomed with his brother-in-law, Peyton Randolph, and George Washington, until he left to take command of the Continental Army in June. On July 5, 1775, Harrison was one of the signers of the Olive Branch Petition, albeit reluctant. The two had a war of words during the debate. Dickinson remarked he disapproved of only one word in the petition, "congress." Replied Harrison, "There is but one word in the paper, Mr. President, of which I do approve, and that is the word 'congress.'" The King rebuffed the chance of reconciliation.

That October, Peyton Randolph died suddenly from a heart attack while dining with Thomas Jefferson. This left Harrison alone in his Philadelphia residence. Harrison now kept busy with military affairs, corresponding with his former roommate. In November, he traveled with Washington, Benjamin Franklin, and Thomas Lynch to Cambridge to inspect the army's condition. Congress now realized the need to increase the number of troops and to increase their pay.

Nearing July 1776, Harrison was chairman of the Committee of the Whole, presiding over the final debates of the Lee Resolution, expressing a desire for independence. Harrison oversaw the amendments of the Declaration of Independence after the Committee of Five presented the draft of the Declaration of Independence. Harrison reported the approved final form of the document on July 4, giving its final reading. Congress then unanimously adopted it. Harrison was one of the signers the next month. At that event, many of the signers were nervous. Benjamin Rush described a "pensive and awful silence" as the delegates believed they were signing their death warrants. He then described how Harrison, known for his sense of humor, lightened the mood. Rush wrote that the corpulent Harrison approached the slender Elbridge Gerry when he was about to sign and said, "I shall have a great advantage over you, Mr. Gerry, when we are all hung for what we are now doing. From the size and weight of my body, I shall die in a few minutes and be with the angels, but from the lightness of your body, you will dance in the air an hour or two before you are dead."

During 1777, Harrison was named to the Committee of Secret Correspondence for the Congress, whose objective was to communicate securely with colonial agents in Britain. He was also named the Chairman of the Board of War, overseeing the army's movements and the exchange of prisoners. During this time, he had a spat with Washington over the commission of the Marquis de Lafayette. Harrison insisted the position was only honorary and without pay. He also endorsed a controversial idea that the Quakers had the right not to bear arms based on their religious beliefs.

In September 1777, Congress fled Philadelphia, stopping briefly in Lancaster before heading to York, Pennsylvania. There, they debated the Articles of Confederation. Again, Harrison argued for greater representation for the larger states, like Virginia. Concerned about his properties back home and not making headway with the Articles, Harrison headed back to Virginia in October. There, he returned to the Virginia House and was elected Speaker. There, he focused on providing for the defense and western land interests.

In January 1781, Benedict Arnold, now on the British side, led an invasion of the James River in Virginia. Harrison arranged for his family to flee Berkeley before Arnold arrived and destroyed most of Harrison's possessions and a large portion of his house. Arnold also burned all the family portraits so that no likeness of the family would survive. Fortunately, the Harrisons escaped with their lives. Soon after the British left, the Harrisons returned and began rebuilding. Harrison returned to his duties, helping supply the army.

Following the victory at Yorktown in October 1781, Harrison was elected the fifth Governor of Virginia. During this time, he focused on the financial difficulties the state was facing at that time. This included negotiating with the native tribes rather than warring with them. This did not please George Rogers Clark, who wanted to secure more western territory. Harrison served as governor through 1784, after which he returned to the House of Delegates.

Elizabeth Harrison, Harrison's wife of over forty years, died in September 1787. In June 1788, Harrison was named to the state constitutional convention to ratify the new US Constitution. Harrison spoke against it because it did not clarify the rights for which they had fought. He voted against its ratification, but when it was known that reforms would be included after all the states passed it, Harrison became a supporter.

Harrison, suffering from chronic gout and other ailments, continued in his service in the Virginia House until his death at Berkeley on April

24, 1791, while celebrating his re-election. Harrison was laid to rest in the family burial ground at Berkeley.

As mentioned previously, Harrison's youngest son, William Henry Harrison, became the 9th President of the United States in 1841. He served only one month before he died. In 1846, Harrison's heirs asked the US government to reimburse the family for pay, bounty land, and other expenses incurred by Harrison from the American Revolution to his death. Harrison's great-grandson, Benjamin Harrison, served in the US Senate from Indiana (1881–87) and as the 23rd President of

The grave of Benjamin Harrison.

the United States (1889–93). His great-great-grandson, William Henry Harrison (1896–1990), served in the US House of Representatives (1951–55, 1961–65) as a Republican from Wyoming. A residence hall at the College of William and Mary is named for Harrison. Also, a bridge spanning the James River near Hopewell, Virginia, bears his name.

In the foreword of the book *The Harrisons* by Ross F. Lockridge, the author writes, "The Harrison family is justly believed to have given more distinguished men to American history than any other family."

William Hooper
(1742–1790)

A Tory in the Continental Congress

Buried at Hillsborough Old Town Cemetery,
Hillsborough, North Carolina.
Partially reinterred at Guilford Courthouse National Military Park,
Greensboro, North Carolina.

Declaration of Independence

Like many Americans at the time, William Hooper saw no compelling reason to support a revolution and break with England. He came from an environment of privilege and was a successful lawyer and politician in North Carolina. While serving in the North Carolina General Assembly, his support for the colonial government began to erode. He slowly became a supporter of the American Revolution and independence, served as a delegate in both Continental Congresses, and signed the Declaration of Independence.

William Hooper was born in Boston on June 28, 1742, the first of five children born to William Hooper and Mary Dennie. His father was a Scottish minister who studied at the University of Edinburgh before immigrating to Boston. Valuing education, the father saw that young William received a grand education for the times, attending the prestigious Boston Latin School and in 1757 entering Harvard College. Three years later, at the age of eighteen, he was awarded a bachelor of arts degree. Three years after that, he was granted a master's degree

William Hooper (1742–1790)

William Hooper

in theology, but much to his parent's disappointment, he refused to enter the clergy and instead chose to study law under James Otis, one of Massachusetts's leading attorneys. Many biographies have stated that Otis's passionate stands for colonial rights influenced the young Hooper. He studied under Otis until 1764 when he passed the bar exam and left Massachusetts for Wilmington, North Carolina. He became the circuit lawyer for Cape Fear and became very popular and respected by the planters and lawyers. By June 1766, he was unanimously elected Recorder of the Borough.

In August 1767, Hooper married Anne Clark, a North Carolina native and daughter of the sheriff of New Hanover County. The couple would have two sons and a daughter.

In 1769 the North Carolina Governor William Tryon named Hooper the Deputy Attorney General of the Salisbury district and the following year named him Deputy Attorney General for the entire colony. It was during this time that Hooper came in conflict with a group called the "Regulators." These farmers opposed excessive colonial government taxation, excessive legal fees, and the corruption of the royal government's officers. They took up arms and rioted to show their bitterness. In 1770, a group of Regulators reportedly dragged Hooper through the streets in a riot in Hillsborough. Hooper urged the governor to use force to end this rebellion. The governor took his advice, and at what became known as the Battle of Alamance in May 1771, routed the Regulators, and the movement was destroyed. It is considered by some to be the opening salvo of the American Revolution. At that point, it certainly appeared that Hooper was a firm supporter of the royal government.

Things started to change when in 1773, Hooper was elected to the North Carolina legislature. He became an opponent of a bill pushed by the colonial governor that would regulate the court system. He wrote a series of essays that he anonymously signed as "Hampden." Although now lost to history, it was one of the first times media was used to oppose proposed legislation. The outcome was that most of the provincial courts were closed and that Hooper, once his authorship became known, was disbarred from practicing law for one year. This episode soured his reputation among loyalists.

During his time in the Assembly, Hooper slowly became a supporter of the American Revolution and independence from Britain. The governor soon disbanded the Assembly, and Hooper helped organize a new colonial assembly without the Royal Government's consent. His loyalist father was so displeased he disowned his son.

In early 1774 Hooper was one of the leaders of the anti-British agitation in North Carolina. He was appointed to the Committee of Correspondence and Inquiry to coordinate activities with other colonies. In June of 1774, the port of Boston was closed by the British, and Hooper took the lead in mustering aid and support for his native city. Two shiploads of provisions and 2000 pounds in currency were sent for relief. Later that year, he was chosen as one of the delegates to the First

Continental Congress. Some delegates, including Thomas Jefferson, believing that he still harbored loyalty to the Crown, referred to Hooper as the "Tory in the Continental Congress." He served diligently on numerous committees and was elected to the Second Continental Congress. There he served honorably in the assembly where Jefferson drafted the Declaration of Independence. Much of his time was split between Congress and working on forming a new government in North Carolina. Due to this, he missed the vote approving the Declaration of Independence on July 4, 1776; however, he arrived in time to sign it on August 2, 1776. He was the youngest signer at 34.

In 1777 due to financial difficulties, Hooper resigned from Congress and returned to North Carolina to resume his law career. Throughout the revolution, he was sought by the British as a traitor for signing the Declaration of Independence. They targeted him to show others the consequences of his actions. In 1780 the British invaded North Carolina. Hooper moved his family from Finian, his country home, into Wilmington for safety, but in January 1781, while he was away, Wilmington fell to the enemy, and Hooper was separated from his family. The British burned his estates in Finian and Wilmington, forcing Hooper to rely on friends for food and shelter and nursing him back to

William Hooper's monument.

health after contracting malaria. His wife Anne and his children were forced to flee to Hillsborough, where her brother found shelter. After nearly a year of separation, Hooper was reunited with his family, and they settled in Hillsborough, where he continued to work with the North Carolina assembly until 1783.

After the war, Hooper's popularity waned as he was lenient towards loyalists. In 1787 and 1788, he campaigned heavily to ratify the new United States Constitution, although he refused election to the convention that ultimately ratified the document. He was appointed a federal judge in 1789 and served for one year before his bad health forced him to retire. His recurrences of malaria and his alcoholism contributed to his death on October 14, 1790, at 48. He was quietly buried in the garden of his estate, which later became a part of the Old Town Cemetery in Hillsborough. Later, in 1894 his remains were reportedly reinterred in the Guilford Courthouse National Military Park in Greensboro, North Carolina, where a huge marker was placed over his grave. Many historians believe that much of his remains are still in his original grave. His home in Hillsborough was declared a National Historic Landmark in 1971.

Francis Hopkinson
(1737–1791)
The Patriot Renaissance Man

Buried at Christ Church Burial Ground,
Philadelphia, Pennsylvania.

Declaration of Independence

In 1924 a Pennsylvanian historian wrote that this founder was a poet and a scientist. As it turns out, that description is an understatement. He was also a mathematician, mechanic, musician, composer, inventor of musical instruments, a lawyer by profession, and a signer of the Declaration of Independence. He was a man who could indeed be termed a Jack of many arts and perhaps a master of some. His name was Francis Hopkinson.

Hopkinson was born in Philadelphia on September 21, 1737. His father, Thomas Hopkinson, was a close friend of Benjamin Franklin. The duo was so close that they co-founded the University of Pennsylvania. It is not surprising that Hopkinson himself was a member of the first class educated by the college his father helped establish. He graduated in 1757 and received a master's degree in 1760.

After college Hopkinson studied law under Benjamin Chew, who was the Attorney General of the province. He was admitted to the bar in 1761 and was considered an able lawyer. However, his many interests encroached on both his ability and time to practice law. In the same year, he was admitted to the bar he was called upon to perform his initial act of public service. He served as secretary to a conference held on the banks of the Lehigh

Francis Hopkinson

River between the Indians of that area and Governor James Hamilton. He wrote a poem titled "The Treaty" that was inspired by this experience.

In 1766 he sailed for Europe where he lived for approximately a year in Ireland and England. When he returned to America, he resumed his law practice and opened a dry goods business in Philadelphia. In 1768 he married a Jersey girl, Ann Borden, and the couple would produce five children including the jurist and statesman Joseph Hopkinson who wrote the lyrics to "Hail Columbia." That song was recognized by many as the de facto national anthem of the United States until the country adopted "The Star-Spangled Banner" when that piece was recognized as the official anthem by Congress in 1931.

After his marriage, Hopkinson moved to Bordentown, New Jersey. When he first entered the practice of law, Hopkinson took legal positions supporting the crown. However, as time passed, he grew to favor American independence, and he resigned from the English colonial government positions. In June of 1776, he was elected to represent New Jersey in the

Second Continental Congress. As a member of Congress, he made enough of an impression on John Adams that the future president conveyed his thoughts on Hopkinson in a letter to his wife, Abigail. Adams wrote, "I met Mr. Francis Hopkinson, late a mandamus councilor of New Jersey, now a member of Continental Congress, who was liberally educated and is now a painter and a poet. I have a curiosity to delve a little deeper into the bosom of this curious gentleman, and may possibly give you more particulars concerning him. He is one of your pretty, little, curious, ingenious men. His head is no bigger than a large apple. I have not met with anything in natural history more amusing and entertaining than his personal appearance, yet he is genteel and well-bred and very social." There is little doubt that Adams was pleased when Hopkinson voted in favor of independence and subsequently signed the document declaring the same.

As a member of Congress, Hopkinson served as the Treasurer of Loans in the young nation's Treasury Department. He also wrote patriotic songs and drew caricatures of other members of Congress. One of the songs he composed titled "The Battle of the Kegs" became the best known of all ballads written during the Revolutionary period. He also worked on designing seals for various agencies of the government and was a member of the committee given the job of designing the Great Seal of the United States.

In 1779 Hopkinson was appointed to the position of Judge of the Admiralty for Pennsylvania. He served in this position until 1789. In that same year, President Washington made him the United States District Judge for Pennsylvania; a position he would hold until his death.

Hopkinson also used his talents to support the ratification of the Constitution. In 1787 he wrote the poem and allegorical essay "The New Roof" to aid in the effort to have the states accept the new form of government that the Constitutional Convention had proposed. In the work, he describes architects who had discovered a weakness in a mansion house composed of thirteen rafters in need of repair. The rafters represented the original colonies. His work ends with the words, "Figure to yourselves, my good fellows, a man with a cow and a horse—oh the battlements, the battlements, they will fall upon his cow, they will fall upon his horse and wound them, and the poor man will perish with hunger. The architects of the new structure (Constitution) would save both the building and the man's possessions."

The grave of Francis Hopkinson.

In 1927 Dr. G. E. Hastings, a professor of English at the University of Arkansas, asserted that Hopkinson and not Betsy Ross was the actual designer of the first American flag. Hastings based his claim on his examination of documents in the archives of the Congressional Library. There he found that Hopkinson had submitted a bill to Congress that requested payment for the work he had done designing the flag. His asking price was "a Quarter cask of the Public Wine." Congress responded by saying that as an employee of the Treasury, his pay had covered any work he had done. While he was never paid, Hastings and other historians have correctly concluded that Hopkinson is the only person in the minutes of the Continental Congress credited with having designed a United States flag.

According to Doctor Benjamin Rush, Hopkinson was "seized with an apoplectic fit" on the morning of May 9, 1791. He died shortly after that and was laid to rest in Philadelphia's Christ Church Burial Ground. As a result of rumors that he wasn't buried in that cemetery, remains were exhumed in the 1930s and inspected by a University of Pennsylvania anatomist. The conclusion was that the remains were Hopkinson's. As his tombstone had deteriorated over the years, when he was reburied, a new memorial was added to the site. Among the credits now listed on the bronze plaque that rests above him is "Designer of the American Flag."

Titus Hosmer
(1736–1780)

Connecticut Lawyer

Buried at Mortimer Cemetery,
Middletown, Connecticut.

Articles of Confederation

Titus Hosmer was a lawyer and leading politician from Connecticut who was thrice elected to the Continental Congress but only attended briefly for one of his terms. He signed the Articles of Confederation.

Titus Hosmer was born in West Hartford, Connecticut, in either 1736 or 1737, the son of Captain Stephen Hosmer and his wife, Deliverance (née Graves) Hosmer. Titus was the third son among eight children. The Hosmer family originated in Kent, England. An ancestor emigrated to Newtown, Massachusetts, in the early 1600s.

Young Titus was educated in local schools as a youth. He then attended Yale College in New Haven. In a speech in 1850, scholar David Dudley said of Hosmer, "While at Yale College, he was distinguished for the acquisition of sciences, excelled in the languages and fine writing. Being graduated in 1757, [he] settled in Middletown about 1760."

Shortly after graduation, Hosmer was admitted to the Connecticut colonial bar and began practicing law in Middletown. The following year, he married Lydia Lord, and the two began a family. Throughout the 1760s, Hosmer gradually increased in stature as a lawyer, working on important estates and dealing with the disposition of debts and creditors. Meanwhile, seven children were born during these years, including

Titus Hosmer

Stephen Titus Hosmer, who would later become chief justice of the Connecticut Supreme Court, and Hezekiah Lord Hosmer, who became a U. S. representative for the state of New York.

As Hosmer became better known, he entered politics, first in local offices such as justice of the peace. Following the collapse of royal rule in Connecticut, Hosmer was elected to the Connecticut General Assembly in October 1773, holding this seat until 1778. A strong advocate for independence, Hosmer was elected speaker of the state House of Representatives in 1777. He also served as a member of the local Committee of Safety.

Titus Hosmer (1736–1780)

As an emerging leader in the Connecticut assembly, Hosmer was elected to the Continental Congress three times: first on November 3, 1774; next on October 12, 1775; and again, on October 11, 1777. However, he only attended in 1778, including when the Congress was in York, Pennsylvania. There is no record as to why he did not attend but a few months, but some have speculated he may have been in poor health. Another possibility is the size of his family and the need to be close to home. Yet another is his attention to duty in the Connecticut Assembly, where he was the speaker and then a state senator beginning in May 1778. Regardless, records show he did attend sessions from June 23 to September 10, 1778, when he returned home.

Hosmer could have been a signer of the Continental Association, and the Declaration of Independence had he been in Philadelphia to fulfill his elected duties. However, it seems he had competing duties and opted to lead locally until the opportunity arose to sign the first constitution for the nation, the Articles of Confederation. The document had been negotiated the preceding two years and was reviewed by Congress during Hosmer's tenure. Starting on July 9, 1778, in Philadelphia, the delegates began to sign the document, after which it went to the states for ratification. Hosmer was one of five Connecticut delegates to sign. The others included Roger Sherman, Samuel Huntington, Oliver Wolcott, and Andrew Adams.

According to two letters written to Connecticut governor Johnathan Trumbull following the signing of the Articles, there was not much to do in Congress. Hosmer complained of the lack of progress with settling the debts of the army. He suggested the idleness was depressing him, and he worried about the continuing disagreements with the Southern States, suggesting the union might not hold together. He also reported on the behavior of some in Congress. Wrote Hosmer,

> ... When we are assembled, several gentlemen have such a knack at starting questions of order, raising debates upon critical, captious, and trifling amendments, protracting them by long speeches, by postponing, calling for the previous question, and other arts, that

Titus Hosmer's grave.

it is almost impossible to get an important question decided at one sitting; and if it is put over to another day, the field is open to be gone over again, precious time is lost, and the public business left undone...

Upon returning to Connecticut, Hosmer continued as a state senator and was then elected as a judge on the maritime Court of Appeals in January 1780. Unfortunately, Hosmer was not able to take the seat.

He died suddenly on August 4, 1780. Obituaries did not mention a cause of death despite his young age of only 43 or 44. He was laid to rest in Mortimer Cemetery in Middletown, Connecticut. Diplomat and poet Joel Barlow wrote a moving tribute to Hosmer entitled "An Elegy." Wrote Barlow:

> Come to my soul, O shade of Hosmer, come Tho' doubting senates ask thy aid in vain; Attend the drooping virtues round thy tomb, And hear a while the orphan'd Muse complain.

Lydia followed Titus to the grave in 1798 and is buried next to him. Besides the sons mentioned previously, a grandson, also named Hezekiah Lord Hosmer, was an accomplished author and the first Chief Justice of the Montana Territory.

Samuel Huntington
(1731–1796)

First President of the United States?

Buried at Colonial Cemetery (aka Old Norwichtown Cemetery),
Norwich, Connecticut.

**Continental Congress • Articles of Confederation
Declaration of Independence**

This founder happened to be the President of Congress on March 1, 1781, when the Articles of Confederation officially went into effect. The Articles essentially brought the individual colonies together and created the United States of America. It is because of his position in the Congress at the time that some point to this founder as the first president. Whether one agrees with that view is not important. The man can and should be remembered for his efforts on behalf and his contributions to the young country. Known for his great dignity and exceptional gentleness, he was described by those who knew him as "a sensible, candid and worthy man." He was among those who risked all by affixing his signature to the Declaration of Independence. His name was Samuel Huntington.

Huntington was born on July 16, 1731, in what is now Scotland, Connecticut. He was the firstborn of Nathaniel and Mehetabel Huntington's ten children. Since he was the oldest of ten children, he was expected to work the family farm. As a result, according to multiple sources, he never received any formal education. However, one researcher

Samuel Huntington (1731–1796)

Samuel Huntington

has written that Huntington graduated from Yale College in 1755. Considering his later success, this is entirely possible. When he reached the age of 16, he apprenticed with a barrel maker while at the same time continuing to assist his father with the farm. He somehow found the time to educate himself by borrowing books from local attorneys and his future father in law, the Reverend Ebenezer Devotion. It appears possible that the studies he undertook on his own could have prepared him for Yale. What is not in dispute is fueled by his industry; he became a practicing attorney after being admitted to the Connecticut bar in 1754.

In 1761 Huntington married Martha Devotion, the daughter of the aforementioned Ebenezer. The couple did not have any children of their own, but when one of Huntington's brothers died, they adopted his two children. Huntington and his wife stayed together until she died in 1794. The couple's adopted son, Samuel Huntington, became the third governor of Ohio.

By the age of thirty, Huntington was one of the most important lawyers in Connecticut. In 1765 he was named the King's Attorney for the colony apposition, making him Connecticut's attorney general. When Huntington first entered politics a year before being appointed as the King's Attorney, as a member of the Connecticut General Assembly, he held conservative views and was loyal to the king. However, as the British Parliament began imposing oppressive measures on the colonies, his position changed, and he became an outspoken critic of the crown and resigned his office. In 1775 he was chosen along with Roger Sherman and Oliver Walcott to represent Connecticut in the Continental Congress. All three members of the Connecticut delegation were ardent advocates of independence. As a member of Congress, he voted for American independence and signed the declaration that proclaimed the separation of the colonies from the British empire.

In terms of his congressional service, in 1846 the historian Robert T. Conrad wrote that Huntington "devoted his talents and time to the public service. His stern integrity, and inflexible patriotism, rendered him a prominent member, and attracted a large share of the current business of the house; as a member of numerous important committees, he acted with judgment and deliberation, and cheerfully and perseveringly dedicated his moments of leisure to the general benefit of the country."

Huntington was not known as a great orator, nor did he write much or very well. He earned the respect of his fellow delegates through his diligence and hard work. When John Jay left Congress to become minister to Spain, Huntington was elected to succeed him as president in 1779. On March 1, 1781, the Articles of Confederation were signed, which made the thirteen colonies the United States of America. Because Huntington was the President of Congress, some point to him as the first President of the United States.

Five months after the signing of the Articles, Huntington was forced to resign from Congress and return to Connecticut due to illness. Despite battling health issues for the rest of his days, he remained active in public affairs. He served as chief justice of the Connecticut Supreme Court and as lieutenant governor of the state before serving as the third governor of the Constitution State. He advocated for religious tolerance, the

Tomb of Samuel Huntington.

abolition of slavery, and the ratification of the United States Constitution under which George Washington served as the generally recognized first president of the country. Huntington presided over the state convention that gathered to debate ratification.

In 1900 Susan Huntington wrote about her ancestor in the *Connecticut Magazine*:

> Among the phalanx of Patriots who fearlessly and unbrokenly resisted the menaces and efforts of the British government to prevent the Declaration of Independence, it is remarkable to observe the great proportion that arouse from the humble walks of life who by the vigour [sic] of their intellect, and unwearied fearlessness compensated the deficiencies of early education and enrolled themselves with honor and capacity among the champions of Colonial freedom. Such a man was Samuel Huntington ... His extreme modesty and the fact that he left no descendants perhaps account

for so little appreciation of the value of his services in these days of revival of interest in all things relating to the American Revolution.

Huntington was serving as governor when he died on January 5, 1796. He was laid to rest just 15 miles away from the place of his birth in the Old Norwichtown Cemetery that is now known as the Colonial Cemetery. In 2003 the citizens of Norwich raised $31,000 and used the funds to exhume both Huntington and his wife. The tomb was restored, and the bodies of the founder and his wife were placed in new caskets and reinterred. There rests a man who went from being a barrel maker to a signer of the Declaration of Independence, to become, at least according to the people of Norwich, the first President of the United States.

Richard Hutson
(1748–1795)

First Mayor of Charleston

Buried at Circular Congregational Church Burying Ground, Charleston, South Carolina.

Articles of Confederation

Richard Hutson was a prominent lawyer, judge, and politician in Charleston, South Carolina. He was elected to the Second Continental Congresses and signed the Articles of Confederation. He also served as the eighth Lieutenant Governor of South Carolina and the first mayor of Charleston. He participated in the state constitutional convention to ratify the U.S. Constitution.

Richard Hutson was born July 9, 1748, in Prince William Parish, South Carolina, to Reverend William Hutson and his wife, Mary (née Woodward or Gibbes). The elder Hutson first studied law in England but disliked it. He came to America and as an actor in 1740, after which he was called to preach. Young Richard studied the classics. He then studied law and graduated from Princeton College in New Jersey in 1765. He was admitted to the South Carolina bar and opened a law practice in Charleston.

The young attorney was an early agitator for independence. He was elected to the provincial assembly in 1776. On January 18, 1777, he wrote Isaac Hayne, his brother-in-law, concerning the mood in South Carolina regarding a state religion:

Richard Hutson

The Dissenters' Petition came before the House on Saturday last. It was introduced and warmly supported by General Gadsden. In order to give you a general idea of the debates, it will be necessary to quote the paragraph, which it was the prayer of the Petition might be inserted into the [state] Constitution. It runs thus: That there shall never be any establishment of any one Denomination or sect of Protestants by way of preference to another in this State. That no Protestant inhabitant of this State shall, by law, be obligated to pay towards the maintenance and support of a religious worship that he does not freely join in or has not voluntarily engaged to support, nor to be denied the enjoyment of any civil right merely on account of his religious principles, but that all Protestants demeaning themselves peaceably under the government established under the constitution shall enjoy free and equal privileges, both religious and civil.

In early 1778, Christopher Gadsden, Arthur Middleton, Henry Laurens, and William Henry Drayton were elected to the Second Continental Congress. Middleton and Gadsden declined the honor, and a subsequent election for the three vacancies selected John Mathews, Thomas Heyward, Jr., and Richard Hutson. Wrote Historian David Duncan Wallace about the elections:

> During the spring and summer of 1778, Congress was considerably strengthened. [On] May 21st Samuel Adams returned from an absence of over six months, which, under the Massachusetts rule requiring three delegates, had deprived the State of her vote; Gouverneur Morris took his seat from New York [on] 20 January 1778; Roger Sherman returned [on] 25 April after a long absence. All the States, even Delaware at last, sent representatives; Laurens, who since the beginning of November 1777, had been the sole attendant from his State, was reinforced [on] 30 March by the brilliant young William Henry Drayton, [on] 13 April by Richard Hutson, [on] 22 April by John Matthews [sic; should be Mathews], and [on] 6 June by Thomas Heyward.

Hutson arrived at the Continental Congress when it was in York, Pennsylvania, having fled occupied Philadelphia. He served from April 13, 1778, until June 27, 1778. At that point, the Congress returned to Philadelphia. Hutson accompanied Elbridge Gerry and Francis Dana to Philadelphia by Wilmington and Chester, avoiding the public inns filled with other delegates and people returning to the city. The group crossed the Susquehanna at McCall's Ferry, southeast of York, and celebrated July 4th at City Tavern in Philadelphia. Hutson then served through February 26, 1779, during which he signed the Articles of Confederation on behalf of South Carolina.

Upon his return to Charleston in 1780, Hutson found himself on the front lines of a British invasion. When Charleston fell, he was captured along with Christopher Gadsden, Josiah Smith, Edward Blake, Jacob Read, and Alexander Moultrie. The group was taken by ship to St. Augustine, where they were held for many weeks.

Following his release, Hutson was elected to the state's Legislative Council, holding the position into 1782. Hutson had served in the South Carolina House of Representatives sporadically throughout the revolutionary years. In 1782, he was elected the lieutenant governor of the state and then, in 1783, was the first elected mayor of Charleston. In 1784, Hutson was elected to a court position, which he held until 1791. In 1788, he was a member of the state constitutional convention that ratified the U.S. Constitution. After 1791, Hutson was promoted to senior judge of the Chancery court.

Tomb of Richard Hutson.

Richard Hutson (1748–1795)

Richard Hutson died in Charleston on April 12, 1795. He was buried in the Perrineau family vault in the Independent Congregational Church Cemetery, now the Circular Congregational Church Burying Ground, located in Charleston. A plaque placed on a wall next to his grave reads:

> Herein Lie the Remains of Richard Hutson 1747–1795. Son of Rev. William and Mary Woodward Hutson. South Carolina Patriot, Statesman, and Jurist. Graduated Princeton 1765. Founding Body the College of Charleston 1772–1794. Member S.C. General Assembly and Legislative Council 1776–1790. Served in Militia and Imprisoned by the British During the Revolutionary War. Delegate to the Continental Congress 1778–1779. Signer Articles of Confederation. Lieutenant Governor 1782–1783. Author of Act Incorporating City of Charleston 1783. First Intendant (Mayor) of Charleston 1783. Judge, Court of Chancery 1784–1794. Senior Judge 1791–1794.

John Jay
(1745–1829)

The First Chief Justice

Buried at John Jay Cemetery,
Rye, New York.

Continental Association • President of Congress
Secretary of Foreign Affairs • United States Supreme Court

This accomplished founder served the young country in multiple positions during his long public career. He was elected to the first and second Continental Congress where, in the latter, he also presided as the President of Congress. During the Revolutionary War, he represented the United States in Spain. He followed that by joining the American team assigned to negotiate the Treaty of Paris with England, which ended the war. Under the Articles of Confederation, he ably filled the position of Secretary of Foreign Affairs. A vocal proponent of a strong national government, he was a co-author of the *Federalist Papers*, which set forth the arguments in favor of the ratification of the United States Constitution. President Washington chose him to be the first Chief Justice of the Supreme Court. While serving in that post, he negotiated the controversial Jay Treaty with Great Britain. He concluded his career as a two-term Governor of New York. His name was John Jay.

Jay was born on December 12, 1745, in New York City. His father, Peter Jay, was a wealthy merchant who traded in furs, timber, and other

John Jay (1745–1829)

John Jay

products. His mother was Mary Van Cortlandt, who could trace Dutch ancestry and whose father served in the New York Assembly and was twice elected mayor of New York during colonial times. The Jays had ten children, seven of which survived to adulthood. Three months after their son John was born, the Jays left New York City and settled in Rye, New York.

Jay was educated at home by his mother until he was eight years of age, when he was sent to continue his schooling under the guidance of an Anglican priest. In 1760, at the age of 14, he entered King's College (now Columbia). Among the friends he made at Columbia was Robert Livingston, a man who would later become one of Jay's staunch critics. After graduating, he studied the law and was admitted to the New York bar in 1768. He and Robert Livingston then agreed to work together as partners. At the time, partnerships among attorneys were rare, but Jay and Livingston believed by working together and utilizing their connections, they were likely to attract more clients. The partnership lasted two years, after which the pair, both feeling they were on a successful path, opened law practices of their own.

During this period, Jay found time for other pursuits besides handling his legal work. According to one of his biographers, Walter Stahr, in his work *John Jay Founding Father*, the young lawyer was a leading member of a group known as the "Social Club" and was the manager of a dancing assembly. Stahr surmises that it was at a dance where Jay met Sarah Livingston in 1772 or 1773. Livingston, the eldest daughter of New Jersey Governor William Livingston, was sixteen years at the time but known for her intelligence and beauty. One of Jay's friends and fellow founder, Gouverneur Morris wrote of her, "never was a creature so admired." Jay married Livingston in the parlor of her father's home on April 28, 1774. The couple would have six children, and Sarah Livingston would be a major support and influence on Jay throughout her life. In his work on Jay, Stahr describes Sarah as "an ardent American patriot, perhaps more vocal than her restrained husband."

As the newlyweds spent their honeymoon in New York's northern counties, there was political activity in New York City. In response to the punitive measures imposed on Boston as a result of the Boston Tea Party, New Yorkers had appointed a committee to "take into consideration the measures of Parliament relative to Boston." When Jay and his wife returned to the city in late May, Jay learned that he had been named to this committee. At the initial meeting of this group consisting of 51 men, Jay was appointed to a subcommittee of four assigned to prepare a response to a letter the New Yorkers had received from Boston. The subcommittee drafted a letter that called for a meeting of delegates from all the colonies to review the situation in Boston and determine how to protect "our common rights." In July, the committee of 51 appointed Jay and four others to represent New York at the Continental Congress.

On September 5, 1774, the delegates to the First Continental Congress met in Philadelphia. The early meetings generally took care of housekeeping items, such as choosing Charles Thomson to serve as their secretary. Early in their initial meetings, an express rider arrived and reported that there had been fighting between British troops and Americans near Boston and that British cannons had begun firing at the city. The delegates viewed this report as an indication that a war with the mother country had started, and many were relieved to learn that the report was false. However, other delegates viewed the concern over the report as an indication that the colonies were ill-prepared to take up arms and that this issue needed to be addressed.

Congress then appointed a committee of 24, including Jay, to prepare a paper detailing the colonists' rights, their grievances with England, and proposals on addressing the problems. With both loyalists and those considered radicals like John Adams, the committee found it difficult to reach a consensus. Although Jay was generally considered a conservative, he sided with Adams during the committee debates. The problem of reaching an agreement was solved when Paul Revere arrived, carrying a copy of the Suffolk Resolves. The Resolves called on the people of Massachusetts to resist "the unparalleled usurpation of unconstitutional power" while at the same time affirming that King George was "our rightful sovereign." After a single day of debate, Congress unanimously approved the Resolves.

As a member of Congress, Jay also took part in the debates that led to the Continental Association. As detailed by Stahr, according to notes taken by John Adams, Jay took the position that "negotiation, suspension of commerce, and war are the only three things. War is by general consent to be waived at present. I am for negotiation and suspension of commerce." Thus, on October 20, 1774, Congress formed the Continental Association effective December 1, 1774, that prohibited both imports and exports with Great Britain, Ireland, and the British West Indies. Jay became one of the signers of the Association.

In April of 1775, Jay was once again one of the New Yorkers elected to represent his state at the Second Continental Congress. As relations between the colonies and England grew worse, he remained as one of the members of Congress who hoped to avoid war and reconcile with Great Britain. In May of 1776, Jay left Congress to spend time with his wife, who was ill, and with his father, who also suffered from poor health. During this time, he served as a member of New York's Provincial Congress. As a result, Jay was not in Philadelphia when Congress voted to approve the Declaration of Independence. Some question whether he would have supported the measure, but John Adams certainly was not one of them. On July 4, 1823, In Quincy, Massachusetts, Adams rose to offer a toast and said to, "the excellent President, Governor, Ambassador and Chief Justice, John Jay, whose name was not subscribed to the Declaration of Independence, as it ought to have been, for he was one of its ablest and faithful supporters."

When Adams called Jay an excellent president, he referred to his service as the President of Congress. Jay was elected to that position in the summer of 1778. During his tenure, Congress had problems due to a high turnover of delegates and their frequent absences. Nevertheless, Jay held this post for ten months, and during this period, he composed more than 500 letters on behalf of Congress. He also had the responsibility to meet with and entertain representatives from foreign countries.

Jay's time as President of Congress was a difficult one for him. According to his biographer, it has been called the "year of division." That same historian concludes that his greatest contribution may have been preventing a quarrelsome Congress from descending into chaos. Jay himself grew in the role. Through correspondence and by supporting the Commander in Chief, he had solidified a friendship with George Washington. In addition, his frustrations turned his thoughts to creating a strong national government. Finally, his knowledge about the views of the major members of Congress would aid him in the tasks he now undertook. First as his country's representative in Spain and then in Paris when he joined the American team whose job was to negotiate a peace treaty with England.

Jay and his wife Sarah set sail for Spain in late October 1779. Congress had given Jay the task of seeking recognition of the United States and hopefully an alliance against England as well as financial support from Spain for the new nation. Knowing he had little to offer the European country in return, he wrote Washington noting that the goals of his mission, "however just, will not be easily attained, and therefore its success will be precarious and probably partial." As it turned out, even these limited hopes proved to be unattainable. Spain refused to receive Jay as the Minister of the United States and declined to recognize American independence because of concerns that such recognition could ignite similar revolutions in their colonies. Nevertheless, Jay successfully obtained a $170,000 loan that the United States government pledged to repay. After this very modest success, he left Spain in May of 1782 and headed to Paris to join in the negotiations with England to end the Revolutionary War.

The American negotiating team included Jay, Benjamin Franklin, John Adams, and Henry Laurens. However, only Jay and Franklin were present in Paris; the other Americans would join them later. David Hartley and Richard Oswald represented England. Congress had directed the American team to keep the French government informed about the progress of the talks. Jay wrote a letter protesting this directive because he believed the Americans could achieve better terms without French involvement. Congress reversed their decision, and a treaty was negotiated with favorable terms for the United States. The Treaty of Paris was signed on September 3, 1783, and included British recognition of the United States as an independent nation and established boundaries that allowed the new country to expand westward. According to Arthur G. Sharp in his work, *Not Your Father's Founders,* the most surprised countries on hearing of the accord were France and Spain. John Adams gave Jay the bulk of the credit for the treaty saying he was "of more importance than any of the rest of us." Adams also noted that the French had bestowed on him the title of 'le Washington of the negotiation.' He called the description a flattering compliment to which he had not a right, saying it "belongs to Mr. Jay."

When Jay returned to New York in July of 1784, he learned that Congress had elected him to the post of Secretary of Foreign Affairs. As detailed by the historian Joseph Ellis in his book *The Quartet,* Jay set certain conditions for accepting the post. He required that he be free to appoint his staff, that he could speak as a representative of the confederation as a collective and (in the words of Ellis) "a rather audacious demand that the Congress move from its current location in Trenton to New York to facilitate his family obligations. It is a measure of Jay's prestige and the delegates' desperation that all the conditions he proposed were found acceptable."

In his new post, Jay sought to establish a strong American foreign policy. He prioritized establishing a stable American currency and paying off the country's Revolutionary War debt. He also worked to secure the recognition of the new nation by the established European powers. Jay also concerned himself with securing Newfoundland fishing rights and setting the country's borders under the best terms available at the time, and protecting American sailing ships from pirates. Unfortunately, his efforts were hampered by a Congress that was often absent or indecisive. Moreover, the country under the Articles of Confederation had neither an army nor a navy, so war may well have been disastrous. So, it may be said that his chief accomplishment when he left this post in 1789 was avoiding any such conflict.

When the Constitutional Convention was held in Philadelphia in 1787, Jay was blocked from joining the New York delegation by Governor George Clinton and his upstate supporters. By this time, Jay was known to be a proponent of a strong national government, which Clinton opposed. Jay had exhibited his preference for a strong executive branch as far back as 1777 when practically on his own he wrote the New York Constitution, which gave more authority to the executive than any other state constitution. As a result, the only member of the New York delegation who was a nationalist was Alexander Hamilton, who was certain to be outvoted by the other two New York delegates who opposed any changes to the Articles of Confederation.

After the convention produced the proposed Constitution, Jay took a leading role in supporting its ratification. He joined Hamilton and James Madison in writing *The Federalist Papers*. The papers were a series of 85 articles aimed at persuading reluctant New York state convention members to ratify the new Constitution. This would be a major task when New York chose its state delegates to consider the matter; only 19 of the 65 elected were known to favor ratification. Jay, of course, was one of them.

The convention met in Poughkeepsie, New York, and Jay proved to be a major force during the debates. Many of those opposed to the

Constitution called for its approval only with amendments that a second Constitutional Convention would be required to consider. Others supported ratification conditioned upon a right to secede from the union. A vote of 31 to 28 defeated the latter proposal.

Jay drafted a letter to address the question of amendments. The letter New York would send to the other states urged them to call another convention to consider proposed amendments. New York did propose amendments, but the state ratified the Constitution without making their adoption or consideration by a second convention a requirement. The vote to ratify was also a close one, 30 to 27. Jay proved successful in using both the carrot and the stick to sway those opposed to his side. The carrot being support for consideration of amendments to the Constitution and the stick being that New York City would secede and form its state if New York failed to ratify. Indeed, Jay's letter may well have been the driving force that resulted in New York joining the Union without conditions.

Once the Constitution had been ratified, it was obvious that George Washington would be the first president. When the president went about assembling his cabinet, he offered Jay the Secretary of State position. This post would have continued his role as Secretary of Foreign Affairs, and he declined the offer instead of accepting a position Washington called "the keystone of our political fabric" Chief Justice of the United States. Washington nominated Jay to the position on the same day he signed the Judiciary Act of 1789, which created the post. Two days later, Jay was unanimously confirmed by the United States Senate. The Jay court's main role was establishing the rules and procedures the court would follow. Jay himself did establish a precedent for the Supreme Court in 1790 when the Treasury Secretary and his old friend Alexander Hamilton wrote to the Chief Justice asking that the Court endorse legislation allowing the federal government to assume state debts. Jay responded that the Court could not endorse legislation, only rule on the constitutionality of cases brought before it. Jay's response predated Chief Justice Marshall's court ruling in the landmark case *Marbury v. Madison* by more than a decade.

In 1792 The Federalist Party nominated Jay as its candidate for Governor of New York. Jay received more votes than his opponent

George Clinton, but his majority was challenged based on vote technicalities in three counties that had delivered Jay his victory. Clinton supporters controlled the State legislature and the state courts, and as a result, enough Jay votes were disqualified to award Clinton the victory.

By the year 1794, the young United States of America was on the verge of another war with England. The former mother country blocked American exports, had failed to leave forts in the northern United States as called for by the Treaty of Paris, and seized American ships and supplies headed for France and impressing American sailors. President Washington gave Jay the task of negotiating a settlement with the English. In Jay's view, his country was totally unprepared for war. He negotiated what came to be known as the Jay Treaty, which ended British control of the northwestern forts but failed to address the country's concern relative to shipping rights and impressment. The emerging political party led by Thomas Jefferson, known as the Democratic-Republicans, denounced the treaty. In the House, James Madison and in the Senate, Aaron Burr, made speeches condemning it. The opposition to the treaty allowed Jay to joke that he could if he wished, make his way from one end of the country to the other by the light of his burning effigies.

Nevertheless, president Washington stood by the treaty, approved by the Senate 20-10, receiving exactly the two-thirds majority required for its adoption. In August of 1795, Washington signed the treaty, and given the fact that while attacking Jay could be done easily, the same was not true when it came to Washington. As a result, the criticisms of the treaty became more moderate in tone. In Jay's view, he had achieved his primary objective, avoiding a war the United States was ill-prepared to fight.

Having been defeated in a disputed election for Governor of New York in 1792, Jay was the obvious Federalist choice for that office in 1795. In May of that year, he was elected Governor, and he resigned as Chief Justice on June 29, 1795. He served as New York's Governor until 1801. His accomplishments as Governor included reforming the prison system, limiting the death penalty and abolishing flogging, constructing canals, and signing a bill that would gradually end slavery in the state.

Despite the measures he took as Governor and the fact that he was a founder of the New York Manumission Society, Jay's record of slavery is mixed. As late as the 1810 census, he is recorded as owning a slave.

John Jay (1745–1829)

John Jay's grave.

He had over the years continued to purchase enslaved people and grant their freedom once he believed their work to "have afforded a reasonable retribution." Yet in the close 1792 election for Governor, his views on slavery cost him votes in upstate New York Dutch areas where slavery was very much practiced. Then in 1794, when he negotiated the Jay Treaty, he angered many southern Americans when he abandoned the demand for compensation for slaves who had been freed and transported to other areas by the British after the Revolution.

In 1801 Jay declined the Federalist nomination to run for another term as Governor. That same year President John Adams nominated Jay, and the Senate confirmed him to return to the Supreme Court as Chief Justice. But, again, Jay declined to serve, opting to retire from public life. Adam's then nominated John Marshall to the post and he became the man who shaped the modern Court and one of the most significant judges in the history of this country.

Jay retired to his farm in Westchester County, New York. His wife Sarah passed away shortly after that. Jay continued to enjoy good health, and with one very notable exception, he stayed out of the political arena. In 1819 he wrote a letter condemning Missouri's bid to enter the union as a slave state. He wrote that slavery "ought not to be introduced nor permitted in any of the new states."

On the evening of May 14, 1829, Jay suffered what probably was a stroke. He passed away three days later and was laid to rest per his wishes in what is known as the John Jay Cemetery in Rye, New York, only open to the public once a year. This is also the only Founder's cemetery protected by barbed wire.

For many years Jay was somewhat of a forgotten founder. Many people had heard of him, but few were aware of the depth of his accomplishments and contributions to the establishment of the United States of America. As the historian, Joseph Ellis has stated, "We can argue about who should be on the top of the list of most important founders until the cows come home, but it's clear he (Jay) should be part of the list."

Fencing with barbed wire protects the Jay Cemetery.

Thomas Johnson
(1732–1819)

One of the Original Supremes

Buried at Mount Olivet Cemetery,
Frederick, Maryland.

**Continental Association • Continental Congress
Military • Supreme Court Justice**

This founder served the young country in multiple positions during both the Revolutionary and post Constitution periods. He was elected to Maryland's colonial General Assembly, a position he held for more than a decade. He was a member of a committee established to study the constitutional rights of colonial Maryland citizens and to offer guidance to the Stamp Act Congress. He was one of the patriots who openly advocated a break with England when many of his contemporaries were urging a policy of reconciliation. He was a member of Maryland's Committee of Correspondence established to maintain communication with the other American colonies. He was elected to represent Maryland in the First Continental Congress. During the Revolution, he served as a brigadier general in the Maryland militia. He then was selected to be Maryland's first governor. After the Constitution's ratification, he became Chief Justice of the General Court of Maryland and then was appointed to be one of the first associate justices on the United States Supreme Court. The name of this accomplished American was Thomas Johnson.

Thomas Johnson

On November 4, 1731, Johnson was born near Saint Leonard's Creek in Calvert County, Maryland. He was the fifth of twelve children born to his father Thomas Johnson and his wife, Dorcas Johnson. When he was a boy, his parents moved the family to Annapolis. He received his education at home, and after studying the law, he was admitted to the colonial bar. He was working in the colonial land office where he met Anne Jennings, his boss's daughter. In 1766 Johnson married Jennings, and the couple would have seven children.

Johnson's initial foray into the political world came in 1762 when he was elected to the lower house of Maryland's Colonial Assembly. He served in that office until 1774. During this period, he also practiced law and invested in an iron furnace with three of his brothers near Frederick, Maryland.

Midway through 1774, a general meeting of representatives from all the colonies was called for with the delegates to meet in Philadelphia that September. Johnson was among the delegates selected to represent Maryland at what became known as the First Continental Congress. On October 20, 1774, Congress established the Continental Association, the colonial answer to the Coercive Acts passed by the British Parliament. These measures aimed to restructure the colonial administration in the American colonies and punish Massachusetts for the Boston Tea Party. The association imposed an immediate ban on British tea and, beginning December 1, 1774, banned importing or consuming any goods from England. Johnson favored these measures and was among the founders who signed the document creating the association.

A year later, Johnson affixed his signature on The Olive Branch Petition. In the petition, Congress made a plea to the British king to address the growing rifts between the mother country and the colonies. By this time, Congress was clearly unaware that the king had already made up his mind relative to the American colonies declaring that "the die is now cast" and that the colonists "must either submit or triumph." On June 15, 1775, as relations with England worsened, Johnson nominated George Washington to be the commander in chief of the Continental Army.

Having served in Congress with Johnson, John Adams offered his opinion that "Johnson, of Maryland, has a clear and cool head, an extensive knowledge of trade as well as the law. He is a deliberating man, but not a shining orator; his passion and imagination do not appear enough for an orator; his reason and penetration appear but not his rhetoric." There can be little doubt that Johnson was a deliberate man or viewed that as a strength. As he once told Adams, "We ought not to lay down a rule in passion."

In January of 1776, Johnson left Congress to serve as a brigadier general in the Maryland Colonial militia. During the winter months at the end of that year, Johnson led his troops to New Jersey to assist Washington during his retreat through that state.

The initial State Constitution of Maryland called for an election of a Governor by the two branches of the state legislature. That vote was taken in February of 1777, and Johnson was elected. He received forty votes compared to nine for Samuel Chase, who was the closest competitor.

Johnson was inaugurated as the state's first governor on March 21, 1777. When in the summer of that year, a British fleet under Admiral Howe's command sailed up the Chesapeake, Johnson issued a proclamation. In it, he called upon the people of his state to repel any possible invasion of Maryland. He noted that "Our wives, our children, and our country implore our assistance: motives amply sufficient to arm every man who can be called a man." The British fleet, for some reason, headed to Pennsylvania and invaded that state instead.

After his term as governor in 1779, Johnson moved to Frederick County, Maryland. A year later, he was elected to the Maryland House of Delegates. The first of three elections that would send him to serve in that body. In 1788 he was a delegate to the Maryland convention called to ratify the United States Constitution. A year later, President Washington appointed him to be the first United States Judge for the District of Maryland, but Johnson declined the appointment. In 1790 he did accept the post of the chief judge of the general court of Maryland. Then, in 1791, Washington chose him to be one of the first associate judges to serve on the United States Supreme Court.

The historian Timothy Hall wrote of Johnson's service on the highest court in the land: "Perhaps no justice ever came to a seat on the US Supreme Court more reluctantly than Maryland's Thomas Johnson, and no justice ever served on the Court for a shorter tenure than he did. By the last decade of the 18th century, age and bodily infirmity persuaded Johnson to retire from what had been a busy public life. But at the request of President George Washington, a longtime acquaintance and business partner, Johnson attempted the post of associate justice, only to discover shortly that 'the office and the man do not fit.' He left his seat on the court for a long retirement leaving little record of his brief presence there."

In August of 1795, following the resignation of Secretary of State Edmund Jennings Randolph, Washington offered the post to Johnson. Writing to his old friend, the president stated, "You know of my wishes of old to bring you into the administration. Where then is the necessity of my repeating them? No time more than the present ever required the aid of your abilities. To have yours would be pleasing to me, and I verily believe would be agreeable to the community at large. It is with you to

Thomas Johnson's grave.

decide." Johnson responded by pointing to his age and his health, saying, "I do not think that I could do credit to the office of Secretary. I cannot persuade myself that I possess the necessary qualifications for it, and I am sure I am too old to expect improvement."

Johnson's final public act was his memorial eulogy following Washington's death in 1799. Johnson passed away on October 25, 1819, at the Maryland estate of his son-in-law. He was laid to rest in the Johnson family vault in the All Saints Parish Cemetery in Frederick, Maryland. In 1913 his remains were moved to Mount Olivet Cemetery, also located in Frederick.

In considering Johnson's contributions to the country's founding, we should consider the words written by Richard Henry Lee's grandson. He called Johnson "one of the ablest men in the old Congress. There did not live in these times which 'tried men's souls' a purer patriot or a more efficient citizen. No Roman citizen ever loved his country more. His private virtues entitled him to veneration and love. Thomas Johnson was, indeed, an honor to the cause of liberty."

William Samuel Johnson
(1727–1819)
The Great Conciliator

Buried at Christ Episcopal Church Cemetery,
Stratford, Connecticut.

U.S. Constitution • Continental Congress • U.S. Senate

William Samuel Johnson was one of the best educated of the Founders and, like others, had strong ties with England, which made renouncing the king personally tricky. He lived in London for four years (1767–1771) and had many good friends in England. Torn by conflicting loyalties, he remained neutral during the revolution, speaking out only against extremism on both sides. Once independence was achieved, Johnson felt free to participate in the government. He thus served in the Confederation Congress, representing Connecticut (1785–1787), and played a significant role as a delegate to the Constitutional Convention. He was one of thirty-nine signers of the Constitution who together represented twelve states. Later he represented Connecticut in the United States Senate and served as the third president of Kings College, now known as Columbia University.

William Samuel Johnson was born in Stratford, Connecticut, on October 7, 1727. His father was a well-known Anglican clergyman and later president of Kings College. His mother was Charity Floyd Nicoll, who was born in Long Island and died in 1758. Johnson received his

William Samuel Johnson (1727–1819)

William Samuel Johnson

primary education at home. He then went to Yale and graduated in 1744. In 1747 he was awarded a master of arts degree from Yale, and an honorary master's from Harvard.

He was under considerable pressure from his father to become a minister but resisted and chose to study law and gained admission to the bar. He set up a practice in Stratford, representing clients from nearby New York as well as Connecticut. Before long, he had established business connections with various mercantile houses in New York City. In 1749 he married Anne Beach, a local businessman's daughter, and they had five daughters and six sons. Sadly, many of them died before reaching adulthood. In the 1750s, Johnson joined the Connecticut militia and earned the rank of colonel.

His political involvement began in the Connecticut legislature. He served in the lower house in 1761 and 1765 and the upper house in 1766 and 1771-1775. He also served on the colony's supreme court in the years 172-1774. In between his service in the legislature from 1767 to 1771, Johnson lived in London, serving as Connecticut's agent in its attempt to settle the colony's claim to Mohegan lands in eastern Connecticut. He won the case and made many friends in England during this time, and Oxford awarded him an honorary degree in 1766. He sharply criticized British policy toward the colonies while there. He had attended the Stamp Act Congress in 1765 and served on the committee that drafted an address to the king, arguing the right of the colonies to decide tax policies for themselves. He also had opposed the Townshend Acts passed by Parliament in 1767 to pay for the French and Indian War. Now his experience in England convinced him that the British policies were shaped more by ignorance of American conditions than through sinister designs of a wicked government as many Patriots alleged.

As the Patriots became more radical in their demands for independence, Johnson was skeptical and found it challenging to commit to it. He thought that an independent America would quickly factionalize and become the easy victim of foreign invaders who would become our new enemy. He decided to work for peace between England and the colonies and to oppose extremism on both sides. He was a very prudent and cautious man who abhorred open conflict and violence. His legal background and his religious practices led him to favor peaceful solutions to disputes. It was by quiet diplomacy that he had become part of Connecticut's political elite. He was so highly thought of he was elected to the First Continental Congress in 1774, but he refused to participate; a move strongly criticized by the Patriots who removed him from militia command. He was also strongly criticized when he visited with British commander General Thomas Gage to end hostilities after Lexington and Concord. That led to his arrest for communicating with the enemy, but the charges were eventually dropped.

Remarkably Johnson's pro-peace activities never seriously damaged his prestige. Once the war was over, he resumed his political career. He served in the Confederation Congress from 1785 to 1787, where it is said he was one of the most popular and influential delegates. He was selected to represent Connecticut as a delegate to the Constitutional Convention in 1787, along with Oliver Ellsworth and Roger Sherman. There he played a significant role. His expressive and eloquent speeches around the topic of representation had great weight in the debate. He favored a strong federal government to protect the rights of Connecticut and other small states from encroachment by their larger neighbors. He supported the New Jersey Plan, which called for a unicameral legislature with equal representation of the states. Later he gave his full support to the Connecticut Compromise, which called for a bicameral legislature with the upper house (Senate) providing equal representation for all states.

Towards the end of the convention, the delegates appointed a committee to revise and arrange the articles agreed upon. Johnson was appointed chair of the committee. Other notable committee members were Alexander Hamilton, Gouverneur Morris, James Madison, and Rufus King. On September 17, 1787, 39 delegates representing 12 states signed the Constitution, including Johnson. Three delegates (Randolph, Mason, and Gerry) refused to sign, and Rhode Island refused to participate. Johnson went on to play an active role in Connecticut's ratification process, emphasizing the advantages that would accrue to the small states under the Constitution.

Johnson became the first president of Columbia College in 1787 and became one of Connecticut's first senators in 1789. Johnson played a significant role in shaping the Judiciary Act of 1789, a critical law that established the federal judiciary system's details. He generally supported Hamiltonian measures that sought to strengthen the role of the executive in the federal government. When the federal government moved from New York to Philadelphia at the end of the first congress in 1791, Johnson resigned to retain his position at Columbia, where he successfully recruited faculty and improved the school's reputation for scholarship.

Johnson retired from Columbia in 1800, a few years after his wife died, and married Mary Brewster Beach, a relative of his first wife. They lived at his birthplace in Stratford, where he died in 1819 at the age of 92. He is buried in Christ Episcopal Church Cemetery in Stratford, Connecticut.

A favorite expression of Johnson's that gives insight into his personality and success is "To keep your secret is wisdom; to expect others to keep it is folly."

William Samuel Johnson's grave.

John Paul Jones
(1747–1792)

"I have not yet begun to fight!"

Buried at US Naval Academy Chapel,
Annapolis, Maryland.

Military

John Paul Jones, along with John Barry, John Adams, and others, is credited with being the "Father of the American Navy." Of Scottish descent, he served on British merchant ships before joining the Continental Navy during the American Revolution. There, he became the most famous naval hero during that conflict. However, after the war, he lost his command in the United States. He then served in the Russian Navy and died in Paris, France. His body was lost for over 100 years before it was rediscovered and ceremoniously returned to the United States in the early twentieth century.

John Paul was born on July 6, 1747, on the estate of Arbigland near Kirkbean in the Stewartry of Kirkcudbright, Scotland, to John Paul Sr., a gardener at the estate, and his wife, Jean McDuff. Kirkcudbright is in the southwest corner of Scotland, on the Irish Sea. The Estate of Arbigland was situated along the coast, owned by William Craik.

At age twelve or thirteen, circa 1760, Paul went to sea as a cabin boy on merchant marine and slave ships, including *King George* and *Two Friends*, plying the Atlantic slave trade between England, America, the West Indies, and Africa. His older brother, William Paul, had married and settled in Fredericksburg, Virginia, and John would visit when he

John Paul Jones

was on that side of the Atlantic. In Jamaica, in 1768, he left *Two Friends* and found passage back to Scotland.

In 1768, aboard the brig *John*, both the captain and first mate died of yellow fever. Paul took control and navigated the ship back to port. The grateful Scottish owners made him master of the ship and crew and gave him ten percent of the cargo. Now a captain, Paul led two voyages before running into trouble.

On the second voyage, 1770, Paul was accused of being unnecessarily cruel when he had a crewman flogged for trying to start a mutiny over wages. Though the claim was dismissed, his reputation was tarnished when the sailor, related to an influential family, died a few weeks later.

Paul was arrested and imprisoned at Kirkcudbright but was released on bail and encouraged to leave the area.

Now the commander of the 22-gun London-registered *Betsy*, John Paul headed out to sea. For nearly two years, he was engaged in trade with Tobago in the West Indies. Once again, Paul got in trouble with his crew. Some crewmen threatened a mutiny and attacked their captain. One of them, a man named Blackton, was killed in a swordfight with Paul. Fearing trouble with the Admiralty Court, Paul left Tobago and headed to Virginia, essentially a fugitive from justice.

In Fredericksburg, he found his brother had died without any immediate family, and he arranged his affairs. He then concealed his identity by appending the last name "Jones" and decided to stay in the colonies.

Now John Paul Jones, as the American Revolution commenced in late 1775, he joined the new Continental Navy as a lieutenant on the 24-gun flagship *Alfred*, thanks to an endorsement from Richard Henry Lee. On this voyage, he was the first to hoist the Grand Union Flag over a naval vessel. The *Alfred* raided military supplies in the Bahamas.

Jones was short in stature, possibly five feet five inches, earning him the nickname "Little Jones" with Thomas Jefferson and others. Unlike many other merchant seamen, he was well-dressed, wore a sword, and behaved nobly. He had a Scottish brogue, and light Celtic features. Though sociable, he was known as a harsh military master. A romantic who wrote poetry and letters and spoke French, he never married. However, he was involved in many romances. Above all, he was fearless.

By May 1776, he was made captain of the 21-gun sloop *Providence*, with which he destroyed British fisheries in Nova Scotia and captured sixteen British ships through the summer. Commodore Esek Hopkins then switched Jones back to captain the *Alfred*. He was ordered to rescue prisoners from Nova Scotia and to raid British shipping. That winter, he captured the *Mellish*, which was carrying winter clothing to General Burgoyne in Canada.

Due to disagreements with Commodore Hopkins about campaign plans, Jones was demoted to a smaller ship, the USS *Ranger*, on June 14, 1777. He sailed to France on November 1, 1777, to aid the American mission there. In France, he advised Benjamin Franklin, Silas Deana, and Arthur Lee regarding naval recommendations. He was promised command of a new vessel, *Indien*, which was being constructed in Amsterdam. However, the British managed to pressure the Dutch to sell it to France, leaving Jones without a command. During this time, he developed a close friendship with Franklin.

After France agreed to enter the war on the Americans' side in February 1778, Jones was back at sea about USS *Ranger*. His was the first American vessel to be formally saluted by the French. In April, he set sail for the familiar Irish Sea, between Ireland and England, and harassed British shipping.

On April 17, 1778, he convinced his crew to attack Whitehaven, England, where he had begun his maritime career. However, the winds drove them toward Ireland. There, they attempted to attack HMS *Drake* anchored at Carrickfergus, Ireland. The sailors balked at attacking in broad daylight, and the night attack was botched by the mate who was to drop anchor when they were next to their target. So, Jones turned *Ranger* out to sea and headed back to Whitehaven. On the night of the 23rd, Jones and two boats of fifteen men attempted to set fire to and sink all of Whitehaven's ships, including merchant and coal transports. While they were able to spike the defensive cannons, they had difficulty starting enough fires. They were forced to retreat when the townspeople were alerted.

Next, crossing to Scotland, he headed to St. Mary's Isle near Kirkcudbright to attempt to capture Dunbar Douglas, the Earl of Selkirk. They found the earl missing and instead negotiated with his wife. The butler handed Jones a bag of coal with some silver on top, fooling the Americans that they had a bag of treasure. The crew had wanted to continue plundering, but Jones wanted to return to the ship. He permitted them to only take a large silver tray with the Selkirk coat of arms, which he later bought at auction and returned to the earl after the war.

Jones then turned *Ranger* back to Carrickfergus to engage the *Drake* again. On the afternoon of April 24, 1778, the two ships battled until the British captain was slain. The Americans captured the *Drake,* and Jones put his lieutenant, Simpson, in charge of it. While returning to

Brest, France, the two ships separated due to Jones chasing another prize. Though both ships reached port safely, Jones filed for court-martial against Simpson for unclear reasons and detained him on the ship. Simpson was ultimately released, however.

Jones was promoted and placed in command of five French and American vessels in 1779. His flagship was now the 42-gun USS *Bonhomme Richard*, named in honor of Benjamin Franklin's character Poor Richard. In August, Jones's squadron set sail for the Irish Sea, acting as a diversion for a large Spanish and French fleet heading to England. British ships pursued Jones as he broke away and sailed around Scotland into the North Sea. While closing on a merchant convoy, The *Bonhomme Richard* encountered the 50-gun HMS *Serapis* and the 22-gun *Countess of Scarborough*. As the merchant ships escaped, what was known as the Battle of Flamborough Head began. While *Serapis* engaged *Bonhomme Richard*, the American ship *Alliance* fired at *Countess*. Jones brought *Bonhomme* close to *Serapis*. The ships and crews fired at one another, clearing the decks. The *Alliance* then sailed past, firing a broadside that damaged both ships. *Countess* was pulled away to engage one of the other American ships downwind.

Bonhomme Richard was now burning and sinking. *Serapis* came alongside and, seeing the ensign shot away, asked if the *Bonhomme* would surrender. Believing Jones dead, one of the American officers shouted a surrender, but Jones appeared and shouted something like, "I am determined to make you strike." Some heard him say, "I may sink, but I'll be damned if I strike." But he never actually said, "I have not yet begun to fight!"

Things got uglier. The *Serapis'* crew tried to board the *Bonhomme* but were repulsed when a grenade ignited gunpowder on the lower decks of the British attacker. The *Alliance* came around again and blasted both ships. Captain Pearson of the *Serapis*, seeing no chance to escape, struck his colors and surrendered. Most of the crew of the *Bonhomme Richard* then transferred to the British ship. Jones took command. After trying to repair the *Bonhomme Richard* over the next two days proved fruitless, the ship was allowed to sink and Jones and his squadron headed for Texel, Holland.

The following year, while the British saw Jones as a pirate, French King Louis XVI granted him the title Chevalier. He also received a sword and *l'Institution du Mérite Militaire* (Order of Military Merit). With the Revolutionary War nearing its end, Jones was to take command of the new 74-gun USS *America* in June 1782. However, the ship was traded to the French as a replacement for the *Le Magnifique*, which had been lost off Boston that year. Jones was next assigned to collect the prize money due his former crew from the ships captured and left in European ports.

In 1787, when the Continental Congress struck a gold medal honoring him for his "valor and brilliant service," Jones made sure the title Chevalier was used. However, he was without prospects, and on April 23, 1787, entered the service of Empress Catherine II of Russia as a rear admiral aboard the 24-gun flagship *Vladimir*. He participated in the Liman campaign against the Turks in the Black Sea. While victorious, Jones transferred to the North Sea due to other officers' jealousy, some British also serving Russia. Jones was accused of sexual misconduct, allegedly raping a 12-year-old girl, but a French emissary investigated on his behalf and found the charges baseless. Jones admitted to "frolicking with the girl for a small cash payment" but denied he had taken her virginity. During this time, he authored the *Narrative of the Campaign of the Liman*.

On June 8, 1788, the Russians awarded him the Order of St. Anne. Jones next went to Warsaw, Poland, in 1789, where he linked up with Tadeusz Kościuszko, the Polish general who served in the American Revolution. Kościuszko suggested Jones should leave the service of Russia and seek opportunities in Sweden. This, however, never materialized.

Though retaining his position as a rear admiral for Russia, Jones moved to Paris in May 1790. He benefitted from a pension for his service, and he tried numerous times to return to active duty. All were rebuffed.

Jones wrote his memoirs and had them published in Edinburgh. He planned to purchase an estate in the United States and had been appointed the US Consul to Algiers, but neither came to fruition due to his declining health. Jones was found dead lying face-down on his bed in his third-floor Paris apartment, No. 19 Rue de Tournon, on July 18, 1792. He was 45 years old. The cause of death was kidney disease. Frenchman

Pierrot Francois Simmoneau funded the mummification of the body and saw it was preserved in alcohol and interred in a lead coffin "in the event that should the United States decide to claim his remains, they might more easily be identified." Jones was buried at Saint Louis Cemetery in Paris, which belonged to the royal family. After the French Revolution, the property was sold, and the cemetery was forgotten.

Over the ensuing years, Jones appeared in the novel *The Pilot* in 1824 by James Fenimore Cooper. Alexander Dumas followed with *Captain Paul* in 1846. Jones also made a cameo in Herman Melville's novel *Israel Potter: His Fifty Years of Exile*. He appealed to historians and novelists due to his personality ad his accomplishments against the most powerful navy in the world.

The gaudy tomb of John Paul Jones at the US Naval Academy.

GRAVES of our FOUNDERS

US Ambassador to France General Horace Porter, circa 1900, began a six-year search to locate Jones's remains. Using an old Paris map, Porter and his team found the cemetery and located and exhumed five lead coffins. The third coffin, unearthed on April 7, 1905, later proved to contain Jones. The cause of death was analyzed, and his face compared to a bust by Jean-Antoine Houdon.

With great decorum, Jones's body was returned to the United States aboard the USS *Brooklyn*, escorted by three other cruisers. As the ships neared the coast, nine other battleships joined the procession. The following year, the remains were installed at the US Naval Academy in Bancroft Hall. President Theodore Roosevelt presided over a ceremony to honor Jones. In 1913, his remains were interred into a bronze and marble sarcophagus in the Naval Academy Chapel.

Jones has since appeared in many movies, books, and television programs. In 1999, the Port of Whitehaven pardoned him for the raid.

According to biographer Walter Herrick, "Jones was a sailor of indomitable courage, of strong will, and of great ability in his chosen career . . . He was also a hypocrite, a brawler, a rake, and a professional and social climber."

To many, he is also the founder of the United States Navy and emblematic of American courage.

Rufus King
(1755–1827)

The Last Federalist Candidate for President

Buried at Old Episcopal Churchyard,
Jamaica, New York.

Military • Continental Congress • U.S. Constitution

This founder represented two states in his distinguished career. He served as a delegate from Massachusetts in the Continental Congress and in 1787 at the Constitutional Convention. After the ratification of the Constitution, he represented New York in the United States Senate. As a young man, he served in the Continental Army where, by a stroke of luck, he avoided losing a leg. He also served as the United States Minister to Great Britain twice. He was a candidate for national office in unsuccessful campaigns three times. His name was Rufus King.

King was born on March 24, 1755, in Scarborough, Massachusetts, a location that has since become part of the state of Maine. His mother was Isabella Bragdon, and his father was Richard King, a prosperous farmer-merchant and sea captain. This financial success created envy among some of his neighbors, and when rioting broke out after the Stamp Act of 1765, the King household was targeted by a mob that ransacked the house, destroying much of the furniture. King's father became a staunch Tory who again faced an angry mob at his home in 1774. One historian

Rufus King

claims the latter event led to Richard King's death a year later and instilled in his son respect for order and reason.

At the age of twelve, King began his formal education at the Dummer Academy, today known as The Governor's Academy. He then attended Harvard College, and he graduated from that institution in 1777. He began to study law under Theophilus Parsons but suspended that study to join the militia and fight in the Revolutionary War. He served as an aide-de-camp under General Glover, who led a detachment to support a failed attempt to retake Rhode Island.

In his work *Rufus King and His Times*, Edward Hale Brush recounts an incident that occurred one morning when General Glover and his staff were seated around a table for breakfast. At one point, the firing of the British guns increased, and Glover sent King to investigate. King's seat at the gathering was taken by H. Sherburne, who had scarcely seated himself when a cannonball entered through a window and smashed Sherburne's ankle resulting in the amputation of his leg. Later in life, Sherburne's and King's paths would occasionally cross, and King would remark that it was he who should be wearing a wooden leg.

After his time in the military, King returned to the study of law under Parsons. He was admitted to the bar in 1780, and he began his law practice in Newburyport, Massachusetts. In 1783 King was elected to the Massachusetts General Court. He then represented his state in the Continental Congress, serving from 1784 to 1787. At the time, he was one of the youngest members of that Congress. The Congress met in New York City where King met Mary Alsop, the daughter of John Alsop, a wealthy merchant and one of the New York delegates. The couple married on March 30, 1786. The Kings had seven children, five of whom survived to adulthood.

In 1787 King repressed Massachusetts at the Constitutional Convention in Philadelphia, a gathering he had opposed just a year before. At just 32 years of age, he had already earned the reputation of being a brainy legislator and a gifted orator. Although he arrived in Philadelphia opposed to changing the Articles of Confederation, his mind was changed as he listened to the issues being debated. In his work on the convention, the historian Clinton Rossiter described King as "an enthusiastic, sharp-witted, persuasive nationalist, who was the champion Committeeman of the summer."

King was fiercely opposed to slavery, and in the debates relative to how the Constitution would address that issue, he made those feelings clear when he lobbied to halt the spread of that institution in the country. His views made him extremely unpopular with the southern delegates. At least one southern delegate, William Pierce, who left the convention before its conclusion, did not share these views. Pierce described King as "much distinguished for his eloquence and great parliamentary talents," adding that King "ranked among the luminaries of the present age." King would sign the proposed Constitution and then campaign strongly for its ratification.

King Manor historic site.

In 1788, at the urging of his good friend Alexander Hamilton, King closed his Massachusetts law practice and moved his family to New York City. He soon immersed himself in the state's politics, and in 1789 the New York legislature appointed him to be one of the state's original United States senators. As a senator, he was an ardent supporter of the economic policies proposed by the nation's first Secretary of the Treasury, the aforementioned Alexander Hamilton. He also supported the controversial treaty that John Jay had negotiated with Great Britain in 1795. The following year he resigned his senate post after being appointed the United States minister plenipotentiary to England by President Washington. He served in this position until 1803.

Upon returning to the United States, he became the Federalist Party candidate for vice president in the elections of 1804 and 1808. In 1804 the ticket of Thomas Jefferson and George Clinton crushed the Federalists in the electoral college 162-14. It was not much better four years later when James Madison and Clinton defeated Charles Pinckney and King by 122-47.

In 1812 King was once again appointed to the United States Senate, where he led the opposition to President Madison's handling of the War of 1812. Four years later, he was the last Federalist candidate for the Presidency, going up against James Monroe. In that contest, he won the electoral votes of just three states.

He returned to the Senate in 1820, where he strongly opposed the admission of Missouri to the union as a slave state. In a speech that year to an audience of whites and free blacks, he stated, "I have yet to learn that one man can make a slave of another. If one man cannot do so, no number of individuals can have any better right to do it." He lost the battle when the then Speaker of the House, Henry Clay, settled the dispute with the Missouri Compromise.

The worn grave of Rufus King.

King remained in the Senate until 1825 when President John Quincy Adams appointed him to represent the United States in Great Britain once again. He served in that post for a year before ill health forced him to resign and return to the states. At this point, he had represented his country in Great Britain under four different presidents.

In 1827 he passed away at his estate, King Manor, located in Queens County, New York. His manor remains and is open to visitors on certain days. He was laid to rest not far from his home in the Grace Episcopal Cemetery. For more than thirty years, he served the nation as both a diplomat and a politician throughout his public life. He also came to be one of the leaders of one of the first two political parties to rise in the country after the Constitution's ratification.

John Langdon
(1741–1819)

Senator from New Hampshire

Buried at Old North Cemetery,
Portsmouth, New Hampshire.

United States Constitution

John Langdon was a revolutionary leader and one of the first two senators from New Hampshire. He was a successful international trader and owner of merchant vessels and contributed his business acumen and fortune to the independence movement. He served in the militia, the state legislature, the Continental Congress, as governor, US Senator, and as a delegate to the Constitutional Convention, where he signed the historic document. He was the first President Pro Tempore of the United States Senate.

John Langdon was born on his parents' farm in Portsmouth, New Hampshire, on June 26, 1741. He attended Major Samuel Hale's Latin School in Portsmouth and then worked as a clerk in Daniel Rindge's counting-house. Both Langdon and his older brother Woodbury rejected the opportunity to join their father's successful agricultural pursuits, succumbing instead to the lure of the sea. With the idea of entering the sea trade, they apprenticed themselves to local naval merchants. Through Rindge's business, John Langdon went on several voyages to the West Indies. By the age of 22, he was captain of a cargo ship, and within a few years, he would purchase his own ships, and soon he and his brother's company were taking such products as lumber and beef to various ports

John Langdon

and returning with rum and sugar. By 1770 both men were rich and owned considerable property in the Portsmouth area.

The harsh economic measures enacted by England against the colonies, the seizure of a ship, *The Resolution*, which contained property of his, and the general atmosphere of interference in colonists' lives turned Langdon from apolitical to sympathizing with those who desired revolt against British rule. He served on the town committees elected to protest the tax Parliament enacted on the tea trade and to enforce a boycott of British goods organized throughout the colonies. In 1774 he was elected to the New Hampshire legislature, but growing impatient with politics, joined with a group of militiamen who raided Fort William and Mary (later renamed Fort Constitution) to seize munitions for use by the rebels.

John Langdon (1741–1819)

On January 25, 1775, Langdon was elected to a seat in the Second Continental Congress. He immediately aligned himself with those calling for independence. He made significant contributions in his one year in congress by serving on the committee that oversaw the establishment of the Continental Navy. He resigned in June 1776 to become an agent to oversee prize ships—those taken or captured in war—and to supervise the construction of several warships, including the *Ranger*, which was captained by John Paul Jones (see chapter 24, page 145), and the navy's first major warship the 74-gun *America*. Another of his responsibilities as a marine agent was supervising the importation and distribution of arms shipped from France to New England ports. These vital weapons were disguised in a complicated trade deal to maintain the appearance of French neutrality. The efforts to get cooperation and support from different states made Langdon feel strongly about a strong and efficient central government.

Elected again to the state legislature's lower house and rising to the rank of speaker, he devoted much of his energy to reorganizing the state militia into two brigades, one based in eastern New Hampshire and one in the west. Langdon himself took command of an elite company of light infantry in the Eastern brigade. Langdon's company of Light Horse Volunteers was often called a "silk stocking" outfit because it was composed of wealthy citizens selected from other units. Langdon financed the equipping of an expedition against British troops under British General John Burgoyne, and his company participated in the Battle of Bennington in August 1777. These troops played a major role in the victory and went on under General John Stark to force Burgoyne's surrender.

In 1778, Langdon's company participated in the Rhode Island campaign and was disbanded in the fall of that year. That ended Langdon's active military duty. Somehow amidst all this activity, he found time to get married to Elizabeth Sherburne, and the couple had one child, a daughter.

In 1784, he built at Portsmouth the mansion now known as the John Langdon house. Langdon was elected to two terms as President of New Hampshire, the title New Hampshire bestowed on its governor, one between 1785 and 1786 and then again between 1788 and 1789. In 1787 he was appointed to represent the state at the Constitutional Convention in Philadelphia. He was so anxious to attend that he paid his own expenses and that of fellow delegate Nicholas Gilman. At the convention, he soon became noted for his strong support of strengthening the national government. He signed the Constitution on September 17, 1787.

Langdon returned to New Hampshire and served as a delegate to the state convention that ratified the US Constitution. On June 21, 1788, New Hampshire's ratification was the ninth state to do so, putting the Constitution into effect. The vote was 57-47. He soon resigned as governor in 1789 to become one of the first US Senators. He served as the first president pro tempore and presided over the Senate's first session in which the electoral votes that made George Washington president were counted.

He retired from the Senate in 1801 and declined President Jefferson's offer to be Secretary of the Navy. Between then and 1812, he was active in New Hampshire politics. He was a member of the legislature from 1801 to 1805, twice holding the position of speaker. In 1805 he was elected governor and continued as such until 1811, except for a one-year hiatus in 1809. In 1812, due to his age and health, he refused the

The tomb of John Langdon.

Democratic-Republican vice-presidential nomination to run with James Madison. He chose instead to retire from public office.

John Langdon died in Portsmouth on September 18, 1819, at 78. He was interred at the Old North Cemetery in Portsmouth. Langdon, New Hampshire, is named after him, as is Langdon Street in Madison, Wisconsin.

Edward Langworthy
(1738–1802)

An Orphaned Founder

He was initially buried at the Old Episcopal Church in Baltimore, Maryland. The church was demolished in 1891, and the location of his remains is unknown.

Articles of Confederation

This founder's parents were likely among the first colonists shipped to Georgia. This conclusion is because he was born within five years of James Oglethorpe recruiting those in poorhouses and debtors' prisons to be the first to settle in the region. It appears his parents died when he was very young as he was raised in the Bethesda Orphan House in Savannah. Despite these challenging beginnings, he would rise to represent Georgia in the Continental Congress during the American Revolution and sign the Articles of Confederation. This document officially united the thirteen colonies as a country. Described by Burton Alva Knokle in *The Georgia Historical Quarterly* as a patriot, teacher, statesman, editor, writer, historian, and eminent citizen of two states, this founder's name was Edward Langworthy.

Langworthy was born in Savannah circa 1738. It appears his parents died when he was relatively young as he was raised and educated in Savannah's Bethesda Orphan House. He took his studies seriously as he became one of the instructors at the orphanage. At one point, he took out an

Edward Langworthy (1738–1802)

advertisement in a Georgia newspaper which read, "The subscriber having taken a convenient House, proposes to board eight young gentlemen at 22 per annum, and to instruct them in the Latin and Greek Languages. The greatest care will be taken to improve them in the English language and to accustom them to a just and agreeable manner in pronunciation and reading. Young ladies may be taught English Grammar, Writing, &c. privately." It appears that teaching as a profession appealed to him since he would take up the profession again later in life.

Edward Langworthy

In 1774, when the fires that became the American Revolution were already burning, Langworthy remained loyal to the British crown, as evidenced by his signing the Loyalist protest of the Savannah Resolutions. His Loyalist leanings did not last long as, within a year, he reversed his position entirely and was chosen secretary to the Revolutionary body known as the Council of Safety. Two months later, he became a member of the Georgia Provincial Congress, where he was appointed secretary of that body. In this position, Langworthy signed the initial delegates' credentials to represent Georgia at the Continental Congress meeting in Philadelphia. Among the credentials he signed was one for a good friend of his, Button Gwinnett. Gwinnett would affix his signature to the Declaration of Independence.

On June 7, 1777, the Georgia legislature elected Langworthy to serve as a delegate to the Continental Congress. As a representative from Georgia, he signed the Articles of Confederation on July 24, 1778. The Articles formally brought the thirteen states together, forming the United States of America. He was not a vocal member of Congress as he is not recorded as ever having made a motion though he did second on two occasions. He was among the representatives who spent time in York, Pennsylvania, when the Congress was moved there after the British army occupied Philadelphia. Based on a letter he wrote at the time, he had little liking for the city. After completing his service in Congress, Langworthy returned to Georgia, where he may well have begun the research on the state's first history, which he would work on for years but never complete. His papers involving this project have never been recovered.

In 1785, Langworthy moved to Baltimore, where he became part owner and the editor of the *Maryland Journal & Baltimore Advertiser*. The newspaper flourished and proved to be a successful business venture. In one open letter to the paper's readers, Langworthy and his co-owner, William Goddard, stated, "It would perhaps be to little Purpose to descant on the many Advantages derived from the Art of Printing; that the present Age is esteemed an Enlightened One, and that we are in the enjoyment of Political Independence, and Perfect Freedom in the important Concerns of Religion, may, in a great Degree, be ascribed to the Liberty of the Press."

When Langworthy was busy with his newspaper, the Baltimore religious heads of the Catholic, Episcopalian, and Presbyterian churches established the Baltimore Academy. The institution's purpose was to provide the young men in the area an opportunity to pursue a higher education without leaving home. Langworthy was chosen to head the school where he also taught the classics. It is not clear how long he labored at the Academy. It is known that he sold his interest in the newspaper on January 1, 1787, and that in March of that year, he completed his memoir of General Charles Lee. In 1792 this work was published in both New York and London.

In 1795, Langworthy was appointed to the post of Baltimore's Clerk of Customs. He would serve in this position until he died on November 2, 1802. He had impressed many in the Baltimore area relative to his conduct and life in his adopted second city.

His obituary stated, "After a severe illness of six days . . . the spirit of Edward Langworthy, Esq. deputy naval officer of the port of Baltimore, took its flight for 'another and a better world.' To eulogize the defunct is not the intention of the writer of this paragraph, suffice it to say, that his public and private walks in life were such as many may endeavor to imitate, but a few will attain to equal perfection."

Langworthy was laid to rest in the yard of Baltimore's Old Episcopal Church. That church was demolished in 1891, and the records of the graveyard were lost.

Robert Livingston
(1746–1813)

The Chancellor

Buried at St. Paul's Episcopal Church Cemetery,
Tivoli, New York.

Continental Congress • Committee of Five • Diplomat

Robert Livingston played several roles in the founding of the United States. He was a very prominent political figure in New York, where he served as the first Chancellor of New York, which was then the state's highest judicial officer. He held that office for 24 years. He was elected to the Continental Congress and was appointed to the Committee of Five, charged with drafting the Declaration of Independence. He administered the oath of office to George Washington in 1789, served as Minister to France in the Jefferson Administration, and negotiated the Louisiana Purchase.

Livingston was born on November 27, 1746, in New York City, the eldest son of Judge Robert Livingston and Margaret Beekman Livingston. The Livingstons were rich land barons and heavily involved in the governing of the colony of New York. Young Robert entered King's College (now Columbia University) at the age of 15. There he met and became close friends with John Jay (see page 124). Amid the rumblings of rebellion, Robert graduated from King's College in 1765 and immediately entered a legal apprenticeship with his father's cousin and later governor

Robert R. Livingston

of New Jersey, William Livingston. He was admitted to the bar in 1770 and that same year married Mary Stevens, the daughter of Continental Congressman John Stevens. He practiced law with John Jay and, in 1773, was appointed Recorder for New York City. He held that position until 1775, when his revolutionary sympathies made him unacceptable to the crown. He was immediately elected to the Continental Congress.

On June 11, 1776, Livingston became a member of the Committee of Five with Thomas Jefferson, Benjamin Franklin, John Adams, and Roger Sherman. They were tasked with drafting the Declaration of Independence. This appointment was seemingly a political maneuver designed to encourage New York into making a firm commitment to independence. Livingston felt that independence was desirable and inevitable but did not think that the time had yet come. Accordingly, he was one of the principal advocates of postponing the issue. He neither contributed to the draft nor signed the document.

The year 1777 was eventful for Livingston. He, John Jay, and Gouverneur Morris drafted New York's Constitution, which was submitted and approved. On July 30 of that year, he became the first Chancellor of New York, a position the new constitution had created and the highest judicial officer in the state. He held the position until 1777. That year, Livingston's home near Clermont, New York, was burned to the ground by the British Army under General John Burgoyne, in retribution for his siding with the Patriots. He rebuilt it between 1779 and 1782. The house is now a New York State Historic Site and a National Historic Landmark.

In 1781 Livingston became the Secretary of the Department of Foreign Affairs under the Articles of Confederation. During the two years he served in that position, he did all he could to strengthen America's alliance with France.

On April 30, 1789, Livingston, by being Chancellor of New York, administered the presidential oath of office to George Washington at Federal Hall in New York City, which was then the nation's capital. Washington appointed his friend, John Jay, to be Chief Justice of the Supreme Court. Alexander Hamilton was named Secretary of the Treasury. Despite Livingston's involvement, he was not rewarded with an office.

Perhaps for this reason and because he disagreed with Hamilton's federal assumption of state debts, Livingston turned anti-Federalist and entered a political alliance with members of the Jeffersonian opposition. In 1798 he ran for Governor of New York against John Jay, who had resigned from the Court, and lost. When Jefferson became President on March 4, 1801, he appointed Livingston the U.S. Minister to France. In that post until 1804, and aided by James Monroe's arrival, he negotiated the Louisiana Purchase, one of the country's greatest diplomatic coups. Overnight the size of the United States doubled. After signing the agreement on May 2, 1803, Livingston made this statement: "We have lived long, but this is the noblest work of our whole lives . . . the United States take rank this day among the first powers of the world."

The tomb of Robert Livingston.

During his time as U.S. Minister to France, Livingston met Robert Fulton. He developed the first viable steamboat, the *North River Steamboat* of Clermont, whose home port was the Livingston family home in Clermont, New York. On her maiden voyage, she left New York

City with him as a passenger, stopped briefly at Clermont, and continued up the Hudson River to Albany. The trip, which previously took nearly a week, was completed in just under 60 hours. In 1811 both men were appointed as members of the Erie Canal Commission funded by New York to explore a canal route to Lake Erie.

Robert Livingston died on February 26, 1813, a happy man having lived a full and successful life. He was buried in the Clermont Livingston vault at St. Paul's Church in Tivoli, New York. When the authors visited the grave, we were dismayed by the lack of memorialization at St. Paul's. There was no signage, no flag, no stone, nor any mention of his achievements or role in history. Today, both a bust in the United States Capitol and the name of New York's Masonic Library memorialize Robert Livingston as The Chancellor. Also, both Livingston County, Kentucky, and Livingston County, New York, are named for him.

Thomas Lynch Jr.
(1749–1779)
Youngest Signer of the Declaration to Die

Lost at Sea

Declaration of Independence

Thomas Lynch Jr. was both the second youngest person to sign the Declaration of Independence and the youngest signer at his death. Elected to the Continental Congress from South Carolina to replace his ailing father, Lynch arrived in time to sign the document in Philadelphia. Less than four years later, he and his wife were lost at sea.

Thomas Lynch Jr. was born August 5, 1749, in Prince George's Parish, South Carolina, to Thomas Lynch Sr. and his first wife, Elizabeth (née Allston). The family lived on the Hopseewee plantation near Winyah Bay, South Carolina, (now Georgetown) northeast of Charleston, where they raised primarily rice. Thomas had two older sisters, Sabina and Esther. After his mother, Elizabeth, died in 1755, Thomas's father married Hannah Motte, with whom he had another daughter named Elizabeth.

Young Thomas attended a local school in Georgetown before going to England to attend Eton College, where he graduated with honors, and then Cambridge. Law studies at the Middle Temple in London followed. After completing his studies in 1772, he returned to South Carolina. At that point, it was clear to Thomas he did not wish to pursue the law and followed his father in agriculture, taking over a nearby plantation named Peach Tree up the North Santee River in St. James Parish.

Thomas Lynch Jr. (1749–1779)

Thomas Lynch Jr.

On May 14, 1772, Lynch married Paige Shubrick, whom he had known at Georgetown. The couple lived at Peach Tree but never had any children.

Lynch, like his father, became involved in politics. On February 11, 1775, he was elected to the Provincial Congress in South Carolina, along with Charles Cotesworth Pinckney, John Rutledge, Charles Pinckney, Henry Laurens, Christopher Gadsden, Rawlins Lowndes, Arthur Middleton, Henry Middleton, Thomas Bee, and Thomas Heyward Jr. The group formed a constitution for the colony.

In June 1775, Lynch was elected as a captain of the 1st South Carolina Regiment, against the best wishes of his father, who urged him to wait for higher command. While out recruiting soldiers, Lynch became ill with bilious fever, which nearly killed him and left him sickly for the remainder of his days. He was unable to fulfill his military command.

In early 1776, Lynch's father suffered a stroke while serving in the Continental Congress. This inhibited his abilities, and on March 23, 1776, the South Carolina General Assembly elected Lynch to the Continental Congress as an additional delegate who would also assist his father. Lynch arrived in Philadelphia in time to sign the Declaration of Independence. His father was unable to. Arthur Middleton, Thomas Heyward Jr., and Edward Rutledge (the youngest signer by three months) also signed the document on behalf of South Carolina.

The Lynches were the only father-son duo to serve simultaneously in the Continental Congress. They were together in Philadelphia for a few months recuperating from their ailments before leaving for South Carolina late in the year. En route, the elder Lynch suffered another stroke and died in Annapolis, Maryland. Lynch buried his father there before returning to Peach Tree.

Back in South Carolina, Lynch's stepmother married South Carolina Governor William Moultrie, a very influential figure. Thomas's sister Sabina married James Hamilton. Their son, James Hamilton Jr., later became governor of South Carolina in 1830.

Lynch was sickly and retired from his duties in 1777. He spent two years in seclusion, attempting to recover. Unfortunately, there was nothing to be done, and the doctors suggested, despite the war in progress, for Lynch and his wife to sail to Europe to seek a cure. In late 1779, the couple boarded a ship in the West Indies bound for France. They were never heard from again. At the age of thirty, Lynch was the youngest signer to die.

As his father's heir and with no children of his own, Lynch stipulated in his will that the heirs of his sisters' families change their name to Lynch to inherit the estate. Sabina did so, and she and her husband managed the estate until their son, John Bowman Lynch, was of age. When Sabina died, the estate passed to the youngest sister.

In his 1829 book *The Lives of the Signers of the Declaration of Independence*, author Reverend Charles A. Goodrich wrote of Lynch:

> Although the life of Mr. Lynch was thus terminated, at an early age, he had lived sufficiently long to render eminent services to his

country, and to establish his character as a man of exalted views and exalted moral worth. Few men possessed a more absolute control over the passions of the heart, and few evinced in a greater degree the virtues which adorn the human mind. In all the relations of life, whether as a husband, a friend, a patriot, or the master of the slave, he appeared conscious of his obligations, and found his pleasure in discharging them. That a man of so much excellence, of such ability and integrity, such firmness and patriotism, so useful to his country, so tender and assiduous in all the obligations of life, should have been thus cut off, in the midst of his course, and in a manner so painful to his friends, is one of those awful dispensations of Him whose way is in the great deep, and whose judgments are past finding out.

William Maclay
(1737–1804)
The First Democrat

Buried at Paxton Presbyterian Churchyard,
Harrisburg, Pennsylvania.

Military • United States Senator

This founder fought as a soldier in both the French and Indian War and the American Revolution. In the latter conflict, he participated in the Battles of Trenton and Princeton. He wed Mary McClure Harris who was the daughter of John Harris who founded the city of Harrisburg. He served as the clerk of courts for Northumberland County and as a surveyor laid out the town of Sunbury. After the Constitution was ratified, he was one of Pennsylvania's first two men elected to represent his state in the United States Senate. As a Senator, he opposed any movement toward the monarchical tendencies of the Senate a position that often put him at odds with Vice President John Adams and Alexander Hamilton. He fiercely opposed Hamilton's plan to get the young country on solid financial footing. His fervent embrace of Jeffersonian Republicanism earned him the title of the earliest Democrat. His name was William Maclay.

Maclay was born on July 20, 1737. His parents sent him to the classical school run by the Reverend John Blair, and he proved to be an industrious student. He decided to study law, and in 1760 he was admitted to the York County Bar. During this period he served as a lieutenant in the

William Maclay (1737–1804)

William Maclay

French and Indian War. He distinguished himself as both a soldier and a leader in this conflict. It was as a direct result of his military service that his practice of the law was curtailed. Much of his time and energy went into surveying lands that had been allocated to officers who served in the war. It was this experience that led to his role in surveying Sunbury, a town where he lived for many years, with his wife, Mary McClure Harris. Between 1770 and 1787 the couple would produce eleven children eight of which survived infancy.

When the American Revolution began, Maclay was working for the colonial government. Despite this, he took an active part in favor of independence. In addition to serving in the Continental Army and fighting in the crucial battles of Trenton and Princeton, he worked on equipping and recruiting troops for the Continental Army.

In 1778, during the "Great Runaway" which followed the Wyoming Massacre, Maclay and his family fled Sunbury for Harris Ferry now known as Harrisburg. In letters to the president of the Executive Council he described in detail the distress felt in the area as a result of the attacks by the British Tories and their Indian allies. In 1781 he was elected to the Assembly where he served at various times as a member of the Supreme Executive Council, Judge of the Court Of Common Pleas And deputy coroner.

In 1789 he was elected as one of the first two senators representing Pennsylvania in the United States Senate. It was as a Senator in the first Congress that Maclay earned the moniker the "First Democrat." The historian Frederic A. Godcharles credited Maclay with being "the original promoter and later the actual founder of the Democratic Party." He was unafraid and unapologetic about voicing his disagreements with the Washington administration. He objected to the President being present while the Senate was conducting business. Yet the presence of America's first President did not deter him from voicing his disagreements with Washington and often with his Secretary of the Treasury Alexander Hamilton.

While serving as a senator, Maclay kept a diary that has been reprinted and titled *The Private Journal of Senator William Maclay, United States Senator, 1789-1791*. That journal is widely regarded as one of the most important political diaries in American history. It recounts his life as a member of the First Congress. He also details Senate debates, the politics of the time, and comments on his fellow members of Congress.

Maclay's diary makes one thing abundantly clear; he probably disliked Vice President John Adams more than any other member of Congress. The feeling was mutual. Adams viewed Maclay as an uncooperative troublemaker. Maclay described Adams as "a monkey just put into Breeches." The feud came back to hurt Maclay during his efforts to have the nation's capital placed in the town of Columbia, Pennsylvania which is located on the Susquehanna River. After a tie vote in the Senate on where to place the capital, Adams was in the position of casting the tie-breaking vote. The decision was on whether the nation's home would be along the Potomac or in Pennsylvania either along the Susquehanna or in Germantown. According to Maclay, Adams flattered the Virginians by praising the Potomac before making less than flattering remarks about the Susquehanna before casting his vote in favor of Germantown. Thanks to James Madison, the Senate bill failed to pass the House without amendment and as a result, was returned to the upper house where it was postponed until the next session of Congress. When the matter was finally settled, the Virginians made a deal with Alexander Hamilton which resulted in Washington, D.C. being the nation's capital. The deal also resulted in the passage of Hamilton's financial plan, which Maclay viewed as an "accursed thing which I fear future generations will hate."

Maclay was hardly a silent Senator. He often spoke during floor debates. He found himself at odds with his colleagues and in the minority on many issues. These included Senate rules, the jurisdiction of the federal judiciary, and the relationship between the legislative and executive branches. In opposing Hamilton's financial plan, he also lost respect for President Washington. He viewed Washington as being "in the hands of Hamilton the Dishclout of every dirty speculation, as his name goes to wipe away blame and silence all murmuring." As a direct result of his failure to support Hamilton's financial plan, the Pennsylvania Assembly refused to re-elect him to the Senate.

Maclay returned to Harrisburg where as a member of Jefferson's Democratic-Republican Party he lost a bid for a seat in the House of Representatives. From 1795 to 1798 he represented Dauphin County in the State House Of Representatives. As a member of this body, he supported a constitutional amendment which limited the terms of United States Senators to three years. He voted against an address expressing regret at the retirement of President Washington and introduced a resolution declaring Pennsylvania's opposition to war and with France specifically. This final act was not a popular position, and he lost a bid for re-election in 1798. He was re-elected five years later in 1803. On April 16 of the following year, he passed away in Harrisburg. He was laid to rest in Harrisburg's Paxton Presbyterian Churchyard.

At the time of his death the political party he helped found controlled the country. In looking back at his life, he may have viewed it much as he viewed his two years in the Senate. On the night he served his last day as a Senator he wrote, "As I left the hall, I gave it a look with that kind of satisfaction which a man feels on leaving a place. Where he has been ill at ease, being fully satisfied that many a culprit has served two years at the wheelbarrow—a punishment for felons—without feeling half the pain and mortification that I experienced in my honorable station." This founder may have been too hard on himself or, on the other hand, he may have just been a little ahead of his countrymen.

There is a street in Harrisburg named for Maclay, and his former home still stands alongside his beloved Susquehanna River. The Pennsylvania Bar Association are the current owners. The house contains a modern portrait of Maclay based on a miniature that was owned by one of his descendants.

The grave of William Maclay.

Henry Marchant
(1741–1796)

Liberty Lawyer

Buried at Common Burial Ground,
Newport, Rhode Island.

Articles of Confederation

Henry Marchant was an attorney from Newport, Rhode Island, who served as the attorney general of that state and a member of the state legislature. As a delegate to the Continental Congress, he signed the Articles of Confederation. He supported the U.S. Constitution and was appointed the first federal judge for the U.S. District Court of Rhode Island.

Henry Marchant was born on April 9, 1741, in Edgartown, on the island of Martha's Vineyard, in Massachusetts, the son of Huxford Marchant, a sea captain, and his wife, Sarah (née Butler) Marchant. The Marchant family descended from John Marchant, born in 1571, in Yeovil, Somerset, England. Sarah Marchant died in 1745 when Henry was a toddler. His father then married Isabel Ward, the daughter and sister of the governors of Rhode Island, Richard Ward and Samuel Ward. When Huxford Marchant died while in Liberia or the West Indies in July 1747, stepmother Isabel remained to raise her young stepson in a world of wealth and privilege.

When Henry was of school age, Isabel sent him to a prestigious academy in Newport. He then went to Philadelphia College (now the University of Pennsylvania), where he was introduced to Benjamin

Henry Marchant

Franklin. Marchant graduated in 1762. Next, he studied law in the offices of Judge Edmund Trowbridge of Cambridge, Massachusetts.

Following his legal training, Marchant was admitted to the Rhode Island bar and opened a practice in Newport. He was the only "liberty lawyer" in the colony but was well-connected with local officials and the church. Marchant was the personal attorney for his uncle Samuel Ward.

On January 8, 1765, Marchant married Rebecca Cooke at Trinity Church in Newport. The couple had four children between 1766 and 1771: Sarah, Henry, William, and Elizabeth. Only Sarah and Elizabeth lived to adulthood.

Marchant then got involved in local politics. On December 4, 1767, he was elected to the Council of Newport. About three years later, Marchant was elected the attorney general for the colony, serving from October 1770 to May 1777.

Marchant was a bright young man, curious about science, and mathematically inclined. In 1769, he assisted Dr. Ezra Stiles, a well-known intellectual, Congregationalist pastor, and founder of Brown University, in observing and plotting the transit of Venus. Stiles was a member of the American Philosophical Society in Philadelphia and later became the president of Yale University.

In 1771, Marchant was named an agent for Rhode Island in England, and he visited the mother country for eleven months seeking recompense for the colony for a couple of court cases. He had quite a send-off, as recounted by David Lovejoy in the *William and Mary Quarterly*:

> Henry Marchant's departure for England on July 8, 1771, was a significant occasion in the social life of Newport. Nearly a score of friends, reluctant to see him leave, accompanied him in chaises and on horseback as far as Bristol Ferry, eight miles northward on the way to Providence and Boston. His well-wishers included his wife, of course, and his "honord Mother in Law," but also Joseph Clarke, General Treasurer of the colony; William Ellery, later member of the Continental Congress; Josias Lyndon, former Governor; and the Reverend Ezra Stiles, Marchant's minister. (Stiles had good reason to be pleasant since Marchant had tucked three guineas "gratuity" into his pocket before they left Newport.) At Bristol Ferry, there was "heavy parting from such good Friends"; several crossed over to the mainland with him and after a "Repetition of parting Feelings," dropped by the wayside at the homes of relatives. Richard Olney accompanied young Marchant to Providence; Mrs. Marchant prolonged her leave-taking and stayed with her husband all the way to Boston, where he was to embark.

Marchant kept a descriptive journal of his thoughts and encounters while in London. He conducted business before the Privy Council in London and traveled through Scotland with Ben Franklin, traveling in the highest intellectual and political circles. In Scotland, the two dined together often and met with David Hume. They toured the universities in Edinburgh and Glasgow. Marchant also participated in the sixty-sixth birthday party for Franklin. Back in London, Marchant was introduced to the historian Catharine Macaulay, and the two had numerous dinners together, discussing English history and the politics of the time. He maintained correspondence with Macauley, who was a radical thinker. Macauley later visited the United States, calling on Richard Henry Lee, George Washington, and others.

With the burning of the *Gaspee* off Rhode Island in June 1772, Marchant's business became more difficult. He bade farewell to Franklin, who was "ill of the Gout in one Foot," and headed home in late July 1772. The voyage turned out to be difficult when, in mid-ocean, a fire consumed the ship's galley thanks to a pot of boiling pitch left unattended. Fortunately, the fire did not reach the thirty barrels of gunpowder in the hold, and Marchant was safely back in Boston on September 20.

By May 1773, Marchant was active in the heated political discussions of the time, fresh off his experiences in England. As tensions mounted with Great Britain, Marchant was a member of Rhode Island's Sons of Liberty and Committee of Correspondence. A son, William, was born in 1774.

When Marchant's term as attorney general concluded, the Rhode Island General Assembly appointed him to the Continental Congress on May 7, 1777. He was then re-elected twice, serving until November 30, 1779. During his tenure, he was interested in military and naval matters. An interesting episode involved the proposed creation of a black battalion in the Rhode Island militia created from purchased slaves who had been freed. Marchant and William Ellery, his counterpart in Congress, were asked to petition Congress to raise funds to reimburse the slave masters. Ultimately, despite their best efforts, Marchant and Ellery could not convince Congress, citing the lack of funds.

Marchant was present in York, Pennsylvania, for the discussions and negotiations that resulted in the Articles of Confederation. He then signed the document on July 9, 1778. Marchant was again elected to Congress in 1780 and 1783 but did not attend. When he came up for election in 1784, he resigned his seat. That year, he was back in local politics as a member of the Newport Town Council. He was elected Recorder for the city and, in 1785, was elected to the state General Assembly. In 1788, Marchant was active with the committee that approved the U.S. Constitution in Rhode Island.

On April 22, 1790, during the early days of the first Washington administration, Marchant was nominated as the first federal district judge in Rhode Island. The Senate confirmed him on July 2, 1790. Early in his term, Marchant presided over *West v. Barnes* in 1791, which was the first case appealed to U.S. Supreme Court.

Marchant served as a federal judge until he died in Newport on August 30, 1796, at age 55. A local newspaper said he was "much lamented." After a well-attended funeral, he was buried in the Common Burying Ground in Newport. His tombstone reads, "The Honorable Henry Marchant. Member of the Revolutionary Congress and U.S. Judge for the District of Rhode Island. Died Aug. 30, 1796."

Rebecca Cooke Marchant died in 1819. Son William Marchant inherited the Henry Marchant Farm, a historic site located in South Kingstown, Rhode Island.

The stone of Henry Marchant.

Francis Marion
(1732–1795)

Swamp Fox

Buried at Belle Isle Plantation Cemetery,
Berkeley County, South Carolina.

Military

Francis Marion, nicknamed the "Swamp Fox," was an officer in the South Carolina militia and the Continental Army during the American Revolution known by the enemy for his irregular methods of warfare. He was best known for his resistance to the British occupation of South Carolina late in the American Revolution. Marion is considered one of the fathers of modern guerilla warfare. He has been portrayed in books and movies since as an American hero.

Francis Marion was born in 1732, at Winyah near Georgetown, South Carolina, to Gabriel Marion, a country planter, and his wife, Esther Cordes. The Marions were of Huguenot ancestry who had been in the colonies since the 1600s. Francis was the youngest of seven children. According to Parson Weems, Marion was born so small; he was the size of a New England lobster.

Marion was not formally educated. As a teenager of fifteen or sixteen, he joined a West Indies-bound schooner. Likely an apocryphal tale, a few days out of Charleston, like an episode in *Moby Dick*, the ship was battered and sunk by a whale. Marion was among six crew members who drifted at sea for a week in a lifeboat. Two died before they were rescued by a passing ship. Marion then focused on terrestrial pursuits

Francis Marion (1732–1795)

Francis Marion

at the family plantation, near the Santee River, about 45 miles north of Charleston.

As the French and Indian War commenced, Marion and his brother, Job, were recruited by Captain John Postell on January 1, 1757. In 1759, when the Cherokee rebelled against the British, Marion was elevated to a first lieutenant in a light infantry company. At the climactic Battle of Etchoe in June 1761, Marion led 30 men in an uphill flanking assault against a strong Cherokee position. Two-thirds of his men fell dead or wounded, but the attack secured a decisive victory and made Marion a hero.

Marion served as a local official after the war. In 1773, he built his plantation home, Pond Bluff, a few miles south of Eutaw Springs, South Carolina. The site is now beneath the waters of Lake Marion. In 1775, Marion was elected to the First Provincial Congress of South Carolina.

At the beginning of the American Revolution, in June 1775, Marion was commissioned a captain and company commander in the 2nd Continental Regiment of South Carolina under William Moultrie. His ability to train raw recruits into a disciplined unit resulted in his promotion to major, second in command of the regiment.

During the early years of the Revolution, Marion participated in the major campaigns in South Carolina and Georgia. He took part in the capture of Fort Johnson in September 1775. At Sullivan's Island on June 28, 1776, Marion and 400 South Carolinians under Moultrie successfully defended against nine British warships in Charleston Harbor. This was especially remarkable since the fortification, built of palmetto logs, was only partially completed. The Continental Congress promoted Marion to lieutenant colonel in September 1776.

Three years later, in the summer and fall of 1779, Marion and his regiment were part of a French American force sent to retake Savannah, Georgia, from the British. His Second Regiment took part in a costly frontal assault against well-entrenched British and loyalist soldiers. The attack failed.

The British under Henry Clinton then moved on Charleston in the spring of 1780. Just before the British cut the last roads leading inland, Marion attended a party where the host locked his guests in until they were drunk. Marion, who was beyond his limit, decided to leave the party by jumping from a second-story window. The fall fractured his ankle, and he went home to recover. When Charleston fell, Marion was healing at home and was not captured. Meanwhile, Clinton returned with most of the army to New York, leaving Lord Cornwallis and a smaller force in the Carolinas.

The British, under Cornwallis, then began scouring the countryside. Despite his crippling injury, Marion fled to Horatio Gates's new American army assembling in North Carolina with a few fellow officers and comrades from his regiment. Gates found Marion an utterly unimpressive figure—short, scrawny, homely, taciturn, and so crippled by a poorly healed ankle fracture that his black manservant had to help him dismount from his horse. Before Gates engaged the enemy at Camden, Marion received a request from the residents of Williamsburg County, South Carolina, to come and help defend them. Marion, now a brigadier general in the militia, was permitted to go home and gather a small force. Colonel Otho Williams, Gates's adjutant, recorded afterward that the northern troops derided the appearance of Marion and his men. Gates seemed only too happy to send Marion and his ragtag group back to South Carolina. He ordered Marion to destroy all the watercraft along the Santee River below Camden before turning east to reach his destination above Charleston. Gates hoped that Marion's small force could frustrate British efforts to reinforce Camden and prevent their retreat after they were defeated. Unfortunately, Gates was defeated convincingly, and now Marion was on his own along the coast.

Between August and December 1780, Marion gained recognition for his actions across the region. While the British looted, burned, and forced captured rebels to switch sides, Marion countered with guerilla tactics and rough treatment of loyalists. Rarely did Marion make frontal assaults but instead relied on surprise attacks to harass and bewilder the enemy before disappearing into the swamp. The British's harsh treatment only increased the opportunities for groups led by Marion, Sumter, and Pickens to recruit and find supplies. Unlike the Continental troops, Marion's Men served without pay and supplied their own horses, arms, and food.

They fought at Great Savannah on August 20 and Blue Savannah on September 4. On September 24, learning that a force of Tories was constructing a small fort at Shepherd's Ferry on Black Mingo Creek, about 30 miles north of Georgetown, Marion planned a night attack. When the clatter of their horses' hooves on a bridge alerted an enemy sentry, Marion hurried his men across the stream, split them into three parties, and attacked from as many directions. But the Tories had received sufficient warning to deploy, and their initial volley caught part of Marion's force crossing an open field and inflicted severe casualties. A sharp fight ensued before one of Marion's other detachments attacked the Tories from the rear, killing and wounding many and scattering the rest.

After this battle, most of Marion's men returned to their homes to bring in the harvest while he was based at Snow's Island, located on the west side of the Great Pee Dee River, just below its confluence with Lynches River. It was further protected by a creek, a lake, and broad belts of cypress swamp and dense canebrakes. Marion used this naturally moated refuge as a supply depot, recruiting station, and sanctuary for the next six months. A British officer who was sent to arrange a prisoner exchange was picked up by Marion's men, blindfolded, and taken to the swampy hideout. There, Marion invited him to share his dinner of roasted sweet potatoes served upon plates of bark. "But surely, general," the officer objected, "this cannot be your ordinary fare."

"Indeed, sir, it is," Marion dryly replied, "and we are fortunate on this occasion, entertaining company, to have more than our usual allowance."

By late October 1780, enough men returned from the harvest so that Marion could resume operations. First up was a Tory recruiting base near the Black River. Marion took 150 men, covered 40 miles, crossed three rivers, and took the enemy's camp by surprise at midnight on October 25 at Tearcoat Swamp. When the Tories fled, Marion's men seized 80 new muskets and an equal number of horses and saddles.

There were also actions at Georgetown on November 15 and Halfway Swamp in mid-December 12–13.

Cornwallis was so concerned about Marion; he sent Banastre Tarleton's 800-man brigade out to capture him. Hearing this, Marion, realizing the long odds, released his men to their homes and headed to North Carolina.

Lieutenant Colonel Banastre Tarleton, known by the patriots as "The Butcher" and "Bloody Ban," led a force known as the British Legion. Tarleton was known for brutal tactics, often killing troops taken prisoner. He came after Marion with his legion and nearly blundered into Marion's brigade on the evening of November 9 at Richardson's Plantation near the Santee River. Each side discovered the other at the same moment. Marion's force was about half the size of Tarleton's, so he ordered a hasty retreat. The chase ensued through the night and onto the following day, November 10.

After riding 33 miles through swamps, creeks, thickets, and forests, Tarleton and his legion were now on the banks of Ox Swamp, near the town of Manning, with no sign of Marion. Frustrated, he turned to his officers and said, "Come, my boys! Let us go back, and we will soon find the gamecock [Sumter], but as for this damned old fox, the devil himself could not catch him." Thus, Marion's famous nickname, "Swamp Fox," was born.

Wrote Lord Cornwallis to General Clinton in early December, "Colonel Marion had so wrought the minds of the people, partly by the terror of his threats and cruelty of his punishments, and partly by the promise of plunder, that there was scarcely an inhabitant between the Santee and the Pee Dee that was not in arms against us." The British turned their attention to protecting their communication lines between Charleston, Camden, and the frontier settlement known as Ninety-Six. They erected Fort Watson on the east side of the Santee, and Fort Motte, farther north, just west of the juncture of the Congaree and Wateree rivers. At this point, South Carolina's governor, John Rutledge, promoted Marion to brigadier general of state troops.

In early 1781, Marion was paired with "Light Horse" Harry Lee's Legion under Major General Nathanael Greene, who had replaced Horatio Gates. Unlike Thomas Sumter, Marion coordinated effectively in the field with the Continental Army. But Marion and Lee were an odd pair. At 25, Lee was outgoing and dashing. Marion was nearly fifty, hook-nosed, swarthy, bowlegged, and reserved. He drank a mixture of vinegar and water and was so indifferent to his appearance; he continued to wear his old leather 2nd Regiment cap even after it was partially burned.

After a failed raid on Georgetown, Lee rejoined Greene's army. This left Marion's brigade alone in March 1781 when Colonel Francis, Lord Rawdon, who had taken over when Lord Cornwallis moved north to pursue Greene's army, planned an attack on Snow's Island. Lieutenant Colonel John Watson and a force of 500 loyalists proceeded east from Fort Watson. Lieutenant Colonel Welbore Doyle and his 300 loyalists were sent east from Camden to cut off Marion from retreating to North Carolina. On March 7, Watson and Marion clashed at Wiboo Swamp, the British getting the worst of it. As they tried to outflank him, Marion anticipated their moves and caught them at a bridge over the Black River two days later. Seventy mounted riflemen destroyed the bridge before the British arrived and then shot at them from the trees, frustrating their attempts to cross. Watson ordered a retreat and headed to a nearby plantation, where he remained for ten days.

On March 15, Watson asked Marion for passes to remove his wounded to Charleston. Marion obliged but kept pressing. By March

20, Watson's troops were out of food, but Marion's riflemen prevented them from foraging. Facing a dire situation, Watson and his men bolted for Georgetown, thirty miles away. Marion sent a party of horsemen ahead to destroy the bridge on the Sampit River. Watson's men desperately plunged into the stream and splashed across as Marion's main force arrived. The Tories lost 20 killed and 38 wounded. Marion only lost a single man. The remnants of Watson's command limped into Georgetown the next day, its wagons loaded with wounded. Unfortunately, while battling Watson in what was known as "the Bridges Campaign," Colonel Doyle and his men destroyed Snow's Island and took all the weapons and ammunition. Doyle then retreated to Camden rather than face Marion.

After the Battle at Guilford Courthouse, General Greene turned his army back to South Carolina and reunited Lee and Marion. He ordered them to attack the British forts between Charleston and Camden. The first target was Fort Watson in April 1781. This same fort had withstood an attack by Thomas Sumter six weeks earlier. Without any cannons, the patriots laid siege for eight days and cleverly built wooden towers from which the sharpshooters could fire into the fort. Realizing their situation was hopeless, the British surrendered. Nathanael Greene wrote to Marion just after Fort Watson's fall, noting that Marion, despite fighting against superior foes, had kept "alive the expiring hopes of an oppressed militia. To fight the enemy bravely with the prospect of victory is nothing, but to fight with intrepidity under the constant impression of defeat, and to inspire irregular troops to do it, is a talent peculiar to yourself."

On April 25, Greene defeated Lord Rawdon at Hobkirk's Hill. After Lee and Marion took Fort Motte on May 12, Lord Rawdon ordered Camden abandoned, burning many of its buildings and supplies that he could not take. This broke the line of communications in the region for the British and further accelerated their collapse. After three more forts were captured, Marion and his men began to dig in at Georgetown, expecting a confrontation, but the British and loyalist garrison boarded three ships and sailed to Charleston, abandoning the town. This was a bloodless victory for Marion, who finally cleaned himself up and obtained a fresh uniform.

Marion continued to harass the British around Charleston through the summer. He commanded South Carolina militia in advance lines along with Brig. Gen. Andrew Pickens at the Battle of Eutaw Springs in September 1781, the last major battle in the Carolinas. The British suffered so many casualties they ceased further inland campaigning.

Over the next fifteen months, there were skirmishes between foraging parties on the outskirts of Charleston. In January 1782, Marion took a seat in the new South Carolina state assembly. He supported measures to foster reconciliation with the state's loyalists, on one occasion preventing his men from lynching a notorious Tory commander. Marion was very reluctant to attack the enemy for fear of losing another man wisely preferred to wait out the British. He said, "If ordered to attack, I shall obey, but with my consent, not another life shall be lost . . . Knowing, as we do, that the enemy are on the eve of departure, so far from offering to molest, I would rather send a party to protect them." The British evacuated Charleston in December 1782. The war ended with the Treaty of Paris.

The war had ruined Marion financially. His plantation had been burned, and his slaves had run away. He borrowed money to purchase more and restart planting. On April 20, 1786, he married his wealthy cousin, Mary Esther Videau. The two lived a comfortable life, but the two had no children.

Marion was awarded a gold medal, a full colonelcy in the Continental Army, and command of Fort Johnson in Charleston harbor. He served in the state Senate from 1783 to 1786, 1791, and 1792 to 1794. He was elected to the state constitutional convention in 1790. Marion also continued as a brigadier general in the militia until his retirement in 1794. At that point, he owned upward of eighteen hundred acres and seventy-three slaves.

Francis Marion died at Pond Bluff, his estate, on February 27, 1795. He was buried in the family plot at Belle Island in St. Stephen's Parish, Berkeley County, South Carolina. A plaque on his tomb aptly describes him as a "noble and disinterested" citizen and a soldier "who lived without fear and died without reproach."

GRAVES of our FOUNDERS

The life of Francis Marion became somewhat legendary due to early biographies and novels that exaggerated his exploits. Marion was presented in the 1955 television show "The Swamp Fox," an episode of the *Cavalcade of America* series. Walt Disney then produced an eight-episode miniseries entitled *The Swamp Fox*. It aired from 1959 to 1961 and starred Leslie Nielsen. Marion was the inspiration for Benjamin Martin, played by Mel Gibson, in the 2000 movie *The Patriot*. Many historians criticized the many oversights and exaggerations in the film, television show, and early biographies.

Numerous towns, counties, parks, hotels, ships, and monuments were named or raised in Marion's honor. Congress approved a national monument to Francis Marion in 2008. Though the park was selected, the monument was never built due to some residents opposing a monument to a slaveowner. The authorization expired in 2018.

The tomb of Francis Marion, the Swamp Fox.

Hugh Mercer
(1726–1777)

The Hero of Princeton

Buried at Laurel Hill Cemetery,
Philadelphia, Pennsylvania.

Military

Hugh Mercer, known as the Hero of Princeton, was a brigadier general in the Continental Army who was a close friend of George Washington. A doctor by trade, he was born in Scotland and served in the British military before emigrating to the colonies. During the American Revolution, Mercer died from his wounds at the Battle of Princeton and was immortalized in famous paintings depicting the scene.

Hugh Mercer was born on January 16, 1726, at the manse of Pitsligo Kirk, near Rosehearty in Aberdeenshire, Scotland. Mercer was the son of the Pitsligo Parish Church of Scotland minister Reverend William Mercer and his wife, Ann Monro. He began studying medicine at only fifteen years of age, attending Marischal College at the University of Aberdeen and later graduating as a doctor at only nineteen.

Mercer then served as an assistant surgeon in the army of Charles Edward Stuart, also known as Bonnie Prince Charlie, who was a pretender to the British throne and who led the Jacobite uprising to restore the Stuarts to power. When the rebellion was crushed at Culloden on April 16, 1746, the Hanoverian line under George II was preserved, and Scotland was forced down the path of integration into the United

Hugh Mercer fighting for his life at Princeton.

Kingdom. Many of the surviving Jacobites were hunted down and killed, and Mercer feared for his life. In 1747, after months of hiding from authorities, Mercer boarded a ship and moved to North America. He settled first in Franklin County, Pennsylvania, near the village of Black Town, now called Mercersburg in his honor. He practiced as a doctor there for the next eight years, far away from Philadelphia and any officials who might still be hunting Jacobites.

In 1755, at the outset of the French and Indian War, some claim Mercer was with Braddock when he was defeated at Fort Duquesne. Others claim he treated the many wounded from that debacle, but there is no record of Hugh fighting for the British until the following year, 1756.

That year, he was commissioned a captain in the Pennsylvania militia under Lt. Col. John Armstrong. The colonel led an expedition of 300 Pennsylvania provincial troops in September against the Indian village of Kittanning, forty miles northeast of modern-day Pittsburgh, Pennsylvania. During the raid, a victory for the provincials, Mercer was severely wounded and separated from his unit. He walked over 100 miles to Fort Shirley in (now) Huntingdon County, Pennsylvania, about fifty

Hugh Mercer (1726–1777)

The Death of General Mercer at the Battle of Princeton January 3, 1777 by John Trumbull.

miles west of Carlisle, living off the land for a fortnight. Upon his return, Mercer was promoted to colonel and soon met another colonel, George Washington, with whom he became close friends.

Mercer and Washington accompanied General John Forbes during the second attempt to capture Fort Duquesne in 1758. On November 25, the burned fort was occupied, and Forbes set about to construct a new fort to be named Fort Pitt after the British Secretary of State. The nearby settlement was dubbed Pittsburgh.

This whole time, General Forbes was in poor health and became gravely ill. In early December he returned to Philadelphia and left Mercer in command. Mercer first built a temporary fort, called Mercer's Fort, at the two forks in the Ohio River to prevent the return of the French. Today this site is a parking lot between Point State Park and the Pittsburgh Post-Gazette building.

Back in Philadelphia, General Forbes passed away on March 11, 1759, and was buried at Christ Church. Mercer continued his duties to secure the area for construction of Fort Pitt. Mercer was commended by the Commander-in-Chief of the British Army in North America, Sir Jeffrey Amherst, for his professionalism. Said Amherst, "Some such men as Colonel Mercer amongst the Provincials would be of great service . . ."

After the war, in 1760, Mercer relocated to Fredericksburg, Virginia, where there was a thriving Scottish community. There, he set up as a doctor and opened an apothecary which is now a museum at 1020 Caroline Street. Mercer became a prominent man in the community, purchasing tracts of land and becoming a member of the Fredericksburg Masonic Lodge of which he was soon Master. This same lodge also claimed George Washington and James Monroe as members as well as other generals during the American Revolution: George Weeden, William Woodford, Fielding Lewis, Thomas Posey, Gustavus Wallace, and (in 1824 as an honorary member) the Marquis de Lafayette. Mary Washington, George's mother, became a patient of Mercer's and he saw many other prominent members of the community.

Mercer married Isabella Gordon and had five children with her: Ann (who married Patton), John, William, George Weeden, and Hugh Tennant. In 1774, George Washington sold his childhood home, Ferry Farm, to Mercer who envisioned creating a town where he and his family would settle.

As tensions increased between the colonies and Great Britain, Mercer became a member of the Fredericksburg Committee of Safety in 1775. The day after Lexington and Concord in Massachusetts, the Royal Governor Dunmore of Virginia ordered the seizing of gunpowder in Williamsburg. This riled the local militias and Mercer was among those urging action. Though initially excluded for a military post by the Virginians due to being Scottish (Jacobite), on September 12, he was appointed a Colonel of the Virginia Minute Men covering Spotsylvania, King George, Stafford, and Caroline Counties, known as the Third Virginia Regiment. George Weedon was appointed lieutenant colonel. James Monroe and future Chief Justice of the United States John Marshall were officers under his command.

In June 1776 the Continental Congress appointed Mercer brigadier general and ordered him to report to New York. Mercer left his family and headed north to take on his new duties reporting to his friend, George Washington. That summer, while Washington was building Fort

Hugh Mercer (1726–1777)

Washington on the New York side of the Hudson River, Mercer oversaw the construction of Fort Lee on the New Jersey side. Unfortunately, this fort fell during the British attacks that November. As the beaten Continental Army retreated to New Jersey, the army was in crisis and in danger of being further decimated due to the large number of enlistments that were ending on January 1, 1777.

With only days until many of the troops would go home, it is said Mercer hatched the plan to cross the Delaware River and surprise the Hessians at Trenton. Certainly, Mercer was a significant contributor to its execution. Due to the victory on December 26, 1776, many of the soldiers agreed to stay on for ten more days provided they received a monetary bonus. This provided the window of opportunity for the Second Battle

Memorial to Hugh Mercer.

of Trenton, also known as the Battle of Assunpink Creek, on January 2, 1777, when Washington defeated Cornwallis's 5000 troops. Mercer was tasked with helping defend the city from potential British capture.

With Cornwallis's forces split between Trenton and Princeton, Washington attacked the latter the following day, January 3. Mercer's brigade of 350 men was sent to destroy the Stony Brook Bridge but engaged with two British regiments and a mounted unit under Colonel Charles Manwood at Clarke's Orchard. Mistaken for George Washington, Mercer's horse was shot from under him, and he was surrounded and ordered to surrender. Mercer refused and drew his saber, and a struggle ensued that devolved to hand-to-hand combat as the men fought to secure the heights of a nearby hill. Unfortunately, most of Mercer's men did not have bayonets on their muskets like their counterparts. They began to fall back, but Mercer desperately rallied them with a cry of "Forward! Forward!" The Brits eventually got him to the ground and stabbed him seven times, leaving him for dead. According to legend, this occurred at a white oak tree which became known as the "Mercer Oak" which later became the seal of Mercer County, New Jersey.

With Mercer on the ground, the colonials retreated but ran into Washington who immediately rallied them upon learning of his friend's fate. They pushed back the British and recovered Mercer, who lay dying from the bayonet wounds and blows to his head. The mortally wounded Mercer was carried to the field hospital at the Thomas Clarke House, now a museum at 500 Mercer Road. Doctor Benjamin Rush attended to him, but Mercer succumbed nine days later, on January 12, 1777. He was initially buried at Christ Church in Philadelphia but was moved to Laurel Hill Cemetery in 1840.

Washington's army was victorious at Princeton, and Mercer's valiant effort became the rallying cry for the colonials whose enlistment problems abated. Following the victory, Washington camped in Morristown, and the Americans secured French arms and supplies. Cornwallis pulled his forces back to New York, stunned by the defeats. Back in London, British public support for the war began to wane.

Two famous paintings of the Revolution portray Mercer at Princeton. John Trumbull used Hugh Mercer, Jr., as the model for *The Death of General Mercer at the Battle of Princeton*. Charles Willson Peale painted

The original tombstone of Hugh Mercer.

the mortally wounded Mercer in the background of his *Washington at the Battle of Princeton*. This painting is a prized possession of Princeton University.

Many Mercer descendants have distinguished themselves. His grandson, John Mercer Patton, was a governor of Virginia. His sons were Confederate officers Lt. Col. Walter T. Patton and Col. George Smith Patton. The latter was the grandfather of General George S. Patton, Jr., of World War II fame. Another grandson of Mercer, Hugh Weedon Mercer, was a Confederate general. The songwriter Johnny Mercer was a descendant as was Sergeant Christopher Mercer Lowe of the U.S. Army, who was recently killed while serving in Afghanistan.

Besides the Mercer Oak, Mercersburg, Pennsylvania, and Mercer County, New Jersey, Mercer's name has been affixed to five other counties across the country, to the town of Mercerville, New Jersey, and to a street in New York City. An elementary school in Fredericksburg, Virginia is also named after him. There is also a prominent statue of Mercer in that town.

Daniel Morgan
(1735/6–1802)

Victor at Cowpens

Buried at Mount Hebron Cemetery,
Winchester, Virginia.

Military

Daniel Morgan was one of the most respected battlefield tacticians of the American Revolution, serving with George Washington, Benedict Arnold, Horatio Gates, and Nathanael Greene during most of the war's major campaigns. Morgan's Riflemen were an elite unit of sharpshooters under his leadership. Morgan was best known for his victory over Banastre Tarleton at the Battle of Cowpens in South Carolina. This served as an inspiration for the fictional character Benjamin Martin in the 2000 film *The Patriot* starring Mel Gibson.

Morgan's origins have always been sketchy. He was never one to speak of it, and anyone who asked was bluntly discouraged from the inquiry. What he did tell people who came to know him is he was of Welsh stock who had emigrated to Philadelphia and settled along the Delaware River. As a young man of seventeen, circa 1752, he headed across Pennsylvania to Carlisle, where he worked a few weeks, before continuing to Winchester in the Shenandoah Valley. There he was a laborer and then a sawyer in a sawmill. He was also a teamster.

Biographers have estimated his birth year as 1735. Some link him to Pennsylvania and others to New Jersey. One biographer states Morgan was the fifth of seven children of James Morgan (1702–1782) and Eleanor Lloyd (1706–1748). Morgan apparently left home after a fight

Daniel Morgan (1735/6–1802)

Daniel Morgan

with his father and headed off into the wilderness. He was well-equipped for it, exhibiting all the skills needed for pioneer life. However, he was not educated and may have been illiterate.

Over two years, Morgan saved enough from his labors to purchase his own team and extra wagons. Soon, he had a thriving business. During the French and Indian War, he was a civilian teamster helping supply the British Army along with, according to one source, his cousin Daniel Boone. Morgan was a teamster in the ill-fated Braddock Expedition and survived the attack. At some point, while retreating or after, Morgan had a confrontation with a British officer who had insulted him. Morgan, ever the country tough, hauled off and punched the man, knocking him out cold. This led to the severe punishment of 500 lashes. According to Morgan, he counted the lashes and realized they had stopped one short. He decided not to point out the error as he took the punishment with a grin. The officer, seeing the apparent cheerfulness of Morgan during the beating, later apologized to him. Morgan attributed this treatment to his growing disdain for British authorities.

By the early 1760s, a local merchant noted that Morgan had three different women buying sundries on his credit. One of them was Abigail Curry, who soon moved in with him. In time, Abigail gave birth to two daughters, Nancy and Betsy. Meanwhile, Morgan served as a rifleman, protecting settlements in the wilderness of Pennsylvania and New York from Indian raiders. Outside Fort Ashby, now West Virginia, Morgan and his companion were ambushed by Indians. He was struck by a musket ball that transited the back of his neck, crushing his left jaw as it exited his cheek. He lost all his teeth on that side of his mouth but survived. He carried the scars with him for the rest of his life. Another time, he led a force that rescued Fort Edward in New York and directed its defense.

After the French and Indian War, Morgan purchased a farm in Virginia between Winchester and Battletown, now Berryville. In 1774, he served in Dunmore's War, participating in raids on Indian villages in western Pennsylvania and northern Virginia. He was made a captain in the Frederick County Militia.

As the American Revolution began in the spring of 1775, Virginia agreed to send two of the ten rifle companies requested by the Continental Congress. The Committee of Frederick County unanimously selected Morgan to form and lead one of them, dubbed Morgan's Riflemen. These men were armed with long rifles with a range of 300 yards compared to the standard musket range of only 80 yards. Morgan recruited 96 men and had them assemble on July 14, 1775, in Winchester. Hugh Stephenson raised another company in nearby Shepherdstown. They had planned to meet Morgan's company at Winchester but found them gone. On what was called the "Bee-Line March," Morgan and his men traversed 600 miles to Boston, Massachusetts, in only 21 days, arriving August 6. Stephenson and his men arrived five days later. Morgan's men, who were sharpshooters, took to the woods and began sniping British officers and soldiers, killing ten a day. This outraged the British Army. They also wore hunting shirts as part of their uniforms. This eventually struck fear in British soldiers because of the known accuracy of the riflemen wearing such shirts.

Later in 1775, Morgan was chosen to lead three rifle companies in the invasion of Canada, and he led the advance party. In the assault on Quebec, when his superior, Colonel Benedict Arnold, fell injured,

Morgan took command of the assault and penetrated the city. When General Richard Montgomery fell dead, Morgan was the senior officer on the field. Despite his outstanding leadership, his forces were overrun, and he was taken captive. He handed his sword to a priest, refusing to give it to the British commander, General Guy Carleton. He remained a prisoner of war until he was exchanged in January 1777.

While Morgan was a prisoner in Canada, George Washington wrote to the Continental Congress to recommend his promotion to succeed Colonel Hugh Stephenson as the rifle unit commander. Congress then appointed Morgan to the rank of colonel in the Continental Army. When Morgan rejoined the army in early 1777, he was surprised to hear he had been promoted for his bravery in Quebec. He then raised the 11th Virginia Regiment of the Continental Line, a new unit. On June 13, 1777, Morgan took command of 500 riflemen from Virginia, Maryland, and Pennsylvania called the Provisional Rifle Corps. Washington ordered them to harass General William Howe's forces as they withdrew from Philadelphia, across New Jersey, back to New York. Morgan and his men disguised themselves as Indians and used guerilla maneuvers against the British.

In September 1777, some of Morgan's regiment, including Morgan, was assigned to Horatio Gates for the Saratoga campaign. Morgan and his riflemen were instrumental in Burgoyne's surrender there. At Freeman's Farm on September 19, Morgan's men ran into the advance wing of Burgoyne's force. In the initial volley, all the British officers in the advance party were killed, and the British retreated. As the British force returned to the field, the two sides fought to a stalemate.

On October 7 at Bemis Heights, one of Morgan's riflemen killed British General Simon Fraser at the urging of Benedict Arnold. This helped to turn the tide of the battle. Arnold and Morgan then turned a counterattack from Burgoyne. That night, Burgoyne withdrew to the village of Saratoga, New York (now Schuylerville). As Burgoyne's forces dug in over the following week, Morgan's men harassed British patrols, convincing them further retreat was not possible. Burgoyne then surrendered. Gates heaped praise on Morgan and his unit. Morgan is depicted in the painting by John Trumbull entitled *The Surrender of General Burgoyne*.

After Saratoga, throughout 1778, Morgan was in New Jersey with Washington, harassing British supply lines. He was not at the Battle of Monmouth and did not receive an expected promotion to brigadier general. Instead, he was made colonel of the 7th Virginia Regiment, a lateral move, likely due to his lack of political connections in the Congress. Citing his aggravated legs and back from the abuse he took in Quebec, the frustrated Morgan accepted an "honorable furlough" to resign from the army in early 1779.

General Gates, who had taken command of the Southern Department, called up Morgan to return to the army in June 1780. Morgan saw that an opportunity for higher command was not on the table and declined the offer. When Gates then suffered a resounding defeat at Camden, South Carolina, Morgan reconsidered and joined Gates at Hillsborough, North Carolina. There, he supported the state militias until Congress elevated him to brigadier general in November.

Nathanael Greene then assumed command of southern American troops. He met with Morgan on December 3, 1780, at Charlotte, North Carolina, and granted Morgan command over a portion of his forces. They were tasked with harassing the enemy in the South Carolina backcountry while avoiding direct conflict. British General Cornwallis then sent Colonel Banastre Tarleton and his legion to track down Morgan. Learning of this, Morgan disobeyed Greene and decided to rally the militia to attack.

On January 17, 1781, the two forces met at Cowpens, South Carolina. Along with militia under Andrew Pickens and dragoons under William Washington, Morgan confronted a superior force of Tarleton's Legion, supplemented by other troops. Morgan took advantage of Tarleton's disdain for the militia and his riflemen's accuracy to lure the British into a trap. As Tarleton's forces advanced confidently, believing they were attacking militia firing and retreating, they were subject to the bullets from the sharpshooters. In less than an hour, over 90% of the British troops were killed, wounded, or captured as well as all their supplies and equipment. Tarleton managed to escape with a small number of troops. Morgan's plan was considered a tactical masterpiece and touted as one of the most successfully executed double envelopes (attacks on both flanks) in all modern warfare. This turned the tide of the war in the South.

Back in Virginia, the commonwealth granted him a forfeited Tory estate. Given the constant pain of his sciatica during the damp, chilly campaign, Morgan returned to Virginia on February 10, 1781. He was back on the field briefly that July pursuing Tarleton with Lafayette, but the Legionnaire escaped. Three months later, at Yorktown, Washington found Cornwallis significantly weakened thanks to Morgan's victory.

Morgan settled into land investing. He accumulated an estate of over 250,000 acres. In 1782, he built a house near Winchester dubbed Saratoga using Hessian labor. In 1790, Congress awarded him a gold medal commemorating his victory at Cowpens.

President Washington called him out of retirement in 1794 to assist General "Light-Horse Harry" Lee with suppressing the Whiskey Rebellion in western Pennsylvania. At this point, he was promoted to major general. The massive show of force helped to end the rebellion without a shot fired. Morgan, who lost his run for the US House of Representatives, remained until 1795, commanding the remnant of the army that stayed to enforce the peace. Among them was Meriwether Lewis.

In 1796, Morgan ran again for the US House of Representatives and won 70% of the vote. He was a Federalist, defeating the Democratic-Republican Robert Rutherford. Morgan held the seat for one term until early 1799, retiring due to his declining health. A doctor who was attending Morgan noticed the welts on his back from his punishment in his youth. Morgan's body was battered from his many engagements. Morgan died at his daughter's home in Winchester on July 6, 1802. He was buried at the Old Stone Presbyterian Church but was later moved to Mount Hebron Cemetery in Winchester after the Civil War. Wife Abigail followed him into the grave in 1816. She is buried in Logan County, Kentucky.

Numerous states have counties named in his honor. Morganton, North Carolina, and Morganfield, Kentucky, are named after him, as are numerous squares, streets, and schools. Likewise, many statues of Morgan have been erected. Confederate General John Hunt Morgan claimed to be a descendant.

An attempt was made in 1951 to reinter Morgan's body at Cowpens, South Carolina, but the Frederick-Winchester Historical Society blocked this. In 1973, his home Saratoga became a National Historic Landmark. In 2000, Morgan was the basis for the character Benjamin Martin in the movie *The Patriot*.

Memorial to Daniel Morgan.

Gouverneur Morris
(1752–1816)

The Penman of the Constitution

Buried at Saint Ann's Episcopal Churchyard,
Bronx, New York.

Articles of Confederation • U.S. Constitution • Military • Diplomat

He was a founding father who hailed from New York City. He argued with his family over the issue of American independence. He served in the army during the Revolutionary War. He signed both the Articles of Confederation and the United States Constitution. He is credited with writing large sections of the latter document including the preamble. He was also a United States Senator from 1800 to 1803. His name was Gouverneur Morris.

Morris was born on January 31, 1752, in what is now called the Bronx section of New York City at the family estate known as Morrisania Manor. As a boy, he exhibited a keen intellect. So keen in fact that, at the age of twelve, he enrolled in King's College which is now known as Columbia University. He began his studies in 1764 and graduated in four years. Since he was too young at age sixteen to start a career, he stayed at King's and received his Master's degree in 1771. Next Morris studied under the noted New York law scholar William Smith. It was through Smith, who opposed British tax policies in the colonies, that Morris met patriots such as John Jay and Alexander Hamilton.

Gouverneur Morris

In 1775, Morris was elected to the New York Provincial Congress. This Congress was organized by patriots who were seeking an alternative to the Province of New York Assembly, which was the official pro-British body. It was during his service in the Provincial Congress that Morris began supporting turning the colony of New York into an independent state. This put him at odds with both his family and his mentor William Smith who had turned away from the patriot cause when it moved towards pursuing independence.

When the Revolutionary War began, Morris favored reasoning with those Americans who stayed loyal to the king. This is hardly surprising since this group, known as Tories, included his mother and his half-brother. His mother gave the family estate to the British army to be used for military purposes. As the war went on, Morris changed his views on the treatment of Tories and favored tarring and feathering, whippings and the confiscation of property.

In 1778, Morris was appointed to be a delegate to the Continental Congress. He was placed on a committee charged with reforming the Continental Army. Upon visiting the army at Valley Forge, he was so affected by the conditions that he became a spokesman for the military in Congress and was instrumental in reforms in training, methods, and financing. That same year, the Conway Cabal took place. Its purpose was to remove George Washington as Commander-in-Chief of the army. Morris cast the deciding vote that kept Washington in his job. In 1779, Morris was defeated in an election that cost him his seat in Congress. Most likely the defeat was caused by his support for a strong central government, a view not popular in New York at the time. After his defeat, he left New York and moved to Philadelphia.

In 1780, Morris shattered his left leg, and it had to be amputated. He said he had done it by getting his leg stuck in the spokes of a carriage he was driving. However, Morris had a reputation for having affairs with both married and unmarried women. There was gossip that the accident occurred while a jealous husband was chasing him.

In Philadelphia, he served as superintendent of finance from 1781 to 1785. He also worked as a merchant who put him in contact with the financier and founding father, Robert Morris (no relation). With the support of both George Washington and Robert Morris, he was appointed to be a Pennsylvania delegate to the 1787 Constitutional Convention.

Morris certainly made his presence known at the Convention. According to Catherine Drinker Bowen in her book *Miracle at Philadelphia*, Morris has been described as the most brilliant man at the Convention. She noted that he often spoke, giving 173 speeches, while never saying anything foolish or tedious. She describes his tactics as abrupt, first an eloquent explosive expression of his position and then cynically waiting for the Convention to catch up with him. He continued to favor a strong central government. He said, "When the powers of the national government clash with the states, only then must the states yield." Many others at the Convention, including Washington, shared his desire for a strong central government. Morris served on the Committee of Style and Arrangement who drafted the final language of the proposed constitution. Bowen called Morris the Committee's "amanuensis" meaning that he was responsible for most of the draft, as well as its final form. Also, Morris was one of the few delegates at the convention who spoke openly against slavery. According to James Madison's notes, Morris attacked slavery calling it a nefarious institution. After the Constitution was adopted, Morris was proud to put his signature on it. He then moved back to New York.

Morris went to France on business in 1789. He would not return for a decade. He served as Minister Plenipotentiary to France from 1792 to 1794. His diaries from this period have become a valuable resource concerning the French Revolution. They also help to document his ongoing affairs with women. He was openly critical of the French Revolution which led to a request from the French government to recall him which the United States eventually did.

Upon his return to the States, he resumed his law practice and entered politics. In 1800 he was elected to the United States Senate as a Federalist representing New York. He would serve until 1803. During this time, he championed improving transportation from the eastern part of the country to the interior. After being defeated in his reelection bid, he became Chairman of the Erie Canal Commission from 1810 to 1813. The canal was instrumental in transforming New York into a financial capital. That much was clear to Morris when he said: "The proudest empire in Europe is but a bubble compared to what America will be, must be, in the course of two centuries, perhaps of one."

Morris married at the age of 57. His wife was Ann Cary Randolph, the sister of Thomas Mann Randolph who was the husband of Thomas Jefferson's daughter Martha. Morris and his wife had one son, Gouverneur Morris Jr., who became a railroad executive.

On November 16, 1816, Morris passed away after causing himself internal injuries while using a piece of whalebone to clear a blockage in his urinary tract. He was laid to rest in Saint Ann's Episcopal Churchyard Cemetery along with his brother Lewis Morris who signed the Declaration of Independence.

Morris's grandson, William Walton Morris, a graduate of West Point, was a brevet Major General during the Civil War. He is also buried at Saint Ann's.

Monument to Morris in the Bronx. His grave is beneath the church nearby.

During the early twentieth century, a great-grandson, also named Gouverneur Morris (1876–1953), authored novels and short stories. The Lon Chaney film *The Penalty* (1920) was adapted from one of them.

Morris was a substantial landowner in St. Lawrence County in upstate New York. There, the town and village of Gouverneur are named for him. During World War II, the liberty ship S.S. *Gouverneur Morris* was named after him.

In *Pennsylvania History* in July 1938, Philip Wild summed up Morris's life:

> Endowed with all that aids a man to achieve much for the common good, namely sterling character, wisdom, worthwhile place and wealth, Morris, on the contrary, chose to use these gifts to advance and strengthen the position of the small group of property men to which he belonged, instead of setting for his goal, the securing of the greatest good for all the people. His narrow conservatism led to his failure to secure political gifts from the people about whom he so often manifested his lack of faith. Lacking political backing, Morris became embittered and adopted positions which have brought rather caustic criticisms to him from historians. But it must be remembered that in public office, his efforts controlled as they were by the more liberal tendencies of his higher officers, produced much of significance for the United States.

Thomas Nelson Jr.
(1738–1789)

The Governor Who Was All-In

Buried at Grace Episcopal Churchyard,
Yorktown, Virginia.

Declaration of Independence • Military

Thomas Nelson Jr. was a wealthy planter, soldier, and statesman who served many terms in the colonial Virginia General Assembly and in the Continental Congress, where he signed the Declaration of Independence. He was governor of Virginia in 1781 and fought in the militia during the Siege of Yorktown. He used his assets to prop up Virginia and the state militia during the American Revolution, only to see his property destroyed by the British and his fortune ruined.

Thomas Nelson Jr. was born December 26, 1738, in Yorktown, Virginia, the oldest son of William Nelson Sr. and his wife, Elizabeth (née Burwell). The elder Nelson served twice as the royal governor of Virginia in 1770 and 1771. Nelson's maternal grandfather, Robert "King" Carter, was one of the wealthiest Virginians and a royal governor. On his father's side, Nelson was the grandson of Thomas "Scotch Tom" Nelson, an early pioneer at Yorktown who emigrated from Cumberland, England. One genealogist stated these Nelsons were distant relations of Lord Horatio Nelson.

Nelson was tagged as a junior due to his uncle by the same name. He attended private schools in Virginia before heading to England to study at Hackney, near London. He then attended Christ's College at

Thomas Nelson Jr.

Cambridge University in May 1758. He graduated in 1760 and returned to Virginia the following year. In 1762 Nelson married Lucy Grymes, a wealthy widow, with whom he eventually had eleven children, including Hugh Nelson, who served in the US House of Representatives from 1811 to 1823. Grymes's first husband was Carter Burwell, and she was the niece of Peyton Randolph, who was a brother-in-law of Benjamin Harrison V. Grimes's aunt was the mother of "Light-Horse Harry" Lee.

Nelson was primarily a planter, helping his father manage his various plantations and the estates owned by his two minor stepsons. He also entered politics and was first elected by York County voters to the Virginia House of Burgesses in 1761, replacing Robert Carter Nicholas. He served six more terms and was also on His Majesty's Council in 1764.

By 1774, after the Stamp and Sugar Acts, Nelson turned against the Crown. At Williamsburg on March 20, 1775, Nelson voted for the measure proposed by Patrick Henry to arm Virginians to fight the British. It was Nelson who introduced a resolution in the Virginia House to declare independence from England. As tensions with the mother country escalated, Nelson was appointed a colonel in the militia's 2nd Virginia Regiment. On August 11, 1775, before Nelson could become engaged in the military, he was elected as a member of the Virginia delegation to the Continental Congress.

Nelson arrived to attend the opening of the Continental Congress on September 11, 1775. According to the diary of John Adams, "Thomas Nelson, Esq., George Wythe, Esq., and Francis Lightfoot Lee, Esq., appeared as delegates from Virginia. Nelson is a fat man, like the late Colonel Lee of Marblehead. He is a speaker, and alert and lively for his weight." Nelson served through February 23, 1776, when he returned home. There, he attended Virginia's constitutional convention that spring.

Nelson returned to the Continental Congress on June 9, 1776. He was one of thirteen members appointed to the committee on June 12 to begin work on what ultimately became the Articles of Confederation. In July, Nelson voted for independence from England and signed the Declaration to that effect. Nelson served in the Congress until May 8, 1777, traveling back and forth from Virginia. During this time, Nelson was appointed a brigadier general and the commander-in-chief of all of Virginia's forces in the Continental Army. Nelson took command and raised an army. He marched them to Philadelphia, which had been invaded by the British. However, Congress was unable to pay the troops and ordered them disbanded.

On December 10, 1778, Nelson was again appointed to the Continental Congress, serving from February 18 to April 22, 1779. Due to a bout of illness, he returned to Virginia, where he financed the state's activities and the militia, acting as the commander-in-chief. By 1781, Nelson succeeded Thomas Jefferson, following William Fleming's nine days as acting governor). During this time, the British invaded Virginia and took Nelson's home, Nelson House, as a headquarters for Cornwallis.

Wrote a descendant, Channing Moon Thompson, in 1898, "In June 1781 [Nelson] was chosen Governor of [the] State of Virginia & took part in the siege of Yorktown as Major General in the American Army. His force of 3000 men was raised and equipped at his own expense. At the time of the siege, his own house was his headquarters, & later, during an engagement, he ordered it to be fired into, saying to General Lafayette 'Spare no particle of my property so long as it affords comfort or shelter to the enemies of my country.'" According to another source, Nelson offered five guineas to the first man to hit his house.

Though victorious at Yorktown, Nelson was under a tremendous financial strain, having utilized much of his personal and family fortune in sustaining the state and the army. He was now in debt. Despite these issues, Nelson continued as a member of the Virginia House of Delegates, representing York County through 1788. Thomas Nelson Jr. died at his son's home in Hanover County, Virginia, on January 4, 1789, and was buried at the Grace Episcopal Churchyard in Yorktown. Wrote Colonel James Innes in tribute:

> The illustrious General Thomas Nelson is no more! He paid the last great debt to nature, on Sunday, the fourth of the present month, at his estate in Hanover. He who undertakes barely to recite the exalted virtues which adorned the life of this great and good man, will unavoidably pronounce a panegyric on human nature. As a man, a citizen, a legislator, and a patriot, he exhibited a conduct untarnished and undebased by sordid or selfish interest, and strongly marked with the genuine characteristics of true religion, sound benevolence, and liberal policy. Entertaining the most ardent love for civil and religious liberty, he was among the first of that glorious band of patriots whose exertions dashed and defeated the machinations of British tyranny and gave United America freedom and independent empire. At a most important crisis, during the late struggle for American liberty, when this state appeared to be designated as the theatre of action for the contending armies, he was selected by the unanimous suffrage of the legislature to command the virtuous yeomanry of his country; in this honourable employment he remained until the end of the war; as a soldier, he was indefatigably active and coolly intrepid;

Thomas Nelson Jr. (1738–1789)

The grave of Thomas Nelson Jr.

resolute and undejected in misfortunes, he towered above distress, and struggled with the manifold difficulties to which his situation exposed him, with constancy and courage. In the memorable year 1781, when the whole force of the southern British army was directed to the immediate subjugation of this state, he was called to the helm of government; this was a juncture which indeed 'tried men's souls.' He did not avail himself of this opportunity to retire in the rear of danger; but on the contrary, took the field at the head of his countrymen; and at the hazard of his life, his fame, and individual fortune, by his decision and magnanimity, he saved not only his country, but all America, from disgrace, if not from total ruin. Of this truly patriotic and heroic conduct, the renowned commander in chief, with all the gallant officers of the combined armies employed at the siege of York, will bear ample testimony; this part of his conduct even contemporary jealousy, envy, and malignity were forced to approve, and this, more impartial posterity, if it can believe, will almost adore. If, after contemplating the splendid and heroic parts of his character, we shall inquire for the milder virtues of humanity, and seek for the man, we shall find the refined, beneficent, and social qualities of private life, through all its forms and combinations, so happily modified and united in him, that in the words of the darling poet of nature, it may be said: His life was gentle: and the elements so mixed in him, that nature might stand up And say to all the world—this was a man.

Nelson House, in Yorktown, Virginia, is a National Historic Landmark maintained by the US National Park Service at the Colonial National Historical Park. Nelson Counties in Virginia and Kentucky are named in his honor, as is the Thomas Nelson Community College and the Thomas Nelson High School.

Robert Treat Paine
(1731–1814)

The Objection Maker

Buried at Granary Burying Ground,
Boston, Massachusetts.

Declaration of Independence

Robert Treat Paine was a Massachusetts delegate to the Continental Congress, a prosecutor in Boston of the British troops involved in the Boston Massacre, and a signer of the Declaration of Independence.

Paine was born on March 11, 1731, in Boston, the fourth of five children of Reverend Thomas Paine, pastor of the Congregational Church at Weymouth, Massachusetts, and Eunice Treat. Paine has an impressive family history. The Treats were prominent in the British colonies, and the Paines can trace a lineage back to the *Mayflower*. Reverend Thomas Paine left the full-time ministry in 1730, moved the family to Boston, and entered business as a merchant.

Robert grew up in Boston near the prestigious Boston Latin School, which he attended. He finished at the top of his class and entered Harvard College at the age of fourteen. Just as he was graduating in 1749, his father lost his fortune and moved to Nova Scotia, leaving Robert to make his own way.

In 1750 Robert took a position as a teacher in the town of Lunenberg, Massachusetts. He moved back to Boston in 1751 and went to sea as a

Robert Treat Paine

merchant selling manufactured goods. He traveled to the southern colonies, mainly North Carolina, the Azores, and Spain. These endeavors were not very successful, and as a result, Paine briefly tried whaling in Greenland. This also failed, and in 1755 he began to study law with his relative Judge Samuel Willard in Lancaster, Massachusetts. When Willard was appointed colonel for the Crown Point expedition during the French and Indian War, Robert tried for an officer's commission but failed and served as chaplain of the regiment. He was encamped at Lake George for three months at the end of 1755. He moved back to Boston in the fall of 1756 and resumed the study of law under Benjamin Prat, later chief justice in New York. In May 1757, he was admitted to the bar. His father died that same month, leaving Robert with many debts and family responsibilities. Instead of setting up a practice, he was forced to go from town to town looking for business, called "circuit riding." In 1758, Paine qualified for practicing before the Superior Court. He moved to Taunton in southern Massachusetts and advanced his legal career, rising to a justice of the peace and barrister.

In 1766, he began to court Sally Cobb, the daughter of a leading merchant in Taunton, and married her on March 15, 1770. The couple had eight children together.

Paine's dedication to the patriot cause began as early as 1766 when he spoke out against the Stamp Act. In 1768, he served as Taunton's delegate at the provincial convention held in Boston to discuss the landing of British troops in Boston. While he decried the measures that the British were using against the colonies, he still believed, at least at this point, that separation from England would not be necessary.

The atmosphere changed in March 1770 when a clash between some Bostonians harassing British troops stationed in the city led them to open fire on the crowd killing five men. Paine was selected to prosecute the troops who were charged with murder. Defending the soldiers was John Adams, thus pitting two of Massachusetts' most eminent attorneys and future signers of the Declaration of Independence against one another. For both sides, trying the case required a great deal of delicacy and diplomacy. Nine soldiers were on trial, including their captain, Thomas Preston. Paine expressed that the core issue was whether the British Parliament could legally quarter an army in a town without its consent.

Following one of the first trials in American history to last for several days, even the crowd seemed exhausted. Testimony after testimony had been used to show both sides of the "Massacre" story. If the troops were assaulted at all, it constituted a provocation for which the law reduces the offense to manslaughter. All nine men were found not guilty of murder, while two were found guilty of manslaughter.

The trial did much to enhance Paine's reputation and popularity. In 1773, based on his work at the trial, he was elected to the House of Representatives from Taunton. That same year, Sam Adams formed a Committee of Correspondence to discuss the colonists' grievances, and he asked Paine to serve on the panel. He continued to represent Taunton in Massachusetts' Provincial Congress in 1774 and 1775.

Also, in 1774 he was elected to attend the First Continental Congress. He served there from October 5 to October 26, 1774, and on December 5 was elected to serve in the Second Continental Congress. Paine was among the members who were hesitant to cut ties entirely with their mother country and hoped that the formation of the Second Continental Congress would show the British a united colonial front, thereby leading them to negotiate. Even after Lexington, Concord, and Bunker Hill, he

The crypt of Robert Treat Paine.

Robert Treat Paine (1731–1814)

hoped that peace could prevail, and in July 1775, he signed the Olive Branch Petition that was sent to King George III as a final attempt to avoid war. The King's rejection proved to be a turning point for many colonists. Paine may not have been among the original supporters of a war with England, but after the Olive Branch Petition rejection, he acknowledged its inevitability.

Paine was a vocal and involved member of the Continental Congress, often to the chagrin of others. Benjamin Rush nicknamed him the "Objection Maker" because, according to Rush, he seldom proposed anything but opposed nearly every measure proposed by other people. The record shows that he served punctually and faithfully on many congressional committees and chaired the Committee on Ordnance. He pressed hard for the domestic manufacture of gunpowder, muskets, and artillery. After signing the Declaration of Independence, Paine returned to Massachusetts and remained involved in government at the state level. He represented Taunton in the Massachusetts House of Representatives. He served as its speaker in 1777, a member of the Executive Council in 1779, and a member of the committee that drafted the state constitution in 1780. He became Massachusetts' first attorney general, serving from 1777 to 1790. He prosecuted the treason trials following Shay's Rebellion.

In 1783 Paine was offered a place on the State Supreme Court bench but initially declined, preferring to remain attorney general. He eventually accepted his friend Governor John Hancock's offer of an associate justiceship in 1790 and served until 1804, when he retired due to his increasing deafness. He enjoyed a peaceful retirement and died in 1814. He is buried in the Granary Burying Ground in Boston, two short blocks from his birthplace. The plaque over the vault of his grave reads, "One of the signers of the Declaration of Independence."

Edmund Pendleton
(1721–1803)

"Here Comes the Judge!"

Buried in the Bruton Parish Church Sanctuary,
Williamsburg, Virginia.

Continental Association

Edmund Pendleton was a long-time member of the Virginia House of Burgesses in colonial times who was also the speaker of that body. He was elected to the First Continental Congress, famously riding on horseback from Mount Vernon, Virginia, to Philadelphia with George Washington and Patrick Henry. There, Pendleton signed the Continental Association. He later contributed resolutions for the Declaration of Independence in the Virginia Assembly, some of the ideas which Thomas Jefferson incorporated. Pendleton then served many years as a judge in Virginia, including in the state supreme court. He was the uncle of fellow Continental Congress delegates Nathaniel Pendleton and John Penn, a signer of the Declaration.

Edmund Pendleton was born on September 9, 1721, in Caroline County, Virginia, the seventh child of Henry Pendleton and his wife, Mary Bishop (née Taylor) Pendleton. Henry's grandfather, also named Henry, emigrated from Norwich, England, in the late 1600s. Henry Pendleton never got to see baby Edmund as he died four months before his son's birth. James Taylor, Mary's father, was a plantation owner in

Edmund Pendleton (1721–1803)

Edmund Pendleton

Rappahannock County who helped the widow and her children until she married Edward Watkins in 1723.

The Watkins stepchildren grew up under meager circumstances. At 14, young Edmund became apprenticed to Colonel Benjamin Robinson, the Clerk of the Caroline Court. Pendleton became exposed to politics and the law. He began reading law books and learning legal procedures. In 1737, at 16, he became the Clerk of the Vestry of St. Mary's Parish in Caroline. He used the money he made to purchase law books and read them diligently. By 1741, at 20, Pendleton was licensed as an attorney. On January 21, 1741, he married Elizabeth Roy, but she died in childbirth on November 16, 1742. The infant son did not survive. On June

20, 1743, Pendleton married Sarah Pollard, the daughter of Joseph and Priscilla Pollard. The couple had no children.

Pendleton worked first in county courts and then as the prosecuting attorney for Essex County. This allowed him to join the general court bar in October 1745. He then accepted an appointment to justice of the peace for Caroline County in 1751. Pendleton trained his nephews, John Penn (a future signed of the Declaration of Independence) and John Taylor (a future U.S. Senator). From 1752 until 1776, Pendleton represented Caroline County in the Virginia House of Burgesses until dissolved at the outset of the American Revolution.

When the Stamp Act was enacted and the distributor of the stamps resigned, Pendleton encouraged as much legal activity as possible without using stamps, such as recording wills. In 1766, when his mentor, John Robinson, who was speaker of the House of Burgesses, died, Pendleton was appointed one of the executors. He helped uncover a scandal involving Robinson's incredible debt, who was assumed to be very wealthy. This controversy lasted for over forty years until it was settled.

As tensions arose with England, Pendleton was on the Virginia Committee of Correspondence in 1773. In August 1774, he attended the convention in Williamsburg to choose delegates to the First Continental Congress. The following delegates were selected from Virginia: Peyton Randolph, Richard Henry Lee, George Washington, Patrick Henry, Richard Bland, Benjamin Harrison, and Edmund Pendleton. He then rode to Philadelphia on horseback with Patrick Henry and George Washington. There, on October 14, 1774, he signed the Continental Association. The following year, on July 8, he signed the Olive Branch Petition. Around that time, in the Second Continental Congress, he proposed a resolution stating, "The ground and foundation of the present unhappy dispute between the British Ministry and Parliament and America, is a Right claimed by the former to tax the Subjects of the latter without their consent, and not an inclination on our part to set up for independency, which we utterly disavow and wish to restore to a Constitutional Connection upon the most solid and reasonable basis."

Back in Williamsburg on December 1, 1775, Pendleton, as President of the Committee of Safety, was president of the convention held to discuss Virginia's disposition. During the convention, there was a call to draft a declaration of independence from England. They asked that all the colonies adopt it. It was the first such declaration in the colonies. The convention also debated George Mason's Virginia Declaration of Rights, which later served as a model for the Declaration of Independence. Pendleton won the support of slave owners for the measure by suggesting that universal rights exclude slaves.

On May 6, 1776, another convention was called in Williamsburg, and Pendleton was again elected the president. Pendleton addressed the convention: "We are now met in General Convention according to the ordinance for our election, at a time truly critical, when the subjects of the most important and interesting nature require our serious attention. The administration of justice, and almost all the powers of government, have now been suspended for near two years. It will become us to reflect whether we can longer sustain the great struggle we are making in this situation; and the case of criminals confined and not tried, and others who may be apprehended pursuant to our laws, deserves particular notice. Our military and naval arrangements, as well as the funds for supporting them, will call for our revision; and the ordinance prescribing a mode of punishment for the enemies of America in this colony being very defective, will require amendment . . ."

That November, Pendleton, Thomas Jefferson, George Wythe, George Mason, and Thomas Ludwell Lee were appointed to a committee to revise Virginia's laws. Pendleton was also elected as the speaker of the Virginia House of Delegates, the new state legislature. In March 1777, Pendleton fell from his horse and dislocated his hip. This forced him to use crutches for the rest of his life. That year he became a judge of the High Court of Chancery. The following year, he was appointed the president of the Virginia Supreme Court of Appeal, a position he held until his death.

In 1788, Pendleton was unanimously elected president of the Virginia Ratifying Convention for the U.S. Constitution by the 168 delegates. After days of debate open to the public, the Constitution narrowly passed, making Virginia the tenth state to ratify it. Pendleton and his friend George Wythe voted in favor. Friend Patrick Henry was opposed.

The tomb of Edmund Pendleton.

Of primary concern was the addition of a Bill of Rights proposed by George Mason and sponsored by James Madison.

On October 23, 1803, Judge Edmund Pendleton died at his 2300-acre estate "Edmundsbury" near Bowling Green, Virginia. He was initially buried on the grounds of the estate. Due to his former estate's decay in 1907, his remains were exhumed and reinterred within Bruton Parish Episcopal Church in Williamsburg, Virginia. The slab covering his tomb says simply, "Edmund Pendleton of Caroline."

Pendleton left no descendants. His nephew, the son of his brother John, was named Edmund Pendleton, Jr., and became the principal heir. His nephew Nathaniel Pendleton, Jr., distinguished himself as an aide to General Nathanael Greene. Many Pendletons in succeeding generations became judges in Virginia. A relative, Philip Pendleton Barbour, served on the U.S. Supreme Court and as Speaker of the House. James Barbour, Philip's brother, served as governor of Virginia, in the U.S. Senate, and as secretary of war. Other Pendleton relations served in the military, including for the Confederacy during the Civil War.

Pendleton counties in West Virginia and Kentucky are named in honor of Edmund Pendleton.

Israel Putnam
(1718–1790)

Old Put

Buried at Putnam Monument,
Brooklyn, Connecticut.

Military

Israel Putnam, known as "Old Put" to many, was a general in the Continental Army during the American Revolution. Though aggressive and courageous, many questioned his military acumen. He first served notably during the French and Indian War as an officer in Rogers' Rangers. During the Revolution, he was most famous for his service at Bunker Hill, where he is credited with ordering, "Don't fire until you see the whites of their eyes!"

Israel Putnam was born in Salem Village (now Danvers), Massachusetts, on January 7, 1718, the son of Joseph Putnam and his wife, Elizabeth (née Porter) Putnam. The Putnams were Puritans and successful farmers. Young Israel was named for his maternal grandfather, Israel Porter, who, along with his son-in-law, Joseph Putnam, challenged local authorities during the Salem Witch Trials in the 1690s. The two men intervened on behalf of Rebecca Nurse, who had been accused of witchcraft. Porter and Putnam signed a petition on her behalf, and she was initially found innocent. However, a jury overturned the ruling, and Nurse was convicted and executed. Her sister was also executed during the craze.

Israel Putnam (1718–1790)

Israel Putnam

Regarding Putnam's upbringing, historian Benson J. Lossing wrote in 1869, "His education was neglected, and he grew to manhood with a vigorous but uncultivated mind." In 1738/39, Putnam married his first wife, Hannah Pope. She was the mother of his ten children. The young family moved to northeastern Connecticut to Mortlake, later part of Pomfret and Brooklyn. There, Putnam became a prosperous farmer.

As a young farmer in 1743, Putnam became a local hero when he killed a wolf that had been menacing his sheep and those of his neighbors. They had tracked the she-wolf to its lair, but their dogs would go no further, some of them injured by the wolf. They attempted to smoke the wolf out of its den using sulfur, but this was to no avail. None of the farmers were willing to enter the cave, and Putnam's servant was likewise inclined to stay out, despite him being handed a torch and gun and ordered to do so. At wit's end, Putnam grabbed the torch and his musket loaded with buckshot and crawled into the cave with a rope around his waist in case he needed to be pulled out quickly. He crawled inside about forty feet, down the narrow passageway, until he saw glowing red eyes and heard the snarl of the beast. He then shot the wolf, killing it, and dragged it out by its ears. The farmers were so delighted; they carried Putnam through the village in a torchlit parade that went late into the night. The nicknames "Wolf Putnam" and "Old Wolf Put" stuck with Putnam for many years afterward. Today in Pomfret, Connecticut, there is a section of Mashamoquet Brook State Park named "Wolf Den," believed to be the event's site.

At age 37, in 1755, after Braddock's defeat, Putnam was summoned into the Connecticut militia and quickly moved up the ranks from private to second lieutenant, captain, major, lieutenant colonel, and colonel. He had natural leadership abilities and charisma and excelled at recruiting men into his regiment. When a captain, Putnam was introduced to Major Robert Rogers, with whom he served in the upcoming expedition to Crown Point, establishing a reputation as a capable frontier fighter. It was said that "Rogers always sent, but Putnam led his men to action."

By 1757, Putnam had seen action at Fort William Henry and was promoted to major. In February 1758, at Fort Edward, along the Hudson River near modern-day Glens Falls, New York, Putnam again exhibited great courage and personal sacrifice. A fire broke out in the barracks near the gunpowder. Fearing an explosion, Putnam got up on the roof and poured bucket after bucket of water on the flames, getting down only when the fire was within feet of the magazine. He then continued to fight the fire until it was extinguished, receiving severe burns and blisters that sidelined him for several weeks.

Putnam was back in action with Rogers' Rangers at the Battle of Fort Carillon, also known as the 1758 Battle of Ticonderoga, on July 8, 1758. He led a regiment into the Valley of Death. Ultimately, the British attack failed, and the French held the fort.

Near Fort Miller on the Hudson, Putnam was alone in a batteau when he was surprised by Indians. He then shot the rapids in his boat,

Israel Putnam (1718–1790)

astonishing the natives. After a fierce skirmish near Fort Ann, New York, Major Putnam was captured by Mohawk Indians on August 8, 1758. They stripped him and tied him to a tree, intending to burn him alive. An early biographer described the natives as they howled and danced around the encroaching flames. Putnam believed his life was at an end and thought of his dear family. Suddenly, a French officer burst through the woods and intervened. He untied Putnam and took him into captivity. After the British victory at Fort Frontenac, later that month, Putnam was exchanged for French prisoners. He was promoted to lieutenant colonel soon after that.

By 1760, the tide had turned in favor of the British. In General Jeffrey Amherst's campaign to successfully take Canada at Oswegatchie, New York, Putnam captured two French ships, boarding them after approaching them in shallow rowboats. As Canada was surrendered to the English, it appeared Putnam's role in the war was at an end. However, after Spain invaded Britain's ally Portugal in May 1762, Putnam took part in an expedition against Havana, Cuba, then a Spanish territory, and was shipwrecked. Not deterred, the assault was successful. Putnam is said to have brought back Cuban tobacco seeds, which he planted in Connecticut, later leading to the Connecticut Wrapper cigar's creation.

During Pontiac's Rebellion, Putnam took up arms again as part of the relief expedition to Detroit in 1764. After the campaign, Putnam returned to civilian life. He joined the Congregational Church in his town.

In 1765, Hannah Putnam died, leaving Putnam a widower alone with ten children. This did not deter him from his public life. Now the owner of a tavern, he became involved in politics. During the Stamp Act crisis of 1765 and 1766, Putnam was vocal against the tax. Putnam was elected to the Connecticut General Assembly and was one of the founders of the local Sons of Liberty. In 1767, he married his second wife, Deborah (née Crow) Lothrop, the widow of Samuel Lothrop.

As the hostilities with Britain began to ramp up, Putnam headed the local Committee of Correspondence in 1774. He was also made a lieutenant colonel in the Connecticut militia. After the British closed the port of Boston, Putnam drove a herd of sheep to the city to benefit the locals. The day after the fighting began the following April at Lexington and Concord, Putnam plowed a field with his son. Upon hearing the news, he unhitched his team, sent word for his regiment to gather, and rode off to the action without changing his clothes. Putnam rode 100 miles in eight hours, arriving in Cambridge the next day. He was named a major general, second in rank to only Artemas Ward, head of the Army of Observation, the Continental Army's precursor. Putnam gathered his troops and conducted numerous sorties against the British, ranging from taunting the British from Charlestown to burning a beached warship. Putnam's goal was to keep his men sharp, anticipating a significant engagement. While discussing the upcoming battle with Joseph Warren and Artemas Ward, Ward suggested a defensive posture, "As peace and reconciliation is what we seek for, would it not be better to act only on the defensive and give no unnecessary provocation?" Putnam, irked by this, turned to Warren and exclaimed, "You know, Dr. Warren, we shall have no peace worth anything till we gain it by the sword!"

While the British troops readied in Boston to attack the colonials at Bunker Hill, Putnam also argued to fortify the adjacent Breed's Hill, closer to Boston. From this point, cannons could threaten the British there, forcing them to attack the hill. Throughout the morning of June 17, 1775, General William Howe began massing roughly 2,300 British troops near Charlestown to attack the freshly dug American defenses. Meanwhile, with Breed's Hill set, Putnam reinforced the forces at Bunker Hill. General Howe ordered the attack at 3:30 PM. Putnam left Bunker Hill to join General William Prescott on Breed's Hill. It is here that Putnam may have ordered Prescott to tell his troops, "Don't fire until you see the whites of their eyes." While it is debated who said these words, the point was to be careful with the precious stock of ammunition.

As the British approached, they were cut down. Putnam rode through the American lines, encouraging his men to hold their positions. Eventually, the Americans ran out of powder and had to retreat. Putnam rallied his Connecticut troops at Winter Hill to make another stand. However, the British stopped their advance. In the end, the tally at Bunker/Breed's Hill was 1054 British casualties, to 449 for the colonials. Wrote General Nathanael Greene to his brother, "I wish we could sell them another hill, at the same price."

On June 14, 1775, before the battle, and unknown to those involved, the Continental Congress voted unanimously for George Washington to be Commander-in-Chief of the army. Putnam was retained as one of the four major generals, the only one to receive a unanimous vote like Washington. Historian Richard Ketchum wrote, "Putnam was five feet six inches tall, powerfully built, and had the face of a cherubic bulldog mounted on a jaw cut like a block of wood." He was regarded as a great soldier based on his reputation during the French and Indian War. Ketchum suggests he was not skilled enough to be a major general, lacking a strategic purview.

Washington placed Putnam in charge of the reserve division for the remainder of the Siege of Boston. Around this time, Washington discussed the siege at length with his officers. Putnam grew tired of all the talk and walked to a window to observe the British. Washington, who noticed Putnam's absence, beckoned him to return. Putnam responded, "Oh, my dear General, you may plan the battle to suit yourself, and I will fight it."

On another occasion, while dining with his fellow officers, Washington offered a toast for "A speedy and honorable peace." A few days later, Putnam offered a contrarian toast for "A long and moderate war." This prompted a laugh from Washington who said to Putnam, "You are the last man, General Putnam, from whom I should have expected such a toast, you who are always urging vigorous measures, to plead now for a long, and what is still more extraordinary, a moderate, war, seems strange indeed." Putnam explained a short war would lead to a divisive false peace. He said, "I expect nothing but a long war, and I would have it a moderate one, that we may hold out till the mother country becomes willing to cast us off forever."

Ultimately, thanks to Henry Knox and Putnam's cousin Rufus Putnam, the British were forced to abandon Boston. At this point, the focus of the war shifted to New York. Putnam was in temporary command of forces there until Washington arrived on April 13, 1776. At Long Island in August 1776, Putnam set the defenses at Guana Heights. General Howe's forces easily outflanked them. The Continental Congress blamed Putnam for the defeat, but Washington did not. Senator Daniel Patrick Moynihan described Putnam's importance, ". . . it could be argued that we owe our national existence to the fortifications which General Israel Putnam threw up in April 1776 on the Buttermilk Channel side [of

Governors Island, New York] . . . [British troops] landed on Long Island and headed for George Washington and his army. He had to flee, and he made it because Putnam's artillery firing on Brooklyn Heights, over the Buttermilk Channel, held Howe back just long enough for Washington to escape to Manhattan and for the Revolutionary War to proceed."

After Long Island, Putnam returned to the Hudson Valley he was familiar with from his earlier days. In October 1777, Putnam was fooled by a feint by General Sir Henry Clinton, which led to Clinton's capture of Fort Montgomery and Fort Clinton on the Hudson. Putnam was brought before a court of inquiry, but it was determined the losses were due to a lack of men and not the commander's fault.

Putnam was not without his controversies. He was known to show favor to captured British officers, especially former comrades. He offered them newspapers and medical attention. He was also against the sale of Tory property, referring to it as embezzlement. This angered many New Yorkers involved in the practice. Washington lost faith in Putnam when he delayed sending troops as ordered. However, this happened around the time word came that Deborah Putnam had been mistaken for dead and buried alive. The casket was exhumed to reveal the error, too late. Washington decided to move Putnam closer to home and gave him recruiting duties in Connecticut and New Hampshire.

During the winter of 1778-1779, Putnam was encamped near Redding, Connecticut, a site now preserved as Putnam Memorial State Park. Here, on February 26, 1779, he was nearly captured by the British. To escape, he rode down a steep slope. A statue of Putnam was erected near this spot. By 1779, Putnam oversaw the troops from Virginia, Maryland, and Pennsylvania. But in December, while riding home to Connecticut, he suffered a stroke, which affected his speech and mobility.

Israel Putnam lingered, incapacitated, for over ten years, succumbing on May 29, 1790. He was buried in the South Cemetery in Brooklyn, Connecticut, in an above-ground tomb. However, over the years, souvenir hunters chipped away at it, making it unfit. An equestrian statue was erected in the town square in 1888, and Putnam's remains were reinterred beneath it.

Israel Putnam (1718–1790)

A captured Hessian once said of Putnam, "This old gray-beard may be a good honest man, but nobody but the rebels would have made him a general." Wrote historian Nathaniel Philbrick, "Israel Putnam was the provincial army's most beloved officer."

Israel Putnam is remembered in many ways with statues, paintings, and historic sites. Nine counties in various states are named after him, as are several towns and many streets.

Impressive equestrian memorial and grave for Ol' Put.

Edmund Randolph
(1753–1813)

Jefferson's Chameleon

Buried at Old Chapel Cemetery,
Millwood, Virginia.

**Military • Continental Congress • Constitutional Convention
Attorney General • Secretary of State**

This founder was born into an influential Virginia family. Benjamin Harrison, who would become the father and great grandfather of two American presidents, considered him "one of the cleverest young men in America." He studied the law and became one of the country's most respected lawyers. His parents remained loyal to the crown, and as the trouble between England and the colonies grew, they returned to the mother country. He served in the Continental Army and represented Virginia in the Continental Congress. After the Revolution, he became the seventh governor of Virginia. He also served as a delegate to the 1787 Constitutional Convention, where he played an influential role but was one of the three members who refused to sign the finished product. President Washington selected him to be the nation's first attorney general. He also served as Secretary of State but was forced to resign from that office because Washington was led to believe that he had revealed sensitive information to France. In 1807 he was part of the defense team that successfully defended former Vice President Aaron Burr in his treason trial. His name was Edmund Randolph.

Edmund Randolph (1753–1813)

Edmund Randolph

Randolph was born in Williamsburg, Virginia, on August 10, 1753. The Randolph's were considered one of the colony's most prominent families of lawyers-statesmen. He received his education at the College of William and Mary and then studied the law at the office of his father, John Randolph, and his uncle, Peyton Randolph. When the American Revolution began in 1775, his loyalist parents returned to England. Their son decided on a different route joining the Continental Army, where he served as an aide-de-camp to General George Washington. In October 1775, his uncle Peyton passed away, and he left the army, returning to Virginia to assume the role of executor of the estate.

In 1776 Randolph served as the youngest delegate to the Virginia Convention that wrote the state's constitution. In August of that year, he married Elizabeth Nicholas, the daughter of Robert Carter Nicholas, Virginia's state treasurer. The couple would have six children, including Peyton Randolph, who would become governor of Virginia in 1811.

Randolph was then elected the Mayor of Williamsburg and became his state's first attorney general. In 1779 he was selected to be one of Virginia's eleven delegates in the Continental Congress. He served in Congress until 1782 and, during this time, maintained a private law practice where he handled numerous legal issues for many noted Patriots, including George Washington. According to Michael Klarman in his book *The Framers Coup,* his contemporaries considered Randolph "one of the most distinguished men in America by his talents and his influence" and as "a young gentleman in whom unite all the accomplishments of the scholar and the statesmen." Enough Virginians shared this view of Randolph to elect him to the governorship of the state in 1786. At this point, he turned his lucrative law practice over to future Supreme Court Chief Justice John Marshall because Virginia law prohibited executive officers from practicing law in the state courts.

In 1787 at the age of 34, Randolph traveled to Philadelphia as a member of the Virginia delegation to attend the Constitutional Convention. As reported by James Madison, Randolph addressed the issue facing the convention, "The true question is whether we shall adhere to the federal plan or introduce the national plan. The insufficiency of the former has been fully displayed by the trial already made . . . A national government alone, properly constituted, will answer the purpose, and he begged it to be considered that the present is the last moment for establishing one. After this select experiment, the people will yield to despair."

Fifty-five delegates attended the convention, which worked from May 29 until September 17, 1787, the day of the signing. Of the delegates, 29 were recorded as having attended every session. The historian Clinton Rossiter in his work *1787: The Grand Convention,* described these 29 as "full-timers." Randolph was one of the full-timers, as was his good friend James Madison. Randolph introduced the idea, for which Madison was mainly responsible, known as the "Virginia Plan." In introducing the plan, Randolph presented it as a response to the deficiencies in the Articles of Confederation. However, he took pains not to criticize the Articles' creators themselves, calling them "wise and great men" who were limited by "the jealousy of the states regarding their sovereignty." The plan Randolph introduced was an outline for a new national government. In his aforementioned work, Michael Klarman stated that the plan and its resolutions "became the convention's first substantive business and would remain its focal point for its duration."

Throughout the convention, Randolph was an active participant in the various debates on the issues raised by the delegates. In his work, the historian Rossiter counts Randolph among a group of attendees that he calls the influentials. Rossiter and other historians give Randolph "considerable credit for the decision to enumerate the powers of Congress." Given the above, one would have expected Randolph to be a supporter of the convention's finished product. This, however, was not the case. Before the vote on the Constitution was taken, Benjamin Franklin urged all present to add their signature to the document. Franklin professed his high regard for Randolph, who had already made it clear that he was unlikely to sign. Randolph motioned that state conventions be permitted to offer amendments to the proposed Constitution and that a second convention be held to act on the state's proposals. Randolph added that if his proposition were not adopted, it would be impossible for him to put his name on the document. Every state voted no on Randolph's motion, and he became one of three delegates who refused to sign the Constitution.

After returning to Virginia, Randolph published a letter explaining his opposition to the Constitution. His chief objections were the provision for equal state representation in the Senate and the absence of a supermajority requirement for commercial legislation. Despite his concerns, he concluded the letter by stating the need for "the establishment of a firm, energetic government." He added that "the most inveterate curse which can befall us is a dissolution of the Union." He stated that if the amendments he favored could not be obtained, he would accept the Constitution as it was written. In 1788 Randolph chaired the Virginia Ratifying Convention, where he supported the ratification of the Constitution. Years later, Thomas Jefferson, who was Randolph's second

The grave of Edmund Randolph.

cousin, offered a less than positive assessment of Randolph's performance calling him, "the poorest chameleon I ever saw, having no color of his own, and reflecting that nearest him."

It appears that President Washington did not share Jefferson's view since when he formed his initial cabinet, he appointed Randolph as the first United States Attorney General. Then when Jefferson resigned as Secretary of State in 1793, Washington replaced him with Randolph. In his new role, he opposed the 1794 appointment of John Jay as the special envoy to England. Jay then negotiated a controversial treaty with Great Britain that Randolph also opposed. In 1795 Washington forced Randolph to resign based on his belief that his secretary of state had shared sensitive information with France. Randolph steadfastly maintained his innocence but recognizing that he had lost the president's confidence, he left office. Modern historians have exonerated Randolph of any misconduct. After his resignation, Randolph was held responsible for $49,000 lost by the State Department during his administration, and he subsequently paid that amount.

Returning to Virginia, he resumed his law practice. His most famous client was former Vice President Aaron Burr. There is little doubt that Randolph's cousin and then-President, Thomas Jefferson, was none too pleased with the successful defense of Burr in his 1807 treason trial.

Randolph had paralysis in his final years, and he passed away at the age of 60 on September 12, 1813. He was laid to rest in the Old Chapel Cemetery in Millwood, Virginia.

The Edmund J. Randolph Award was named in his honor. It is the highest award presented by the United States Department of Justice. It is awarded to persons who make "outstanding contributions to the accomplishments of the Department's mission."

Philip John Schuyler
(1733–1804)

Father-in-Law of Hamilton

Buried at Albany Rural Cemetery,
Menands, New York.

Military • Political

Philip John Schuyler is best known as the father of Elizabeth Schuyler, who married Alexander Hamilton, the military hero, Federalist, and first Secretary of the Treasury. Schuyler was also a major general during the American Revolution and served in the Continental Congress. After the Revolution, he was a senator from New York in the First Congress and later the Fifth Congress. He was also a wealthy landowner and state politician who encouraged the ratification of the US Constitution and was known for his high character and virtue.

Philip John Schuyler was born on November 22, 1733, in Menands, in Albany, New York, to Johannes Schuyler Jr., a merchant, and his wife, Cornelia (née Van Cortlandt) Schuyler. He was the eldest son and heir to the family estate. The family is believed to be connected to a Schuyler who settled in New York, emigrating from Amsterdam in the mid-1600s. They were wealthy and likely belonged to nobility since they were permitted to hang their coat of arms painted upon the local church's windows.

Schuyler's father died in 1741 when he was eight. He was then raised by his mother and grandfather, Johannes Sr., until his death in 1747. Schuyler attended the public school in Albany and was then tutored at the Van Cortlandt family estate in New Rochelle. Next, he studied with a

Philip John Schuyler (1733–1804)

Philip John Schuyler

private tutor, Reverend Peter Strouppe, to learn French and mathematics to go with his Dutch and English fluency. During this time, Schuyler began to suffer from a debilitating illness, similar to gout and arthritis, that would plague him his entire life, often leaving him incapacitated.

Despite his illness, Schuyler was a successful businessman around Albany and interacted in the privileged social circles of his rank. His business interests involved trading with the Indians at Oswego, and he went on many trade missions before the French and Indian War. During this time, he learned to speak Mohawk.

During the French and Indian War, in 1755, Schuyler raised a company and was commissioned a captain thanks to his cousin James DeLancey, the lieutenant governor. Later that year, on September 7,

1755, he married Catherine Van Rensselaer of another well-to-do New York Dutch family. Ultimately, they had fifteen children together, eight of whom lived to adulthood. Schuyler served under Colonel John Bradstreet as a quartermaster at Oswego until the fort fell. He also took part in the battles of Lake George and Oswego River. The following year, he had left the army and was elected to the common council in Albany as a local politician.

In 1758, Schuyler rejoined the army as a major and fought at the Battle of Fort Frontenac. He was then dispatched to England to represent New York regarding settling claims before the British government regarding his quartermaster role. He stayed in England until 1763 when he left the army again and returned home.

He then began constructing his home, known as Schuyler Mansion (now the General Schuyler House). He expanded his business interests to include a lumber concern in Saratoga, New York, and the first flaxseed mill in America. In 1768, he was elected to the New York Assembly, serving there until 1775. During this time, he came to oppose the colonial government and was made a colonel of the militia but was also limited by his chronic illness.

Schuyler was elected to the Continental Congress early in 1775, serving until he was selected as one of the four major generals for the Continental Army under George Washington on June 19. He was given command of the Northern Department and planned the Invasion of Canada but was unable to lead it due to his health failing while on Lake Champlain, on the way to Quebec. Richard Montgomery led the expedition in the field.

In 1777, when the British invaded New York following the failed Canada campaign, they targeted Fort Ticonderoga. After General St. Clair surrendered the fort, both he and Schuyler were court-martialed. In the meantime, Horatio Gates was given command of the Northern Department. This was not before Schuyler had written to advise Washington on handling the forces at Saratoga on his home turf. Some surmise that had Schuyler not advised Washington, Gates and Benedict Arnold might not have been victorious against the British there. Saratoga was a key victory for the Americans. Gates and Arnold were heroes, and

Philip John Schuyler (1733–1804)

Schuyler's home was burned to the ground during the campaign. The following year, Schuyler and St. Clair were acquitted. France, seeing the victory over the British, agreed to join in the fight.

Now no longer in command of the Northern Department and his name cleared, Schuyler left the army on April 19, 1779, and returned to the Continental Congress. He also began rebuilding his homestead. On December 18, 1780, his daughter Elizabeth married Alexander Hamilton before his heroism at Yorktown. In 1781, Schuyler was the target of a failed kidnapping plot. Fortunately, he was tipped off and managed to leave before the kidnappers arrived at his estate.

After the Revolution, Schuyler was one of the founding members of the New York Society of the Cincinnati. From 1780 to 1784, he was a member of the New York State Senate and Surveyor General from 1781 to 1784. He returned to the state senate from 1786 to 1790, supporting the US Constitution's passage. During these years, he expanded his estate near Saratoga to tens of thousands of acres and had many slaves and tenant farmers. He also owned mills, stores, and schooners on the Hudson River.

Upon the passage of the US Constitution, Schuyler was elected to the US Senate representing New York, along with Rufus King, in the First Congress. He served from July 27, 1789, to March 3, 1791. He lost a reelection bid to Aaron Burr in 1791 and returned to the state senate from 1792 to 1797. He was then elected to the US Senate, serving from March 4, 1797, until his resignation on January 3, 1798, due to his chronic illness.

Catherine Schuyler died in 1803, as the couple approached 48 years of marriage. This greatly affected Schuyler. After his son-in-law Alexander Hamilton was killed in a duel with Aaron Burr on July 12, 1804, Schuyler replied to the many letters of condolence. From one of them:

> My warmest and unfeigned acknowledgments are due to the President and members of the St. Andrew's Society, for the delicate and feeling manner in which, they have conducted with me on the irreparable loss I have sustained, in the death of a son, who

had endeared himself to me, by the most tender solicitude; who was the kindest and most affectionate husband to my dear and distressed daughter . . .

Four months later, Schuyler died in Albany on November 18, 1804, from his "lingering illness." Schuyler was buried in Albany Rural Cemetery in Menands, New York. A huge obelisk marks the grave.

One aspect of Schuyler's life that is hard to quantify is his influence in social circles, individually and through his family. He was selected as one of the four lieutenants to George Washington, indicating he was held in high regard by Washington and the Continental Congress. But it is his extended family that further indicates his impact. As discussed, his second daughter, Elizabeth, was the wife of Alexander Hamilton. Schuyler was very fond of his son-in-law, and the two were close. Schuyler's eldest daughter, Angelica, married John Barker Church, who was later a British MP. Daughter Margaret married Stephen Van Rensselaer III, the 8th Patroon of Rensselaerwyck, the estate of the Rensselaers. Son John married Elizabeth Van Rensselaer, Stephen's sister. Son Philip served in the US House of Representatives. Son Rensselaer married Elizabeth Ten Broeck, the daughter of General Abraham Ten Broeck. The younger children also married well.

Philip's cousin Peter commanded the Jersey Blues. Cousin Hester was married to William Colfax of Washington's Life Guards and later the general in charge of the Jersey Blues. His brother-in-law Dr. John Cochran was the Director-General of Military Hospitals for the Continental Army.

Schuyler's name has been used in honor of many places, especially in New York. There are the towns of Schuyler and Schuylerville. There is also Schuyler County in New York as well as Illinois and Missouri. Fort Schuyler was built at the tip of Throggs Neck in the Bronx and now houses the Maritime Industry Museum and the State University of New York Maritime College. The Philip Schuyler Achievement Academy is in Albany, New York, though a name change is soon expected due to his ownership of slaves.

Schuyler has appeared in works of art, including the painting of the *Surrender of General Burgoyne* by John Trumbull hanging in the US Capitol. A bronze statue by J. Massey Rhind was erected outside city hall in Albany in 1925. Due to Schuyler's ownership of slaves, Albany's mayor, in 2020, ordered the statue removed. The mayor of Schuylerville, New York, requested it the next day to be moved to Schuyler House, managed by the National Park Service. Schuyler is also depicted in the play *Hamilton* in a non-speaking role.

Impressive monument to Philip Schuyler.

Charles Scott
(1739–1813)

Head of Intelligence

Buried at Frankfort Cemetery,
Frankfort, Kentucky.

Military • Political

Charles Scott was an early proponent of westward expansion and was best known as the fourth governor of Kentucky. Scott also served in the military for many years. He was a member of the ill-fated Braddock Expedition and then served in the American Revolution, ending the war as a major general. He was a trusted adviser to George Washington and handled his intelligence gathering. After the war, he accepted a grant of land in the west, settled there, and helped to quell the natives as a member of Anthony Wayne's Legion of the United States.

Charles Scott was born in April 1739, in what was part of Goochland County, Virginia, now Powhatan County, to Samuel Scott, a farmer and member of the Virginia House of Burgesses, and his wife. Scott's mother likely died circa 1745, and her name is lost to history. Scott was the second of five children. He had an older brother, John, and younger siblings Edward, Joseph, and Martha. He did not receive much education.

Samuel Scott, a widower, died in 1755, leaving the five children as orphans. Charles apprenticed as a carpenter and was to be placed with a guardian by the court when, at 16, he enlisted in the Virginia Regiment. He was assigned to David Bell's company and rose to the rank of sergeant by the next year.

Charles Scott (1739–1813)

Charles Scott

During the Braddock Expedition and after, Scott served under George Washington, conducting scouting and escort missions. Scott was then part of the Forbes Expedition, after which Washington promoted him to ensign. Around 1759, Virginia's forces were switched to Colonel William Byrd. Scott was elevated to captain and led an expedition against the Cherokee. Before 1762, Scott left the military to return home.

Older brother John Scott died before 1762, making Charles the heir to his father's lands. Scott settled on his inherited farm and married Frances Sweeney of Cumberland County, Virginia, on February 25, 1762. Scott raised tobacco and milled flour with the help of his slaves. In 1766, he was named a captain in the local militia. He and Frances had eight or nine children over the years.

At the outset of the American Revolution, Scott was quick to serve, raising a company of volunteers in Cumberland County. The company was to aid Patrick Henry in a potential clash with Lord Dunmore in Williamsburg in May 1775, but Dunmore abandoned the city. Scott was made the temporary commander-in-chief of volunteers until he was elected a lieutenant colonel in William Woodford's regiment in August. His younger brother Joe served as a lieutenant in the same regiment. On December 9, 1775, this regiment helped win the Battle of Great Bridge, which stopped a British advance and led to the occupation of Norfolk. Lord Dunmore subsequently left Virginia.

In early 1776, the regiment was merged into the Continental Army, and Scott retained his rank. On August 12, 1776, the Continental Congress elevated Scott to colonel of the 5th Virginia Regiment under Adam Stephens, stationed at Hampton and Portsmouth, until Washington ordered them to New Jersey in the fall, where they participated in the successful Battle of Trenton on December 26. The following week, at the Battle of Assunpink Creek, the 5th Virginia slowed the advance of British and Hessian forces marching towards Trenton. A member of Scott's unit, Major George Johnston, later said Scott had "acquired immortal honor" for his performance.

While Washington camped at Morristown, New Jersey that winter, Scott was based at Chatham, from which he led raids on foraging parties. At the Battle of Drake's Farm on February 1, 1777, Scott defeated a superior force of British and Hessian mercenaries. On February 8, Scott's unit raided a force of over 2,000 soldiers at the Battle of Quibbletown, earning some note.

Scott was granted a furlough in the spring of 1777 and returned to his Virginia farm. While there, Congress promoted him to brigadier general. On May 10, 1777, Washington requested Scott's return to duty at Trenton. The following months were difficult for Washington and the Continental Army. At the Battle of Brandywine, Scott's 4th Virginia Brigade fought well against Cornwallis's advancing forces but had to retreat. British General Howe now advanced towards Philadelphia, stopping at Germantown. Scott urged an attack upon Germantown. Washington ultimately agreed, and the attack went forward on October 4, 1777. Scott's troops, however, were a non-factor. They became lost in smoke from muskets and a fire set by the British. Confused, the colonials retreated.

With Howe taking Philadelphia, Scott urged an attack on the capital but instead was ordered to engage in skirmishes near Whitemarsh. The army then settled in at Valley Forge for the winter. Scott stayed at Samuel Jones's farm and did not experience his men's difficulties in the camp. But he inspected the troops daily. Scott was again furloughed from March to May to return home to attend to his farm.

In June 1778, Washington ordered Scott to take 1500 troops and harass the British in New Jersey. He was joined by Marquis de Lafayette and 1000 more men. They expected to launch a major offensive the next day, but there was confusion under Major General Charles Lee's leadership, who oversaw the operation. After several days of delay, Lee finally launched the attack that became the Battle of Monmouth on June 28. However, the forces were not well-organized, and when an artillery unit was seen retreating, though they had only run out of ammunition, Scott ordered his men to retreat, and then other units followed. Lee aborted the offensive, greatly angering Washington, who arrived on the scene to stop the British advance. Lee was later court-martialed for his behavior and was suspended from command.

After Monmouth, the British retreated to New York City. Scott was made Washington's chief of intelligence and conducted scouting missions out of the base at White Plains, New York. There were no significant operations before Scott's furlough in November 1778.

The following spring, Scott was ordered to recruit volunteers. Washington's attention had turned south, and there was confusion about British intentions in Virginia. Scott was retained in Petersburg to defend Virginia should the British attack. By the spring of 1780, it was clear Charleston was the British target, and Scott was sent there just as Clinton laid siege to the city. Scott was captured when the city surrendered on May 12. He was then a prisoner. On January 30, 1781, citing poor health, Scott requested parole from General Cornwallis, who obliged his request. Scott was out of action until he was exchanged for Lord Rawdon in July 1782, missing the Battle of Yorktown.

Washington next sent Scott to assist Peter Muhlenberg in recruiting troops in Virginia. He was then told to report to General Nathanael Greene, but Greene wrote he did not have a position for him and urged him to stay with Muhlenberg. The peace treaty ending the war was signed in March 1783. Scott was brevetted to major general on September 30, 1783, just before leaving the army. He then became a founding member of the Society of the Cincinnati.

Scott, like many soldiers, was granted land in the west by the Virginia legislature. Scott was given over 20,000 acres in Fayette and Bourbon counties. He spent the next two years preparing to settle along the Kentucky River in what would later become the state of Kentucky. In 1787, Scott moved his family to their new plantation near Versailles. He constructed a two-story log cabin and stockade and prepared to raise tobacco. That June, within weeks of moving, Shawnee warriors killed and scalped his son, Samuel, while crossing the Ohio River in a canoe. He watched helplessly from the riverbank. According to later biographers, this was the incentive for Scott's harsh treatment of the natives after that. Scott focused on building his plantation and served one term in the Virginia House of Burgesses.

In 1790, during the early days of the Washington administration, tensions increased with the natives in the Northwest Territory. Scott raised volunteers in Fayette and Bourbon counties to assist Josiah Harmar in a raid against the Western Confederacy. This expedition fought some skirmishes but accomplished little. In June, Harmar and Arthur St. Clair were ordered to lead another expedition against the Indians. Scott did not participate due to his service in the Virginia General Assembly. The expedition failed, and there was great distrust of Harmar among the Kentuckians.

On December 30, 1790, concerned about the failed expeditions, Washington urged Virginia's Governor Randolph to appoint Scott the general overseeing the Kentucky district. The next month, Scott was included in the Kentucky Board of War, which also comprised Senator John Brown, Isaac Shelby, Harry Innes, and Benjamin Logan. They urged a campaign against the Indians along the Ohio River. Washington agreed but selected Arthur St. Clair to lead, much to the disappointment of the Kentuckians. Scott was asked to lead 1000 men under St. Clair, about one-third of the force. Before launching the primary attack, Scott was ordered to take his men and distract the Indians while the main force gathered. He did so, capturing or killing nearly 100 Indians while only losing two men, who drowned in a river crossing. Scott's unit was then discharged.

Encouraged by Scott's prior success in the Wabash region, St. Clair encouraged the Board of War to mount another expedition on June 24, 1791. This time, Scott designated others to mount the raids, which were successful, taking a heavy toll on the Indians. The Weas and Kickapoos later signed a peace treaty in 1792 and moved further west.

St. Clair intended to mount a large initiative despite the Kentuckians' reluctance, many of whom were resisting service. Scott set about recruiting men for St. Clair. Colonel William Oldham was the highest-ranking of the Kentuckians. St. Clair's party headed out on October 1. On November 3, after setting camp, they were attacked before dawn by Indians. Of St. Clair's 1400 men, 600 were killed and 300 captured. St. Clair retreated and was joined by Scott and 200 volunteers. However, Scott's men did not have to fight as the Indians did not attack again. The natives' success further emboldened other tribes in the region.

President Washington now called for creating a 5000-man Legion of the United States to fight the Indians in the Northwest Territory. He considered assigning his friend Scott to lead the legion but decided against it because of Scott's penchant for alcohol. Instead, Washington appointed Anthony Wayne. On June 1, 1792, Kentucky became a state. Three days later, Scott and Benjamin Logan were appointed Major Generals of the state militia. Scott was given responsibility for territory north of the Kentucky River. During this time, there was discussion of Scott running for Congress, but he served only as a presidential elector in 1793.

Wayne arrived in mid-1793 with only 3000 of the 5000 men he intended. Scott's force was merged into the federal army, and Scott was commissioned an officer. However, the rest of the year, there was no significant action, and the men went home for the winter. The following spring, Wayne built Fort Recovery in Kentucky on the site of St. Clair's defeat. This helped raise the Kentuckians' confidence in their federal commander, especially when Wayne had 600 skulls the Indians had dug up reburied.

In June 1794, Wayne built Fort Defiance on an abandoned Indian town. Scott had a role in naming it, saying, "I defy the English, Indians, and all the devils in hell to take it." Wayne then marched to Fort Miami, where he expected to fight the Indians and British. On August 20, Wayne's forces engaged with the Indians at the Battle of Fallen Timbers. The Indians were routed, and the British refused to open their fort to the natives. The campaign ended two months later, in October. The House of Representatives, while commending Wayne on December 4, 1794, thanked Scott for his service. The Treaty of Greenville ended the war in 1795.

For the rest of the 1790s, Scott served as the major general of the 2nd division of state militia. He was highly regarded as a military hero in Kentucky. His daughter Martha married future US Senator George M. Bibb in 1799. In 1800 and 1804, he again functioned as a presidential elector, voting for Democratic-Republicans. Scott's wife, Martha, died on October 6, 1804, after which he sold his farm and moved in with his daughter and son in law in Lexington.

In 1807, as tensions mounted with Great Britain following the Chesapeake-Leopard Affair, Scott suggested to Governor Greenup that he should raise a mounted militia unit. The governor agreed, but Scott remarried on July 25, 1807, Judith Cary (Bell) Gist and did not assemble the unit. Gist was the widow of an old friend from the Revolution, Colonel Nathaniel Gist. Scott and his new wife settled at Canewood, the Gist family plantation.

On February 11, 1808, Scott announced his candidacy for the governorship of Kentucky. His stepson-in-law, Jess Bledsoe, a law professor at Transylvania University, managed the campaign. As the most senior Revolutionary War officer in the state, Scott controlled the veterans' lobby, boosting his candidacy. He won the campaign by a nearly two-to-one margin over his two opponents.

Upon taking the governorship, Scott appointed Bledsoe his Secretary of State. It was Bledsoe who delivered Scott's address to the legislature on December 13, 1808. Later that winter, Scott slipped on the icy steps of the governor's mansion and was permanently injured, requiring crutches for the rest of his life. This made him more dependent on his Secretary of State, who performed many of his official functions.

Rumors of alcoholism followed Scott during his term as governor. He was known to drink heavily and use profanity profusely. On one occasion, while providing feedback on a speech written by Bledsoe, Scott remarked, "Well, Mr. Bledsoe, I know you think you are a damned sight smarter than I am, and so you are in many respects; but this message as it is now, won't do at all; I'll be damned if it will." After Bledsoe asked what was wrong with the speech, Scott replied, "Why, damn it to hell, why don't you put a good solemn prayer at the end of it, and talk about Providence, and the protection of Heaven, and all that?"

The weathered stone of Charles Scott.

As war with Britain again loomed, Scott was a staunch supporter. He backed William Henry Harrison's recruitment of Kentuckians who ultimately fought at the Battle of Tippecanoe. Scott used the newspapers to call for volunteers to fight the British. On August 14, 1812, Scott greeted two regiments at the governor's mansion. As he hobbled among the soldiers with his crutch, he hammered it against the steps and said, "If it hadn't been for you (the crutch), I could have gone with the boys myself." On his last day in office, August 25, Scott made Harrison major general over the Kentucky militia, even though Harrison was not a resident. While unconstitutional, it was a popular move. President James Madison soon made Harrison the supreme commander of the Army of the Northwest.

His term over, Scott retired to Canewood with his wife. By mid-1813, Scott's health began to fail. He died on October 22, 1813 and was initially buried at Canewood. His remains were reinterred at Frankfort Cemetery in 1854. During the ceremony in 1854, a speaker described Scott as "a man of strong natural powers, faithful and constant in his friendships and implacable in his enmities. Somewhat illiterate, he was unpolished in manners and very eccentric."

Scott counties in Kentucky and Indiana are named after Charles Scott. Scottsville, Kentucky, and Scottsville, Virginia, are also named in his honor.

Arthur St. Clair
(1737–1818)

First Governor of the Northwest Territory

Buried at Saint Clair Park Path,
Greensburg, Pennsylvania.

**Military • President of Congress
First Governor of Northwest Territory**

Arthur St. Clair, originally from Thurso, Scotland, was a political and military leader during the American Revolution and the first governor of the Northwest Territory in 1788 that later became Ohio, Indiana, Illinois, Michigan, and parts of Wisconsin and Minnesota.

St. Clair was a delegate to the Continental Congress who became its second to last President. He was also a major general in the Continental Army before losing his command following a retreat from Fort Ticonderoga. Later, in 1791, he was in command when American forces experienced their worst defeat by the Native Americans.

Historian Joseph J. Thompson called him "one of the most unique figures in American history . . . the handsome, polished, accomplished, profound St. Clair. The appearance and conduct of the men we have been considering were influenced by their rugged and rustic surroundings, but St. Clair was the product of culture and fashion."

Arthur St. Clair was born in Thurso, county of Caithness, Scotland in the 1730s. Some have estimated his birth year as 1734, but subsequent research points to March 23, 1736, as a reasonable date, which is 1737

Arthur St. Clair

on the modern calendar. The names of his parents are unknown, though one biographer states they were "probably" William Sinclair, a merchant, and Elizabeth (née Balfour or Hamilton).

It is believed St. Clair attended the University of Edinburgh for a time but then left to study anatomy with Dr. William Hunter, a leading Scottish physician, around 1756. Soon after, he quit and purchased a commission in the British army as an ensign and served in North America during the French and Indian War.

During the war, he served under General Jeffrey Amherst at the capture of Louisburg, Nova Scotia in July 1758. The following spring, he was promoted to lieutenant and served under General James Wolfe at the Battle of the Plains of Abraham resulting in the capture of Quebec City.

After the battle, St. Clair went on leave in Boston where he met his future wife, Phoebe Bayard, the niece of Governor James Bowdoin of Massachusetts colony. St. Clair married her, resigned his commission, and decided to settle in the Ligonier Valley near modern-day Pittsburgh, Pennsylvania using funds from his father-in-law. There he invested in mills and took a position as a surveyor, becoming the largest landowner in the region. Despite not being a lawyer, he was named a local justice and in a 1774 almanac was listed as a prothonotary in Bedford and Westmoreland Counties.

St. Clair was a proponent of Pennsylvania in its disputes with Virginia regarding the Ohio Country and Fort Pitt area. St. Clair worked with the natives in the area to promote the fur trade rather than see them give up their lands to the Virginians. Lord Dunmore's War ultimately settled the boundaries between the settlers and the natives at the Ohio River. St. Clair's actions likely spared the settlers in the Fort Pitt area from native vengeance.

At the outset of the American Revolution, St. Clair was a supporter of the patriot cause. He served on his local Committee of Safety and was the secretary to the representatives from the Continental Congress who negotiated with the Indians of the Ohio Country. In 1775, the Congress appointed him as a colonel in the 3rd Pennsylvania Regiment of the Continental Army and he participated in the attack on Canada at the Battle of Trois-Rivières. Afterward, he was appointed to brigadier general and in August 1776 was sent by Washington to organize the New Jersey militia. During the winter of 1776-77, he was with Washington at the battles of Trenton and Princeton. He crossed the Delaware River with Washington on the night of December 25-26, 1776, and many biographers credit him with the strategy that led to the capture of Princeton. He was promoted to major general in February 1777.

In the spring of 1777, St. Clair was assigned to command Fort Ticonderoga in New York. When the British invaded, knowing he could not hold the fort without heavy casualties, St. Clair abandoned the fort and retreated. George Washington was disappointed he left without a fight. A subsequent court-martial headed by General Benjamin Lincoln, however, found St. Clair innocent of all charges. Despite his exoneration, St. Clair was not given significant commands for the remainder of the war though he was an aide-de-camp to General Washington, who retained a high opinion of him. St. Clair was at Cornwallis's surrender at Yorktown.

After the Revolution, St. Clair was elected to the Continental Congress, serving from November 2, 1785, to November 28, 1787. During his last year in Congress, St. Clair was elected President of

Congress, succeeding Nathaniel Gorham, on February 2, 1787, amid Shay's Rebellion. After the rebellion was put down, the Congress passed the Northwest Ordinance, creating the Northwest Territory (comprising modern-day Ohio, Indiana, Illinois, Michigan, most of Wisconsin, and eastern Minnesota), and assigned St. Clair as the governor. His presidency ended on October 29, 1787, when he took over his new duties.

St. Clair named Cincinnati, Ohio, after the Society of Cincinnati, and made his headquarters there. He formulated Maxwell's Code, named after its printer, as the first written laws in the territory. In 1789, he convinced certain Indians in the area to give up their land claims by signing the Treaty of Fort Harmar. Several chiefs had refused to participate or sign the treaty triggering the Northwest Indian War or Little Turtle's War. St. Clair, proceeded to build forts in western Ohio. He sent General Josiah Harmar and 1500 troops to suppress the Indians, ordering them to destroy the village of the Miami at present-day Fort Wayne, Indiana. Shawnee chief Blue Jacket and Miami chief Little Turtle defeated Harmar's men in October 1790 in what is known as Harmar's Defeat. Harmar retreated to Fort Washington, present-day Cincinnati, and St. Clair then took up command personally.

On March 21, 1791, Secretary of War Henry Knox ordered St. Clair to establish a strong and permanent military presence in the region. Congress commissioned St. Clair to lead two 300-man regiments of regular troops and 1400 ill-trained militiamen to move against the main Miami town, Kekionga.

St. Clair and his men left Fort Washington on September 17. The men marched twenty miles in two days and then built Fort Hamilton. They then advanced forty-five miles northward, where they erected Fort Jefferson. Leading primarily untrained militiamen, St. Clair faced problems with desertion from the beginning of his campaign. Although it was still early fall, his men faced cold temperatures, rain, and snowfall. Due to the scarcity of supplies, many of the men became demoralized. Despite these problems, St. Clair continued to advance against the Miami (in what is present-day Indiana). By November 3, his men had arrived on the banks of the Wabash River, near some of the Miami villages. Little Turtle, Blue Jacket, and Tecumseh, aided by British collaborators Alexander McKee and Simon Girty, surprised the poorly-prepared

Americans at Fort Recovery, Ohio, near the headwaters of the Wabash River, with 2000 warriors on November 4, 1791.

Many of the poorly-trained American militiamen immediately fled. St. Clair led the regular soldiers in a bayonet charge and had two horses shot out from under him. Several bullets passed through his clothing, and one took off a lock of his hair.

The natives surrounded the American camp. After three hours of fighting—the remaining Americans fought through the natives as they began a long retreat. The survivors reached Fort Jefferson late that afternoon and evening but with limited quantities of food and supplies there, St. Clair ordered his forces to Fort Washington.

More than half of the Americans were killed or wounded, and the survivors haphazardly fled back to Fort Washington. The battle has since been known as St. Clair's Defeat, the Battle of the Wabash, the Columbia Massacre, or the Battle of a Thousand Slain. It was the most significant defeat of the U.S. Army by natives in American history. Only about fifty natives were killed. St. Clair was among the wounded. One of the survivors stated, "The ground was literally covered with the dead."

A subsequent investigation exonerated St. Clair, but he resigned his army commission in March 1792 at the request of President Washington. However, he continued to serve as the Governor of the Northwest Territory. Eventually, American forces led by General Anthony Wayne won the campaign, overwhelming the natives and resulting in the Treaty of Greenville in 1795.

St. Clair was a Federalist. He hoped to see two states created from the Ohio Territory to increase Federalist power. However, the Democratic-Republicans led by Thomas Jefferson continued to gain influence in the capital and the territory. Despite St. Clair's resistance, the U.S. Congress sanctioned the Enabling Act of 1802 which gave Ohioans the right to form a constitutional convention on the path to statehood. St. Clair remarked the U.S. Congress had no power to interfere in the affairs of those in the Ohio Territory. He also stated the people of the territory "are no more bound by an act of Congress than we would be bound by an edict of the first consul of France." This led to Jefferson removing St. Clair as territorial governor and prevented him from playing a role in organizing the state of Ohio in 1803.

The grave of Arthur St. Clair.

Following his resignation as governor, St. Clair returned to Pennsylvania where he invested in iron mines in the Pittsburgh area and established a foundry to make stoves and castings. He was very liberal with his money, loaning it to friends and family.

Though Congress did pay him a pension of two thousand dollars on May 1, 1810, it was not enough to save St. Clair from financial trouble. He lost his vast landholdings and eventually moved into a small log cabin on the property of his daughter, Louisa St. Clair Robb, on a ridge between Ligonier and Greensburg. He died there on August 31, 1818.

St. Clair was buried in the Old Greensburg Cemetery which later became St. Clair Park in Greensburg, Pennsylvania. His wife Phoebe died shortly after and was buried next to him. A Masonic monument was later placed over their graves. Said the *National Intelligencer* newspaper at the time, "On the summit of the Chestnut Ridge which overlooks the valley of Ligonier, in which the commencement of the revolution found him in prosper; on this lonesome spot, exposed to winter winds, as cold and desolating as the tardy gratitude of his country, died Major General Arthur St. Clair. The traveler as he passed the place, was reminded of the celebrated Roman exile's reply, 'tell the citizens of Rome that you saw Caius Marius sitting amongst the ruins of Carthage.'"

St. Clair remained a controversial figure for years to come, his reputation attached to the defeat on the Wabash. This historian wonders if his reputation would have been different had George Washington lived longer and been able to remind everyone of St. Clair's contributions at Trenton and Princeton.

Arthur St. Clair has been honored in many ways:
- A portion of the Hermitage, St. Clair's home in Oak Grove, Pennsylvania (north of Ligonier), was later moved to Ligonier, Pennsylvania, where it is now preserved, along with St. Clair artifacts and memorabilia at the Fort Ligonier Museum.
- An American Civil War steamer was named USS *St. Clair*.
- The following places were named after him: Upper St. Clair, Pennsylvania; St. Clairsville, Pennsylvania; St. Clair, Schuylkill County, Pennsylvania; St. Clair Township, Westmoreland County, Pennsylvania; East St. Clair Township, Bedford County, Pennsylvania; West St. Clair Township, Bedford County, Pennsylvania; the St. Clair neighborhood in Pittsburgh, Pennsylvania; St. Clair Hospital, Mt. Lebanon, Pennsylvania; St. Clair Township in Butler County, Ohio; St. Clair Township in Columbiana County, Ohio; St. Clairsville, Ohio; St. Clair Avenue in Cleveland, Ohio; Fort St. Clair in Eaton, Ohio; St. Clair County, Illinois; St. Clair County, Missouri; St. Clair County, Alabama; St. Clair Street in Frankfort, Kentucky; and the three-star St. Clair Hotel in Sinclair St., Thurso, Caithness.

Baron Friedrich Wilhelm von Steuben (1730–1794)

The Prussian General

Buried at Steuben State Memorial Site,
Steuben, New York.

Military

Baron von Steuben was a Prussian military officer who became a major general and Inspector General of the Continental Army. He is credited with developing the military training and manual that greatly improved American troops' performance in the field. Later in the war, von Steuben served as Washington's chief of staff. Baron von Steuben was likely an openly gay man at a time when sodomy laws outlawed such behavior.

Friedrich Wilhelm August Heinrich Ferdinand von Steuben (born Friedrich Wilhelm Ludolf Gerhard Augustin von Steuben, later known as Baron von Steuben, was born on September 17, 1730, in Magdeburg, Kingdom of Prussia (now Germany), to Captain Wilhelm von Steuben, of the Royal Prussian Engineers, and his wife, Elizabeth von Jagvodin. His parents were Protestants, though Jesuits taught von Steuben. From a young age, he accompanied his father on military adventures and may have served at age 14 with his father during the War of the Austrian Succession.

Von Steuben officially joined the Prussian Army when he was 17. He was battle-tested right away and rose through the ranks quickly, from second lieutenant to first lieutenant, to captain. In 1762, he became

Baron Friedrich Wilhelm von Steuben (1730–1794)

Friedrich Wilhelm von Steuben

an aide-de-camp to Frederick the Great and received personal training from the king. However, the following year, when the war ended, he was unemployed. Von Steuben later wrote that "an inconsiderate step and an implacable personal enemy" was the cause of his dismissal. Some historians have speculated he was removed because of his homosexuality. However, he carried with him the knowledge of the finest army in the world at that time, known for its discipline.

Over the next dozen years, von Steuben was the grand marshal of the kingdom of Hohenzollern-Hechingen. In 1771, he accompanied his prince to France and had been granted the title baron. However, Baron von Steuben, who had been born a commoner, was deeply in debt.

In 1777, Baron von Steuben traveled to France to meet with his connection there, the French Minister of War, Count de St. Germain and was introduced to Ben Franklin. A position in the Continental Army was discussed, but the Americans had become tired of foreign mercenaries who demanded high rank. Franklin told the baron he would have to come as a volunteer and present himself to Congress. Von Steuben left the meeting disappointed and returned to Prussia. Upon arriving, he found himself embroiled in a controversy, anonymously accused of having "taken familiarities" with young boys while in the service of the prince of Hohenzollern-Hechingen. The baron realized his potential for continuing his military career in Europe was likely ruined, though he was not prosecuted. Instead, he returned to Paris and took Franklin up on the offer. Franklin likely knew of the baron's alleged issues but overlooked them. Count de St. Germain vouched for the baron's abilities.

The French government paid Baron von Steuben's passage to America. On September 26, 1777, he, his dog Azor, his aide de camp, Louis de Pontiere, and his military secretary, Pierre Ettienne Duponceau, sailed for America, arriving in Portsmouth (now Maine), on December 1. Upon arrival, he was nearly arrested by the locals because they mistook his group's red Prussian uniforms for British. The party then traveled to Boston, where they were extravagantly entertained. They then traveled overland to York, Pennsylvania, where the Congress was seated, arriving on February 5, 1778.

Franklin's letter of introduction to George Washington and Congress was deliberately misleading, exaggerating his credentials. He was introduced as "His Excellency, Lieutenant General von Steuben, Apostle of Frederick the Great," despite von Steuben having been only a captain. In French, von Steuben's title in the Prussian Army was "Lieutenant General Quarters Maitre," which meant he was a quartermaster. Franklin embellished the translation to "Lieutenant General."

Not picking up on Franklin's ruse, Congress accepted the baron's offer to volunteer without pay, though they promised compensation after the war dependent on his contributions. He reported to George Washington at Valley Forge on February 23. Washington rode out to meet him but noticed his small entourage. He found it peculiar, and though he later learned the baron had only been a captain, he approved of him, "He appears to be much of a gentleman, and as far as I have had an opportunity of judging, a man of military knowledge, and acquainted with the world."

Baron von Steuben was a native German speaker and did not know English. Fortunately, he was fluent in French, as were several officers in Washington's camp. Washington's aide-de-camp, Alexander Hamilton, and Major General Nathanael Greene were instrumental in translating for the baron. Washington asked von Steuben to inspect the army and found them short of everything but spirit. He said, "no European army could have held together in such circumstances." He next set about to devise a training regimen.

Wrote one soldier about his first impression of the baron; he was "of the ancient fabled God of War . . . he seemed to me a perfect personification of Mars. The trappings of his horse, the enormous holsters of his pistols, his large size, and his strikingly martial aspect, all seemed to favor the idea. He turned the volunteers into a great army."

The baron worked on camp layouts and sanitation standards that would be used until the early 20th century. The men had been relieving themselves where convenient, and animal carcasses were left to rot nearby. Von Steuben brought order to this, creating quarters for the command center, offers, and soldiers, and placing kitchens and latrines on opposite sides. The latrines were placed downhill.

Impressed by what he had seen, Washington recommended to Congress that von Steuben be made the Continental Army's Inspector General. This was approved on May 5, 1778. Congress assigned the baron the rank and pay of major general. Von Steuben next focused on cleaning up the books regarding the procurement of supplies. He enforced the keeping of meticulous records and performed strict inspections. This eliminated the graft that had been commonplace.

Next, von Steuben focused on the soldiers. He selected 120 men to form an honor guard for George Washington and used them to demonstrate military training to the remaining troops. This train-the-trainer approach was very effective and included the use of bayonets. He wrote the orders in German, which were then translated to French, and then to English. The eccentric von Steuben was also loved and respected by the men as he drilled them twice a day in full military dress. The baron's use of profanity in several languages made him popular with the men. The training was changed to a process whereby new soldiers were trained gradually by their leaders in their regiments rather than just being assigned without traning.

During this period, the baron met Captain Benjamin Walker. Remarked von Steuben, "If I had seen an angel from Heaven, I should not have more rejoiced." Shortly after that, Walker was made the baron's aide-de-camp. It was the beginning of a lifelong relationship.

The baron also socialized with the troops. One of his aides, Pierre-Étienne Du Ponceau, recalled a wild party given at Valley Forge. "His aides invited a number of young officers to dine at our quarters," he wrote, "on condition that none should be admitted, that had on a whole pair of breeches." The men dined in torn clothing and, he implied, no clothing at all.

While homosexual relationships were common during this time, there was no concept of gay marriage or gay pride. There was no language to describe it and no open culture. It was a private matter, generally kept out of the public eye. Sodomy was a crime in many jurisdictions, but romantic relationships between men were tolerated until the 19th century. Only in the 20th century did the U.S. military crack down on homosexual behavior.

The positive impact of von Steuben's training was noticed in the subsequent battles at Barren Hill on May 20, 1778, and at Monmouth in June. At Stony Point, the army won based on von Steuben's bayonet training, their muskets unloaded. That winter, von Steuben's *Regulations for the Order and Discipline of the Troops of the United States*, also known as the "Blue Book," was completed based on the actions at Valley Forge. This book was used by the army until 1814 and impacted drills and tactics until the Mexican-American War in 1846.

After sitting on the court-martial of Major John André in 1780, von Steuben was assigned to Nathanael Greene for the Southern campaign. He was instrumental in Virginia's defense and led a division at the decisive Battle of Yorktown in 1781.

For the next two years, von Steuben moved to New York, to Washington's headquarters at Newburgh, until the army was demobilized.

He aided in planning the nation's defense and, in May 1783, presided over the founding of the Society of the Cincinnati. He was discharged from the military with honor on March 24, 1784.

After the war, the baron was made a U.S. citizen and settled in New York City with his companion, William North. He created a special room for him called the Louvre. Von Steuben also became a prominent figure and elder in the German Reformed Church and served as president of the German Society of the City of New York.

Von Steuben, who lived extravagantly, was out of money and petitioned Congress for more. He was granted properties confiscated from Loyalists in New Jersey. These and the New York City property were used to pay debts while the baron tempered his lifestyle while supporting Walker and North. He then moved to upstate New York, in Oneida County, near Rome, where he was granted a 16,000-acre estate. There, he lived with Walker and North. "We love him," North wrote, "and he deserves it for he loves us tenderly."

Congress awarded him a pension of $2500 a year in 1790, lasting until his death. Baron von Steuben never married and had no children. He adopted Captain Benjamin Walker and Major General William North as his heirs. This was a common practice by gay men in an era before same-sex marriage. However, the historical record is not clear about how close these men were in their relationship and whether it was sexual. These men lived together and managed his finances. John Mulligan, also gay, served as the baron's secretary and also had a relationship with him.

Baron von Steuben died at his Oneida County estate on November 28, 1794. He was buried in a grove at what is now the Steuben Memorial State Historic Site. He left his estate to his companions, Walker and North, with whom he had "extraordinarily intense emotional relationship . . . treating them as surrogate sons." He also considered Mulligan similarly and left him his vast library, map collection, and $2500 in cash. North divided the land among his military companions. Today, the estate is part of the town of Steuben, New York.

In memory of the baron, von Steuben Day is celebrated every September in many cities in the United States, often considered the year's German American event. In New York City, the German American

Steuben Parade is held in September, after which an Oktoberfest celebration begins. Chicago's Steuben Day parade was featured in the movie *Ferris Bueller's Day Off*. Philadelphia also has a smaller parade.

The Steuben Society was founded in 1919 to help German-American communities after World War I. It is one of the largest organizations for German Americans.

Several ships have been named after the baron, the most recent being the U.S. Navy submarine USS *Von Steuben*.

Counties in New York and Indiana carry his name. The city of Steubenville, Ohio, is named after the baron. Several buildings and facilities are also named in his honor, and his former New Jersey home is a historic site.

A statue of the baron in Lafayette Square, in Washington, DC, joins statues from three other European military leaders who assisted the Revolution. There are other statues of von Steuben around the country, including at the Valley Forge Military Park.

The tomb of General von Steuben.

Baron Friedrich Wilhelm von Steuben (1730–1794)

Actors have portrayed von Steuben on television over the years. In 1979, Nehemiah Persoff played the general in the miniseries *The Rebels*. Kurt Knudson played him in the 1984 miniseries *George Washington*. Arnold Schwarzenegger provided the voice of von Steuben in the animated series *Liberty's Kids*. A documentary titled *Von Steuben's Continentals: The First American Army* was released on DVD in 2007. It detailed the improvements made by the general at Valley Forge.

Thomas Sumter
(1734–1832)

Carolina Gamecock

Buried at Thomas Sumter Memorial Park,
Sumter County, South Carolina.

Military • Political

Thomas Sumter, nicknamed the "Carolina Gamecock," was a brigadier general in the South Carolina militia during the American Revolution known by the enemy for his aggressive fighting style. He was initially a member of the Virginia militia and later a planter, politician, member of the US House of Representatives, and a US Senator. Fort Sumter in Charleston Harbor was named in his honor.

Thomas Sumter was born August 14, 1734, in Hanover County, Virginia, to William Sumter, a miller and former indentured servant, and his wife, Patience, a midwife. Sumter spent most of his early years assisting his father at the mill and tending livestock. He received only rudimentary schooling during these years.

As a young man, Sumter was a member of the Virginia militia and survived the ill-fated Braddock Expedition in 1755. During the French and Indian War, he rose to the rank of sergeant. From 1759 to 1761, Sumter participated in the Cherokee War. As that conflict with the natives ebbed, Sumter was selected for a diplomatic mission to the Cherokee nation known as the Timberlake Expedition led by Henry Timberlake and organized by Colonel Adam Stephen. They were accompanied by

Thomas Sumter

an interpreter named John McCormack and a servant. The goal was to renew friendship with the Overhill Cherokee towns.

During the expedition, while they were exploring a cave, their canoes drifted away on an icy stream. Sumter dove in and swam nearly a half-mile to retrieve them. The party was greeted warmly when they reached Tomotley on December 20, 1761. There a chief, Ostenaco ("Mankiller"), offered them a peace pipe. During the following weeks, peace ceremonies were held in surrounding Cherokee towns.

That spring, the party returned to Williamsburg, Virginia, with Ostenaco and several other tribal leaders. While there at the College of William and Mary, Ostenaco requested to meet with the King of England. Thomas Jefferson, who was a student at the time, later recalled Ostenaco:

> I knew much of the great Outassete (Ostenaco), the warrior and orator of the Cherokee. He was always the guest of my father on his journeys to and from Williamsburg. I was in his camp when he made his great farewell oration to his people the evening before he departed for England. The moon was in full splendor, and to her, he seemed to address himself in his prayers for his own safety on the voyage and that of his people during his absence. His sounding voice, distinct articulation, animated action, and the solemn silence of his people at their several fires, filled me with awe and veneration, although I did not understand a single word he uttered.

A voyage commenced in May 1762 with Sumter and others accompanying the Indian delegation. In London, the natives were celebrities and received their audience with King George III. The Cherokee then accompanied Sumter back to the colonies, arriving in Charleston on August 25, 1762.

All was not well for Sumter at this point. He had petitioned Virginia for reimbursement of his travel expenses but was denied. This would seem to indicate Sumter's role in the voyage was not an official one. Without money and now in debt, Sumter was thrown into debtor's prison in Staunton, Virginia. Fortunately, a fellow soldier and friend, Joseph Martin, located him and requested to spend a night in jail with him. That evening, Martin handed Sumter some money and a tomahawk. Sumter then used the money to buy his way out of jail. Sumter then headed for South Carolina to start his life anew and escape any further difficulties with creditors.

Around 1764, Sumter settled in Stateburg, South Carolina, in Orangeburg County, along the Santee River. There, he became a merchant and opened a country store. He prospered and acquired property and slaves. In 1767, Sumter married Mary Cantey Jameson, a wealthy, crippled widow who was many years older than him. They moved in together on her plantation, Great Savannah, where they raised two children and became successful planters.

In 1775, as the Revolution began, Sumter was a member of the local Council of Safety and the provincial congress. He reentered military service as a captain. In December 1775, he participated in the "Snow Campaign" to subdue Loyalist forces. It was called this due to snowy weather.

In 1776, he raised a local militia group and was elevated to lieutenant colonel of the Second Regiment of the South Carolina Line. In June 1776, he served under General Charles Lee in the successful defense of Charleston at the Battle of Sullivan's Island.

From July to October 1776, Sumter was back fighting against the Cherokee with whom he had helped broker peace in the prior decade. He then fought the British in Georgia and St. Augustine from 1777 to 1778 before leaving the army at the rank of colonel on September 19, 1778. He returned to private life and was elected to the first South Carolina General Assembly following the new state constitution.

The British invaded South Carolina and captured Charleston in May 1780. They seemed poised to control the South and were on their way to victory. However, they made a fateful decision when Col. Banastre Tarleton's raiders burned down Sumter's plantation home. Sumter took this personally and immediately returned to the field and organized an army of local backcountry partisans who elected him their general. "Sumter's Brigade" spent the summer of 1780 as the only opposition to the British in South Carolina, engaging the enemy at Rocky Mount on July 30, Hanging Rock on August 6, and Fishing Creek on August 18. While they did not always win, the tough resistance raised the patriots' spirits until Nathanael Greene's army could join them. Sumter's brother William served as a captain during this time.

Recognizing Sumter's contributions, Governor Rutledge appointed him as a brigadier general in the South Carolina militia on October 6. Sumter's forces fought well at Fishdam Ford on November 9 and Blackstock's on November 20. The rebels routed Tarleton's force, losing only three killed and five wounded to nearly 200 casualties for the British. Unfortunately, Sumter was one of the severely wounded, taking a ball in the chest. He was out of commission for three months. After this battle, Tarleton commented that Sumter "fought like a gamecock," and Cornwallis described the Gamecock as his "greatest plague."

While Sumter was convalescing, Washington sent Nathanael Greene to lead the Southern Department, overlooking Sumter. Back in the saddle in February 1781, Sumter led troops at Fort Gransby but did not appreciate the commands he was receiving from on high in the army of Nathanael Greene. Sumter attempted to resign, but Greene did not permit it. Sumter then fought at Orangeburg in May.

In July, Sumter then joined with Greene and led "the raid of the dog days" into the low country of South Carolina, riding with Francis Marion. However, he could not reconcile his differences with leadership, and his resignation was accepted in February 1782, ending his military career.

Sumter remained involved in politics. He served eight terms in the General Assembly of South Carolina between 1776 and 1790. In 1783 he helped to found the town of Stateburg, South Carolina. He promoted it as the site of the new state capital, but this was not to be. After the passage of the new US Constitution, Sumter was a member of the First Congress, serving in the US House of Representatives from 1789 to 1793. During this time, in 1792, Sumter was reunited with his old friend, Joseph Martin, and repaid him the money that had helped him get out of debtors' prison thirty years earlier.

Sumter was reelected to the House of Representatives and served from 1797 to 1801. After being selected by the South Carolina legislature, he jumped to the Senate to replace Charles Pinckney, who had resigned. He served as a US Senator for ten years until December 16, 1810. While in the Congress, Sumter was a Democratic-Republican, backing the Jeffersonians who were friendlier to the backcountry farmers.

Now retired from the Senate in his mid-70s, Sumter watched his son, Thomas Sumter Jr., serve as the United States Ambassador to the Portuguese Court while exiled in Brazil, at Rio de Janeiro 1810 to 1819. Thomas Jr. had married Natalie De Lage de Volude, the daughter of French nobility, sent by her parents to America for her safety during the French Revolution. She was raised in New York City from 1794 to 1801 by Vice President Aaron Burr as his ward, alongside his daughter Theodosia.

Thomas Sumter (1734–1832)

Thomas Sumter's crypt.

Thomas Sumter lived to the age of 97, the last surviving general from the American Revolution. On June 1, 1832, he died at South Mount, his plantation near Stateburg, South Carolina. He was buried at what is now the Thomas Sumter Memorial Park in Sumter County, South Carolina.

Colonel Thomas De Lage Sumter, a grandson of Thomas Sumter, served in the US Army during the Second Seminole War (1835-1842). He later represented South Carolina in the United States House of Representatives.

Fort Sumter, planned after the War of 1812, was erected in Charleston Harbor and named after him. His name would then become forever associated with the opening volleys of the Civil War in 1861.

The town of Sumter, South Carolina, was named after him. They erected a memorial to him, and the town has been dubbed "The Gamecock City."

Four states have counties named after him: Alabama, Florida, Georgia, and South Carolina.

Since 1903, the University of South Carolina's nickname has been "The Fighting Gamecocks."

At the state capitol in Columbia, South Carolina, Sumter shares a monument, erected in 1913, with Francis Marion and Andrew Pickens.

Charles Thomson
(1729–1824)

Secretary of the Continental Congress

Buried at Laurel Hill Cemetery,
Philadelphia, Pennsylvania.

Secretary, Continental Congress

Although few people have heard of Charles Thomson, he was one of America's most significant and influential Founding Fathers. He served as the only Secretary of the Continental Congress for its entire fifteen years. He was a tremendous unifying factor. He kept the minutes of all sessions of Congress, including special minutes of all the secret meetings and deals. His journals and files became the archives of our nation. In all the factional disputes of the Revolutionary period, his judgment was respected. During the rumors and uncertainties of the Revolutionary War, Thomson helped the Continental Congress retain the faith and support of the people by insisting that full and honest reports be issued, under his signature, concerning all battles and engagements whether won or lost. His reputation was such that his reports were in high demand. When a congressional paper appeared containing his signature, the expression was frequently heard, "here comes the truth." Thomson's name was regarded as an emblem of truth.

Charles Thomson was born in 1729 in County Derry, Ireland to Scots-Irish parents. He was one of six children, and his mother died in

Charles Thomson

1739 during or shortly after the birth of his youngest sibling. Within a few months, his father John set out for Philadelphia with Charles and three of his older brothers. John became violently ill and died within sight of the shore. The ship was just off the capes of Delaware. The children were now left to the mercy of the sea captain, who embezzled the money which the father had brought with him and landed the boys ashore at New Castle, Delaware.

There Charles was separated from his brothers. He was placed in the care of a blacksmith who intended to make him an indentured servant. Through good fortune, he was admitted to the New London Academy in Chester County, Pennsylvania. While a student there, Thomson made the acquaintance of Benjamin Franklin and frequently sought his advice regarding the prospects of working in Philadelphia. Franklin, being President of the Board of Trustees of the new Academy of Philadelphia (the forerunner of the University of Pennsylvania), secured a position for Thomson at the school. He started as a tutor there on January 7, 1751.

He served as a tutor until 1755 and left to become head of the Latin department at Philadelphia's Friends Public School. In 1758 he married Ruth Mather, a member of a well-to-do Chester family. In 1760 he left teaching to enter into business. He and Ruth separated in 1769. In 1770 tragedy struck when their infant twins and Ruth died.

While at the Friends School, Thomson joined the Quakers in their opposition to the Penn family's Indian policy. He became the secretary for the Delaware Indians in 1756 at a great council held in Easton, Pennsylvania to resolve their differences with the settlers. The tribe adopted him as a son according to an ancient Indian custom. All during this time, he was allied with Ben Franklin, but they parted politically during the Stamp Act crisis in 1765. He then allied himself with John Dickinson. He worked diligently throughout the Revolutionary period to keep English goods out of Philadelphia. By 1773 he was writing fiery handbills against the importation of tea from the East India Company. During this decade Thomson was the colony's most powerful protest organizer. He became known as "the Sam Adams of Philadelphia." He also became a leader in Philadelphia's Sons of Liberty, a secret organization of landowners throughout the colonies formed to protect the rights of colonists and to fight taxation by the British government.

On September 1, 1774, Thomson married Hannah Harrison, the sister of Benjamin Harrison, who would become a signer of the Declaration of Independence. The following Monday, September 5, the First Continental Congress convened in Philadelphia and unanimously selected Thomson as Secretary.

He served over the next fifteen years as secretary to the first and second Continental Congresses and then to the Confederation Congress. Through those fifteen years, Congress saw many delegates come and go, but Thomson's dedication to recording the debates and decisions provided continuity. The Continental Congress was in some respects one of the most remarkable legislative bodies the world has ever seen. Thomson knew better than any other man the secret history of Congress and the motives which influenced its members. He beheld the development of

Obelisk honoring Charles Thomson.

national consciousness, and he was present at the dawn of independence. Thomson's name appeared on the first published version of the Declaration of Independence as the only non-delegate signature. He signed in his capacity as Congressional Secretary.

Among his many accomplishments as Secretary, Thomson designed the Great Seal of the United States. The United States of America continues to use the Great Seal on all of its official documents. It can be easily found on the reverse side of the one-dollar bill.

Thomson's service was not without its critics, however. In 1780 delegate James Searle, a close friend of John Adams, began a cane fight on the floor of Congress, claiming that Thomson misquoted him in the minutes. Both men were slashed in the face. Thomson's recordings of events frequently led to arguments and fights on the floor of Congress.

Thomson was keenly aware of the slavery problem. He wrote to Jefferson in 1785: "It grieves me to the soul that there should be such grounds for your apprehensions respecting the irritation that will be produced in the southern states by what you have said of slavery. However, I would not have you discouraged. This is a cancer we must get rid of. It is a blot on our character that must be wiped out. If it cannot be done by religion, reason, and philosophy, confident I am that it will be done one day by blood."

Thomson's last official act as Secretary was to inform George Washington of his election. He traveled to Mt. Vernon on April 1789 to tell him officially that under the new constitution he had been elected the first President. By July, Thomson was retired, having turned over the Great Seal of the United States to Washington.

As Secretary of Congress, Thomson chose what to include in the official journals of the Continental Congress. He also prepared a work of over 1000 pages that covered the political history of the American Revolution. After leaving office, he chose to destroy this work, stating his desire to avoid "contradicting all the histories of the great events of the Revolution. Let the world admire the supposed wisdom and valor of our great men. Perhaps they may adopt the qualities that have been ascribed to them, and thus good may be done. I shall not undeceive future generations."

Charles Thomson died on August 16, 1824, at the age of 95. He had been residing in Bryn Mawr, Pennsylvania at Harriton House which still stands today and operates as a museum. He was initially buried there, but in 1838 his nephew moved his remains to Laurel Hill Cemetery in Philadelphia. A large handsome monument marks his grave.

Matthew Tilghman
(1717–1790)

Father of the Revolution in Maryland

Buried at Rich Neck Manor,
Claiborne, Maryland.

Continental Association

Matthew Tilghman was a planter and attorney from the Eastern Shore of Maryland, who served in the First and Second Continental Congresses, and signed the Continental Association. Known as "The Patriarch of Maryland" and "The Father of the Revolution in Maryland," Tilghman was a prominent member of a ruling clique in Maryland that included his cousin, Edward Lloyd, and William Paca, with whom he was related by marriage. Tilghman is credited with guiding the transition of Maryland from the colonial proprietor to statehood.

Matthew Tilghman was born on February 17, 1717 or 1718, at the family's estate, "The Hermitage," on the Chester River, near Centreville, Queen Anne's County, Maryland, the youngest son of Richard Tilghman, a colonial politician known as "Colonel Richard," and his wife, Anna Maria (née Lloyd) Tilghman. The elder Tilghman was the justice of the Provincial Court from 1746 to 1766. The Tilghman family, through blood and marriage, is related to Charles Carroll, William Paca, and Edward Lloyd, all of the Continental Congress, and Rogers Brooke Taney, who served as chief justice of the US Supreme Court.

Matthew Tilghman

The family's plantation, "The Hermitage," was considered one of the greatest in Maryland. It was first settled by Matthew Tilghman's grandfather, Richard Tilghman "The Elder," who was a surgeon in the British Navy in London. He emigrated to Maryland in 1660 with his wife and two children. Here, Matthew was raised and educated by the Reverend Hugh Jones, the rector of the St. Stephen's Parish, in Cecil County, Maryland. In 1733, he went to live with his cousin, Matthew Tilghman Ward, at Ward's "Rich Neck Manor," near the village of Claiborne, Talbot County, Maryland. When "Colonel Richard" died in 1739, Tilghman inherited 2000 acres. Then, when Ward died without any direct descendants in 1741, Tilghman inherited his estate of 2000 acres and 100 slaves. He married his first cousin Anne Lloyd on April 6, 1741, and the two resided at the manor. They had five children. Their oldest daughter, Margaret, married Charles Carroll. The other children were Matthew Ward, Richard, Lloyd, and Anna Maria. Richard was a major in the militia of Queen Anne's County during the Revolution. Anna Maria married her cousin, Tench Tilghman, an aide-de-camp to George Washington.

In 1741, Samuel Oglethorpe, the governor of Maryland, appointed Tilghman as a justice of the peace for Talbot County. He held this post until at least 1746. In 1751, he was elected to the Maryland House of Delegates, serving from 1751 to 1774. Beginning in 1773, Tilghman was the speaker of that body. During the Stamp Act controversy, Tilghman's loyalties first switched away from Lord Baltimore. He and his son-in-law, Charles Carroll, refused appointments to the Lordship's Council.

As the Revolution neared, Tilghman was the prominent leader in Maryland as a member of the committee of correspondence, chairman of the committee of safety, and president of the Annapolis Convention. He was then appointed to the Continental Congress in 1774 and led the Maryland delegation.

Tilghman went to Philadelphia with Samuel Chase, Robert Goldsborough, Thomas Johnson, and William Paca. All but Goldsborough signed the Continental Association in response to the Boston port controversy. Tilghman was sent to the Second Continental Congress while also dealing with the collapse of the colonial government in Maryland. He was president of the committee that drafted the new constitution for the state and was essentially the head of the new government in Maryland. Tilghman also supported the Declaration of Independence, voting for its final approval. However, on June 21, 1776, Tilghman returned to Maryland to attend to affairs there and missed the signing of the Declaration of Independence. Charles Carroll of Carrollton replaced him in that role.

Tilghman's focus was now on his home state of Maryland. In 1777, he was elected to the state senate, serving until 1783, the last three years as the president of that body. Tilghman retired from the senate in 1783, now in his mid-60s, to tend to his plantation at Rich Neck, which had expanded to over 8000 acres, including Sherwood Manor, acquired in 1771.

Matthew Tilghman (1717–1790)

In 1784, Tilghman served as a representative to a meeting of the Protestant Episcopal Church. He died of a stroke on May 4, 1790, at Rich Neck. Said one obituary, "In his public Sphere, he stood high in the Confidence of his Country; and, until Age and Infirmities pleaded for Retirement, his Life might be said to have been one continued Scene of Labour, and Usefulness, in its Service; while he was ever considered as one of the firmest and most zealous Advocates of civil and religious Liberty."

Tilghman was buried in the family plot of Rich Neck which still stands near Claiborne, Maryland. The authors were grateful to the current owners for the ability to visit and photograph the grave, which is on private property in a beautiful location along the Chesapeake Bay.

Matthew Tilghman's grave.

John Walton
(1742–1783)

The Other Walton

Buried somewhere near Augusta, Georgia.

Articles of Confederation

John Walton was a planter from Georgia who served in the Continental Congress in 1778, where he signed the Articles of Confederation. He was the brother of George Walton, who signed the Declaration of Independence.

John Walton was born circa 1742, along the south side of the James River in Goochland County (now Cumberland County), Virginia, the eldest child to Robert Walton and his wife, Sallie (née Hughes) Walton. His father may have been descended from Robert and Frances Walton, who, it is believed, emigrated to Pennsylvania from England with William Penn in 1682.

Father Robert Walton II died either late in 1749 or early in 1750 and left John land on the James River "bought of Sanbourn Woodson—land where I now live," his desk, and a slave named Toby. Until 1757, John and his siblings lived with their mother on the family estate both before and after her remarriage in 1754 to John Winfrey.

In 1757, an event, most likely the death of their mother, occurred, causing the court to appoint guardians for all four of the Walton siblings: John, Robert, Sarah/Sally, and young George. Tucker Woodson, the children's uncle, was appointed John's guardian. At the September Court 1760, John was asked to choose a new guardian, and he chose his Uncle

John Walton (1742–1783)

George and Aunt Martha Hughes Walton. The last account recorded for John Walton, orphan of Robert Walton deceased, was filed by George Walton in August Court 1763, at which time he would have been 21.

It is unclear what education they received, though it is known George became an indentured carpenter's apprentice as a teen. On or about April 22, 1765, Walton sold his inheritance and headed to North Carolina. He then continued to Georgia.

John must have studied law at some point because he is listed as a justice of the peace for St. Paul, St. George, and St. Matthew Parishes in Georgia on February 24, 1768, when he was barely thirty. He had also been "awarded by Royal Grant 859 acres along Uchee Creek above public road laid out for Quakers." That December, according to the *Georgia Gazette*, Walton had been elected to the General Assembly in Georgia but declined to serve. Richard Cunninghame Crooke was elected in his place.

Walton was a tax collector for Augusta and surveyor of roads for St. Paul's Parish. It is known that John took up farming as a young man and became a planter near Augusta, Georgia.

In 1774, at the outset of the American Revolution, Walton signed a public call for liberty against the royal governor. Walton was next a delegate to the Provincial Congress in Savannah, Georgia, on July 4, 1775. He represented St. Paul Parish.

On February 28, 1778, the Georgia legislature elected Walton to a seat in the Continental Congress. His younger brother, George, had served two years earlier and signed the Declaration of Independence. John Walton served briefly, from July 23 to August 4, 1778, and August 31 to November 16, 1778. The Articles of Confederation had been negotiated the previous year in York, Pennsylvania. Now, the Congress was back in Philadelphia, and eight of thirteen states had signed it. Georgia did not have a delegation at the signing ceremony on July 9, 1778. When Walton arrived later that month, he was recognized as a representative of Georgia and affixed his signature on July 24. There is no other record of Walton's activities in Congress or Philadelphia.

After returning to Georgia, Walton was the official surveyor for Richmond County. He died in New Savannah, Georgia, a few miles south of Augusta, circa 1783, and his burial site is unknown. His will is on file in Augusta, Georgia, and is dated June 11, 1778. It was probated on June 24, 1783. His brother George Walton, William Glascock, and Britton Dawson were executors. His wife was named Elizabeth, formerly Claiborne, and was pregnant at the time of his death. Only daughter Elizabeth Martha Walton lived to adulthood and married Colonel Robert Watkins, from whom issued John Walton's descendants.

Walton left considerable land, over 2500 acres, and slaves to his heirs.

Mercy Otis Warren
(1728–1814)

The Muse of the Revolution

Buried at Burial Hill,
Plymouth, Massachusetts.

Poet • Political Playwright • Thought Leader

This founder was undoubtedly ahead of her time. When Benjamin Franklin was writing in *Poor Richard's Almanac*, "Girls, Mark my words and know, For men of sense/ Your strongest charms are native innocence," she was busy with her education, refining her talents and losing that aforementioned innocence. In 1848 she was hailed by Elizabeth Elett as "perhaps the most remarkable woman who lived at the time of the Revolution." Her writings were admired by her friend John Adams whom she would come to call a monarchist. She also argued in print against the ratification of the Constitution unless it contained a Bill of Rights. Her biographer, Nancy Rubin Stuart, referred to her as "The Muse of the Revolution." One hundred seventy-three years after her death, she became the first woman to have her portrait unveiled in Boston's historic Faneuil Hall. This remarkable woman's name was Mercy Otis Warren.

Warren was born on September 14, 1728, in West Barnstable, Massachusetts. She was the third of thirteen children and the first daughter produced by Colonel James Otis and Mary Allyne Otis. Just six of her siblings lived to adulthood. Her father was an attorney who

Mercy Otis Warren

served as a judge for the Barnstable Court of Common Pleas. He was also active in local politics and was elected to the Massachusetts House of Representatives in 1745. It was during this time that Warren's father also became a colonel of the local militia.

In these colonial times, it was unusual, even for well-born girls like Warren, to receive the education afforded to young men. Instead, girls were expected to learn various household duties and assist in keeping up the homestead. Warren found some escape from her chores in books brought into the house by her older brothers, who were being tutored by James Otis's brother-in-law, the Reverend John Russell. Warren pleaded with her father to join her brothers in their studies, and no one knows why he eventually agreed. One popular theory is that when her brother Joseph decided to end his educational pursuits, Warren's father permitted her to take his place with the Reverend Russell.

The Reverend was widely recognized as one of the best-educated men in the local area. Under his tutelage, Warren studied the works of Milton and Shakespeare and learned to write. Her later work would reflect the style and cadence used by Reverend Russell in his sermons. She also studied British history reading, according to her biographer, Raleigh's *History of the World*.

There is no doubt that Warren's growing up in the Otis household also influenced her evolving political views. Her father was a well-known critic of British rule, and he often found himself at odds with the colonial governor Thomas Hutchinson. She and her siblings have been described as raised "in the midst of revolutionary ideals."

On November 14, 1754, at the age of 26, Warren married James Warren. The letters exchanged between the couple over the years illustrate the respect and bond the two felt for each other. In one letter, James wrote, "I have read one Excellent sermon this day and heard two others. What next can I do better but to write to a Saint." Warren's letter in response stated, "Your spirit I admire were a few thousands on the Continent of a similar disposition we might defy the power of Britain." Through the course of their marriage, the couple would produce five sons.

James Warren shared many of his wife's revolutionary views. He also had a successful political career. In 1765 he was elected to the Massachusetts House of Representatives. He would serve as the speaker of this body and as the President of the Massachusetts Provincial Congress. During the Revolutionary War, he also served for a time as paymaster to Washington's army. It was during his political career that he struck up a friendship with John Adams. In 1767 Adams enjoyed a Sunday dinner with the Warrens. Afterward, he wrote to his wife Abigail, "In Coll. Warren and his lady, I find friends." Despite the age differences between the couples, the Warrens were more than a decade older. By 1772 drawn together by their shared views, they were good friends.

In December of 1773, Adams wrote to James Warren relative to the Boston Tea Party. The letter included a request. "Make my compliments to Mrs. Warren and tell her I want a poetical genius to describe a late frolic among the sea nymphs and goddesses. I wish to see a late glorious event, celebrated by a certain poetic pen, which has no equal . . . in this country." The result was Warren's composition titled "The Squabble of the Sea Nymphs or the Sacrifice of the Tuscararoes." Though Warren harbored doubts about the merits of her composition Adams not only arranged for its publication in the *Boston Gazette,* he sent Mr. Warren another letter where he described the poem as "one of the incontestable evidences of real genius."

Warren was more than a poet. She was also a playwright and a historian. Her play *The Adulateur* was published in 1773. It was directed against her father's adversary Massachusetts Governor Thomas Hutchison. The play predicted the Revolutionary War. Hutchinson is represented by the character Rapatio. The fact that this character represented Hutchinson was so thinly veiled that Massachusetts citizens who identified with the patriot cause began referring to him by that name.

The same year that *The Adulateur* was published, Rapatio made another appearance in a play Warren penned titled *The Defeat.* In the biography, *The Muse of the Revolution,* Stuart describes this work as "one of the Revolutionary era's most scorching indictments of the British abuse of colonial liberties." The play contributed to increased resistance to Hutchinson's rule and is believed to have played a significant role in the British decision to replace him in office. Also, these works have been credited to have influenced many colonists to join the patriot cause.

In 1774 Warren sent her husband the first two acts of her latest play titled *The Group.* This satire focused on what would happen if the British monarch eliminated the Massachusetts charter of rights. The play had a second theme, namely championing the rights of married women. Warren cautioned her husband that whatever he did with the piece to make sure that the author's identity was not revealed. She knew that the English authorities would view the piece as treasonous. James Warren sent the work to John Adams in Philadelphia, and Adams immediately had the play published. Soon it was circulated in both Boston and New York and was warmly received by those sympathetic to the patriot cause. John Adams praised the work and writing the author's husband described her as "an incomparable satirist."

Warren herself regularly corresponded with a group of friends that included Abigail Adams, Martha Washington, and the renowned English historian Catherine Macaulay. According to the author Katherine Anthony in her work *First Lady of the Revolution: The Life of Mercy Otis*

Warren Macaulay had "a more profound influence on Warren than any other woman of her era."

When the American Revolution began, Warren began recording the events of the day. These writings would form the foundation for her *History of the Rise, Progress, and Termination of the American Revolution*, published in 1805. This was one of the first nonfiction books written by a woman in the United States. The history was admired by then President Thomas Jefferson, who ordered copies for himself and his

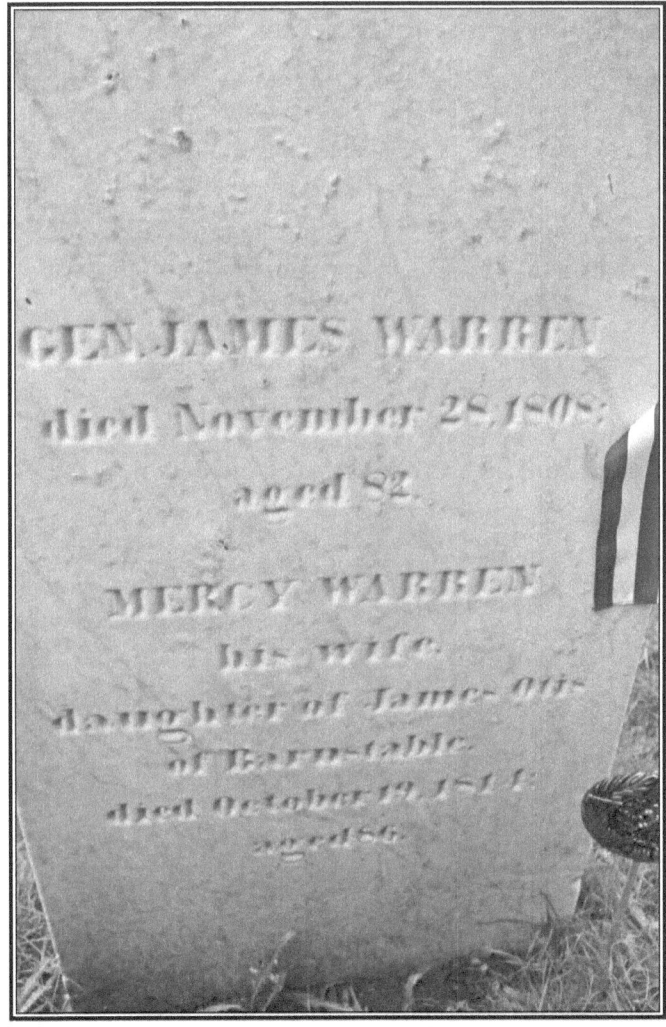

Mercy Otis Warren marker.

cabinet members. John Adams failed to share Jefferson's enthusiasm. The sharp and critical comments on the Adams presidency resulted in damaging their friendship. Among her criticisms was her view that Adams had "forgotten the principles of the American Revolution." Adams remarked that "History is not the province of the ladies." The two continued to argue via letter until they reconciled their differences in 1812.

Before publishing her history in 1790, Warren released the first work bearing her name *Poems, Dramatic and Miscellaneous*. This book was made up of political poems and two plays. Two years earlier, she had written *Observations on the New Constitution*. This piece was critical of the proposed Constitution for failing to include specific provisions for freedom of speech and the freedom of the press. Eventually, ten of Warren's objections would appear in the Bill of Rights. For years Observations was thought to be the work of Elbridge Gerry until one of her descendants found a reference to the piece in a letter sent in 1787 to Catherine Macaulay, which resulted in recognition of Warren as the author.

Warren died at the age of 86 on October 19, 1814. She was laid to rest at Burial Hill in Plymouth, Massachusetts. Alexander Hamilton had Warren in mind when he stated, "In the career of dramatic composition at least, female genius in the United States has outstripped the male."

William Williams
(1731–1811)

Puritan Patriot

Buried at Trumbull Cemetery,
Lebanon, Connecticut.

Declaration of Independence

William Williams was a soldier in the French and Indian War, a merchant, local and state government official, and son-in-law of Connecticut royal governor Jonathan Trumbull, the only governor to convert to the patriot cause. Williams was appointed to the Second Continental Congress, where he signed the Declaration of Independence.

William Williams was born March 29, 1731, in Lebanon, Connecticut, to First Congregational Church minister Solomon Williams and his wife Mary (née Porter). After attending local preparatory schools, Williams entered Harvard College at 16, where he studied theology and law, graduating in 1751.

At the age of 21, Williams was elected to the office of town clerk in Lebanon and later town treasurer. He served as town clerk for 44 years. While performing these duties, Williams planned to become a minister and studied with his father. He was ordained a deacon in his father's church. Yale College awarded Williams a bachelor's degree in 1753 for his previous work at Harvard. Williams then completed a master's degree at Harvard in 1754.

On the verge of becoming a minister, Williams heard the call to arms at the outset of the French and Indian War. He served as an aide under his

William Williams

older cousin, Colonel Ephraim Williams, from Massachusetts, who led ten companies of William Johnson's expedition against the French fort at Crown Point, New York. During the expedition, Johnson renamed *Lac du Saint-Sacrement* to Lake George in honor of his king. During the Battle of Lake George on September 8, 1755, Colonel Ephraim Williams was shot in the head and killed by an ambush of French soldiers and allied Indians. This incident became known as the Bloody Morning Scout. The colonel's body was hidden by his regiment to prevent its desecration. He was then buried nearby, and a stone with his initials and year of death stands at Lake George near a monument erected in his honor. The assets of the colonel's estate were subsequently used to establish Williamstown,

Massachusetts, and Williams College. In the early 20th century, the colonel's body was disinterred at Lake George and moved to the chapel at Williams College. The alumni also funded the monument at Lake George, marking the site of the ambush.

Though the British ultimately won the battle and erected Fort William Henry on the shores of Lake George, this experience caused William Williams to begin to question his loyalty to them. He did not like how the provincials, including his cousin, were treated as inferiors. He began to think the colonies might do better to govern themselves.

After Lake George, Williams returned to Lebanon and opened a retail store called The Williams, Inc. However, politics soon called, and he was elected to the Connecticut General Assembly in 1757, serving until May 4, 1776, when he was promoted to the upper house known as the Council of Assistants. Having left his business behind, Williams was so passionate about his public service, he never missed a session. In addition to his role in the assembly, Williams was a member of the Sons of Liberty and later served on the Committee of Correspondence and Council of Safety in Connecticut. When British soldiers occupied Boston in 1768, Williams voiced his opposition. When the British implemented the Townshend Acts in 1769, Williams strongly opposed them and was a staunch supporter of the colonials' non-importation agreements. When the British repealed the Townshend Acts in 1770, except for the tax on tea, Williams urged merchants to continue to adhere to the non-importation agreements. However, few listened, including Silas Deane, whom Williams never trusted.

Finally, at the age of 40, Williams set aside his duties to marry Mary Trumbull on Valentine's Day, February 14, 1771. Mary was the daughter of Connecticut Royal Governor Jonathan Trumbull, who had also previously struggled at being a merchant. The couple ultimately produced three children: Solomon, born 1772; Faith, 1774; and William Trumbull, 1777. The marriage forged a strong bond between Williams and his father-in-law, who was also a native of Lebanon, Connecticut.

Following the Boston Tea Party, the British parliament implemented the Coercive Acts in 1774. On July 1 of that year, Williams published a satirical address to the king in the *Connecticut Gazette* under a pseudonym. Wrote Williams:

We don't complain that your father made our yoke heavy and afflicted us with grievous service. We only ask that you would govern us upon the same constitutional plan, and with the same justice and moderation that he did, and we will serve you forever. And what is the language of your answer . . . ? Ye Rebels and Traitors . . . if ye don't yield implicit obedience to all my commands, just and unjust, ye shall be drag'd in chains across the wide ocean, to answer your insolence, and if a mob arises among you to impede my officers in the execution of my orders, I will punish and involve in common ruin whole cities and colonies, with their ten thousand innocents, and ye shan't be heard in your own defense, but shall be murdered and butchered by my dragoons into silence and submission. Ye reptiles! ye are scarce intitled [sic] to existence any longer . . . Your lives, liberties, and property are all at the absolute disposal of my parliament.

Williams not only voiced his concerns, he invested over two thousand dollars of his own money in continental currency to support the rebellion. He used his connections as a former merchant to collect blankets and munitions for the cause. He assisted his father-in-law, who was the only royal governor to join the patriots, in preparing to establish the new rebel government in Connecticut. In 1775, Williams was elected speaker of the Connecticut Assembly and then to the Continental Congress to replace Oliver Wolcott on July 11, 1776. That day, word was received of the vote for independence on July 2, nine days prior. Williams hurried to Philadelphia, arriving on July 28. While he was too late to vote for the Declaration of Independence, he signed the document as a representative of Connecticut.

Some have written about Williams's self-righteous attitude. Perhaps he was overly confident as the son-in-law of the governor. In one exchange at a Council of Safety meeting in late 1776, when it looked like the British might prevail, Williams said calmly, "If they succeed, it is pretty evident what will be my fate. I have done much to prosecute the contest, and one thing I have done which the British will never pardon, I have signed the Declaration of Independence." To that, Congressman Benjamin Huntington replied he should be exempt from the gallows

The grave of William Williams.

because he had not signed the document. Williams retorted, "Then sir, you deserve to be hanged for not having done your duty."

Williams, a man of devout faith, was also somewhat puritanical. In a letter to his father-in-law, the governor, regarding the celebration of the first anniversary of the Declaration of Independence, he wrote:

> Yesterday was, in my opinion, poorly spent in celebrating the anniversary of the Declaration of Independence. But to avoid singularity and Reflection upon my dear colony, I thot my duty to attend the public entertainment; a great expenditure of Liquor, Powder, etc. took up a good part of the Day and of candles thro the City, good part of the night.

After 1777, Williams returned to Connecticut and continued his public service. He was a judge of the Windham County Court from 1776 to 1804 and Windham district probate judge from 1776 to 1808. He became an assistant councilor in 1780 and served as assistant and as councilor for 24 years. He returned to the state house of representatives from 1780 to 1784 and was the speaker from 1781 to 1783. In 1787, Williams was a member of the ratification convention in Connecticut for the new U.S. Constitution. At the state's constitutional convention in 1788, Williams represented Lebanon. His only objection was a clause banning religious tests for government officials.

Under the new constitution, brother-in-law Jonathan Trumbull, Jr. was elected to the first three U.S. congresses from 1789 through 1795. During the Second Congress, he was Speaker of the House, sandwiched between two terms when Frederick Muhlenberg had the role. Trumbull was then governor of Connecticut from 1798 to 1809. Another brother-in-law, John Trumbull, was known as the "painter of the American Revolution."

During his later years, Williams was a pastor at the First Congregational Church in Lebanon and a successful merchant. He spent the last years of his life devoted to reading, meditation, and prayer. On August 2, 1811, he died at Lebanon and was interred in the Trumbull Tomb in the East Cemetery in the town, now known as Trumbull Cemetery. His house still stands and is on the National Registry of Historic Landmarks.

James Wilson
(1742–1798)

A Legal Theorist

Buried at Christ Episcopal Churchyard,
Philadelphia, Pennsylvania.

Declaration of Independence • U.S. Constitution
Supreme Court Justice

This founder was born in Scotland. He was educated at several Scottish universities including Edinburgh and Saint Andrews. He came to America in search of the opportunities offered by the new world. He would make his way in the legal profession becoming well known as a brilliant jurist. He would join in the cause of American independence and sign both the Declaration of Independence and the United States Constitution. He was appointed to the United States Supreme Court by President Washington. His name was James Wilson.

Wilson was born on September 14, 1742, in Carskerdo, Scotland. He was a Scottish farmboy who trained for the Presbyterian ministry at prestigious universities though he never graduated with a degree. In 1765 Wilson arrived in America and settled in Philadelphia determined to make his fortune. Initially, he became a teacher at the College of Philadelphia but soon devoted himself to the study of law under John Dickinson. After being admitted to the bar, he moved to Carlisle, Pennsylvania where he set up a successful law practice. Within a decade of his arrival

James Wilson

in the country, Wilson was recognized as one of the outstanding colonial leaders in the struggle against Great Britain.

In 1771, Wilson married Rachel Bird. The couple produced six children. Rachel passed away in 1786, and Wilson married Hannah Gray in 1793. They had one son named Henry who died at the age of three.

Wilson's treatise titled *Considerations on the Nature and Extent of the Legislative Authority of the British Parliament* was published in 1774. Some viewed it as the most learned and far-reaching statement of the colonial case against the mother country. Wilson took the position that Parliament lacked the authority to pass laws relative to the American colonies because the colonies were not represented in that body.

By the year 1776, Wilson was serving as a member of the Continental Congress representing Pennsylvania. As noted by the historian Pauline Maier, Wilson, who she described as having "advanced views on the constitutional structure of the empire," was also "one of Congress's great foot-draggers" on the question of American independence. On January

9, 1776, Wilson proposed that Congress vote to disavow any desire for independence. Those who opposed the proposal were able to postpone the question. On February 13, Wilson put forth an address to the people that was described by Richard Smith as "very long, badly written and full against Independency." According to Smith, the majority rejected Wilson's arguments, and he abandoned his proposal and never raised the subject again. In mid-May, Wilson noted that Pennsylvania had bound its delegates from approving anything that did not further improve relations between the colonies and England. It is evident that by July, things in Pennsylvania had changed and Wilson joined Benjamin Franklin and John Morton voting in favor of independence. Two members of the Pennsylvania delegation voted no, and two other representatives abstained so the three aye votes resulted in a narrow majority. Wilson proudly signed the Declaration of Independence.

Wilson was one of the most active members of the Continental Congress. He served on the Committee of Spies along with John Adams, Thomas Jefferson, John Rutledge, and Robert Livingston. He was also active relative to relations with American Indian tribes. He was described as the most influential delegate in laying down the general outline that governed the affairs of Congress with the border tribes. In 1954 the American historian Page Smith wrote that as a member of Congress Wilson "performed greater services than any other member of that distinguished group of Continental statesmen."

In 1779 Wilson demonstrated his skills as an attorney after the British had abandoned the city of Philadelphia. He successfully defended 23 Tories, those who had remained loyal to the crown, from property seizure and exile by the government of Pennsylvania. A mob motivated by liquor and the speeches of Joseph Reed, President of Pennsylvania's Supreme Executive Council, formed and armed with two cannon marched to the sound of drums to Wilson's home on Third and Walnut Streets. When they reached Wilson's house, they began the assault on what would come to be known as Fort Wilson. Shots were fired from both sides. Only the arrival of the First City Troop saved the lives of Wilson and those who had taken refuge inside. On the street, one boy and one man lay dead, and many in the mob were arrested. Inside the Fort Wilson, one man,

Captain Campbell, was killed and two others were wounded. The arrested members of the mob were subsequently pardoned and released by order of Reed.

By the time the Constitutional Convention convened in 1787, Wilson was one of the most prominent and respected lawyers in America. He once again represented Pennsylvania at that gathering, and his performance did not disappoint. In his book *1787 The Grand Convention*, which is still hailed as among the best accounts of the meeting that produced the Constitution, Clinton Rossiter rates Wilson's performance second only to that of James Madison. Rossiter terms it an honorable second noting that Wilson "debated, drafted, bargained, and voted with unremitting zeal. He did most to give strength to the executive, and to lay the foundations of the new government broad and deep upon the sovereign people of the United States." Similar sentiments can be found in *The Founders Coup: The Making of the United States Constitution* authored by Michael J. Klarman. In this volume, Wilson is said to be one of the three or four most important delegates. In Klarman's view, Wilson was "among the foremost in legal and political knowledge." Klarman points out that Wilson had made the study of government and the political institutions of the world a life long study. The wisdom he shared at the convention cemented his place in history. When the Constitution was adopted, Wilson was once again a proud signer of that historic document.

Wilson was an active participant in the fight for ratification of the Constitution. He is recognized as the leading voice of those who favored ratification in the state of Pennsylvania. As a delegate to the state convention, he answered virtually every argument raised against the Constitution with a clarity and eloquence that was to be expected from one of the great legal minds of his time. The divisions in Pennsylvania relative to ratification were put on display in Carlisle where a mob burned Wilson in effigy after receiving word that the state convention had voted in favor of ratification.

President Washington nominated Wilson to be a Justice on the United States Supreme Court on September 24, 1789. He was confirmed by the Senate and served on the court until 1798. Not unlike some of his fellow founders, Wilson's final days were marked by financial failures.

James Wilson (1742–1798)

He found himself deep in debt as a result of investing in land that became liabilities as a result of the Panic of 1796. He was imprisoned in a New Jersey debtors prison for a short time but was released after his son satisfied the obligation. He then fled to North Carolina to elude other creditors. He was visiting a friend in North Carolina when he suffered a stroke and died at the age of 55. He was initially laid to rest in North Carolina, but in 1906 his remains were reinterred in the Christ Episcopal Churchyard in Philadelphia. Dr. Benjamin Rush, a fellow delegate at the Constitutional Convention, described Wilson's mind as "one blaze of light." That light still shines through the United States Constitution and remains bright in the two centuries that have passed since its ratification.

The grave of James Wilson.

John Witherspoon
(1723–1794)

President of Princeton

Buried at Princeton Cemetery,
Princeton, New Jersey.

Declaration of Independence • Articles of Confederation

John Witherspoon is a hard man to understand. He was a renowned theologian from Scotland who was invited to be president of the College of New Jersey, now Princeton University. He was extraordinarily successful in that role and went on to embrace the revolutionary cause. He was the only clergyman to sign the Declaration of Independence and the Articles of Confederation. He also served at the convention that ratified the U.S. Constitution in New Jersey. He was a highly active member of the Continental Congress and served in the New Jersey state government. Yet Witherspoon owned slaves and lectured *against* the abolition of slavery.

He was born in Gifford, Scotland, and received the finest education available at that time. He attended the preparatory school in Haddington, Scotland, and obtained a master of arts degree from the University of Edinburgh in 1739. He remained at Edinburgh to study divinity. In 1764 he was awarded an honorary doctoral degree in divinity by the University of St. Andrews. In 1743 he became a Presbyterian Minister at a parish in Beith, Scotland, where he married Elizabeth Montgomery. The couple had ten children, with five surviving to adulthood. He remained in Beith until 1758 and, in that time, authored three notable works on

John Witherspoon (1723–1794)

John Witherspoon

theology. From 1758 to 1768, he was minister of the Laigh Kirk, Paisley, a large growing parish church. There he became very prominent within the church.

Witherspoon was aggressively recruited by the trustees of the College of New Jersey in 1766, who needed a first-rate scholar to serve as its president. He was at first unable to accept due to his wife's great fear of crossing the sea. The trustees persisted, particularly Richard Stockton and Benjamin Rush, who visited the Witherspoons and convinced them to accept. He had a comfortable life and was well respected in the U.K., so it was a big decision. They arrived in Philadelphia in early August of 1768.

He enjoyed great success at the college. He turned it into a remarkably successful institution and was extremely popular as a result. He wrote frequent essays on subjects of interest to the colonies. He taught courses and recruited quality staff and students. Moral Philosophy was a required course as he considered it vital for ministers, lawyers, and those in government. Among his students were five delegates to the U.S. Constitutional Convention, including James Madison. Among his students came 37 judges (3 became Supreme Court Justices), 10 Cabinet officers, 12 members of the Continental Congress, 28 U.S. Senators, and 49 Congressmen.

While Witherspoon first abstained from political concerns, he came to support the revolution, joining the Committee of Correspondence and Safety in early 1774. The British referred to his college as a "seminary of sedition." He was passionate about American independence and the necessity of checks and balances for an ethical form of government. Following along the traditions of John Locke, he believed that "because of the depravity of human nature, government power needs to be carefully limited and separated among branches and levels . . . to prevent any one level, any one branch, or any one individual in government from becoming too powerful."

In 1776 he was elected to the Continental Congress, where he voted for Richard Henry Lee's famous resolution for independence and the Declaration of Independence. He was one of the most active members of the Congress, serving on an exceptionally large number (Over 120) of committees, was appointed Congressional Chaplain, helped draft the Articles of Confederation, helped organize the executive departments, and drew up the instructions for the Peace Commissioners. Perhaps his most important contribution during the war happened due to his role on the Committee for Foreign Affairs. Fluent in French, he wrote a letter to a French agent introducing Ben Franklin and explaining the necessity of an alliance between the colonies and France, without which the course of the revolutionists might have been lost.

The year 1777 was tough for John Witherspoon. His son Major James Witherspoon was killed at the Battle of Germantown, and as the fighting neared Princeton, he closed and evacuated the college. The main

John Witherspoon (1723–1794)

Witherspoon bronze at Princteon.

building, Nassau Hall, was severely damaged, and his papers were lost. The school remained closed for several years.

Witherspoon left the Continental Congress in November 1782 to rebuild his beloved Princeton. During the summer of 1783, the Continental Congress met in Nassau Hall, making Princeton the nation's capital for four months. Between 1783 and 1789, he sat for two terms in the New Jersey Legislature and strongly supported the adoption of the Constitution during the ratification debates. In 1789 his wife Elizabeth died. In 1791 the 68-year-old delighted the college community by marrying a 24-year-old widow, Ann Dill, with whom he had two daughters.

Witherspoon's last years were filled with difficulty. He lost one eye on a fundraising trip to Great Britain in 1784 and lost his sight completely in 1792. On November 15, 1794, he died at his farm at the age of 71 and was buried along President's Row in Princeton Cemetery.

An inventory of Witherspoon's possessions taken at his death included two slaves valued at $100 each. This deeply religious man, who required all his students to attend his lectures on moral philosophy, owned slaves and lectured against the abolition of slavery. In 1779 when he moved from the President's House on campus to the newly completed country home called "Tusculum" he purchased two slaves to help him run the 500-acre estate. When helping to draft the Articles of Confederation, Witherspoon sided with Southern states and adamantly opposed the taxation of slaves, comparing slaves to horses as simply another form of

The grave of John Witherspoon.

property. In 1782 he gave lectures disapproving of the slave trade, yet he owned slaves and retained ownership of them.

For all his discussion about the injustice of holding men in bondage "by no better right than superior power," he ultimately concluded that emancipating them was not necessary, stating, "I do not think there lies any necessity on those who found men in a state of slavery, to make them free to their own ruin."

This conclusion conveniently absolved him and other slaveholders of their moral dilemma. Slavery continued in New Jersey until the end of the Civil War.

Sources

Books, Magazines, Journals, Files:
Alexander, Edward P. *Revolutionary Conservative: James Duane of New York.* New York: Ams Press, 1978.
Anthony, Katharine Susan. *First Lady of the Revolution; The Life of Mercy Otis Warren.* Port Washington, N.Y.: Kennikat Press, 1972.
Appleby, Joyce. *Inheriting the Revolution: The First Generation of Americans.* Cambridge, Massachusetts: Harvard University Press, 2000.
Atkinson, Rick. *The British Are Coming: The War for America, Lexington to Princeton, 1775-1777.* New York: Henry Holt & Co. 2019.
Bordewich, Fergus M. *The First Congress: How James Madison, George Washington, and a Group of Extraordinary Men Invented the Government.* New York: Simon and Schuster Paperbacks, 2016.
Boudreau, George W. *Independence: A Guide to Historic Philadelphia.* Yardley, Pennsylvania: Westholme Publishing, LLC. 2012.
Bowen, Catherine Drinker. *Miracle at Philadelphia: The Story of the Constitutional Convention May to September 1787.* Boston, Massachusetts: Little, Brown & Company, 1966.
Breen, T.H, *George Washington's Journey: The President Forges a New Nation.* New York: Simon & Schuster. 2016.
Brookhiser, Richard. *Gentleman Revolutionary: Gouverneur Morris The Rake Who Wrote the Constitution.* New York: Free Press, 2003.
———. *John Marshall: The Man Who Made the Supreme Court.* New York: Basic Books. 2018.
Brush, Edward Hale. *Rufus King and His Times.* New York: N.L. Brown, 1926.
Chadwick, Bruce. *I Am Murdered: George Wythe, Thomas Jefferson, and the Killing That Shocked a New Nation.* Hoboken, New Jersey: John Wiley & Sons, 2009.
Chambers, II, John Whiteclay. *The Oxford Companion to American Military History.* Oxford: Oxford University Press, 1999.
Commager, Henry Steele & Richard B. Morris. *The Spirit of 'Seventy-Six: The Story of the American Revolution as Told by Participants.* New York: Harper & Rowe, 1967.
Cole, Ryan. *Light-Horse Harry Lee: The Rise and Fall of a Revolutionary Hero.* Washington, D.C.: Regnery History. 2019.
Conlin, Joseph R. *The Morrow Book of Quotations in American History.* New York: William Morrow and Company, Inc., 1984.
Daniels, Jonathan. *Ordeal of Ambition.* Garden City, New York: Doubleday & Company, Inc., 1970.

Sources

Dann, John C. *The Revolution Remembered: Eyewitness Accounts of the War for Independence*. Chicago: University of Chicago Press, 1980.

DeRose, Chris. *Founding Rivals: Madison vs. Monroe: The Bill of Rights and the Election that Saved a Nation*. New York: MJF Books, 2011.

Drury, Bob & Tom Clavin. *Valley Forge*. New York: Simon & Schuster. 2018.

Ellis, Joseph J. *Revolutionary Summer: The Birth of American Independence*. New York: Alfred A. Knopf, 2013.

———. *The Quartet: Orchestrating the Second American Revolution, 1783-1789*. New York: Alfred A. Knopf, 2015.

———. *His Excellency: George Washington*. New York: Alfred A. Knopf, 2004.

Fleming, Thomas. *Duel: Alexander Hamilton, Aaron Burr and the Future of America*. New York: Basic Books, 1999.

Flexner, James Thomas. *George Washington in the American Revolution, 1775-1783*. Boston: Little, Brown & Company, 1967.

Flower, Lenore Embick. "Visit of President George Washington to Carlisle, 1794." Carlisle, Pennsylvania: The Hamilton Library and Cumberland County Historical Society, 1932.

Gerlach, Don R. *Proud Patriot: Philip Schuyler and the War of Independence, 1775-1783*. Syracuse, N.Y.: Syracuse University Press, 1987.

Goodrich, Charles A. *Lives of the Signers of the Declaration of Independence*. Charlotteville, N.Y.: SamHar Press, 1976.

Graeff, Arthur D. *Conrad Weiser: Pennsylvania Peacemaker*. Mechanicsburg, Pennsylvania. Distelfink Press. 2019.

Griffith, IV, William R. *The Battle of Lake George: England's First Triumph in the French and Indian War*. Charleston, South Carolina: The History Press, 2016.

Grossman, Mark. *Encyclopedia of the Continental Congress*. Armenia, New York: Grey House Publishing, 2015.

Hamilton, Edward P. *Fort Ticonderoga: Key to a Continent*. Boston: Little, Brown & Company, 1964.

Hocker, Edward H. *The Fighting Parson of the American Revolution*. Philadelphia: Edward H. Hocker. 1936.

Isenberg, Nancy. *Fallen Founder: The Life of Aaron Burr*. New York: Penguin Group, 2007.

Kennedy, Roger G. *Burr, Hamilton, and Jefferson: A Study in Character*. New York: Oxford University Press, 1999.

Kiernan, Denise & Joseph D'Agnese. *Signing Their Lives Away: The Fame and Misfortune of the Men Who Signed the Declaration of Independence*. Philadelphia: Quirk Books, 2008.

———. *Signing Their Rights Away: The Fame and Misfortune of the Men Who Signed the United States Constitution*. Philadelphia: Quirk Books, 2011.

Klarman, Michael J. *The Framers' Coup: The Making of the United States Constitution*. New York: Oxford University Press, 2016.

Langguth, A. J. *Patriots*. New York: Simon and Schuster, 1988.

Larson, Edward J. *A Magnificent Catastrophe*. New York: Free Press, 2007.
Lee, Mike. *Written Out of History: The Forgotten Founders Who Fought Big Government*. New York: Penguin Books, 2017.
Lewis, James E., Jr., *The Burr Conspiracy: Uncovering the Story of an Early American Crisis*, Princeton: Princeton University Press, 2017.
Lockridge, Ross Franklin. *The Harrisons*. 1941.
Lomask, Milton. *Aaron Burr: The Years from Princeton to Vice President, 1756-1805*. New York: Farrar Straus Giroux, 1979.
Lossing, Benson J. *Pictorial Field Book of the Revolution*. New York: Harper Brothers. 1851.
Maier, Pauline. *American Scripture: Making the Declaration of Independence*. New York: Alfred A. Knopf, Inc., 1997.
McCullough, David. *John Adams*. New York: Simon & Schuster, 2002.
Meltzer, Brad & Josh Mensch. *The First Conspiracy: The Secret Plot to Kill George Washington*. New York: Flat Iron Books. 2018.
Middlekauff, Robert. *The Glorious Cause: The American Revolution, 1763-1789*. Oxford: Oxford University Press, 2005.
Miller, Jr., Arthur P. & Marjorie L. Miller. *Pennsylvania Battlefields and Military Landmarks*. Mechanicsburg, Pennsylvania: Stackpole Books, 2000.
Millett, Allan R. & Peter Maslowski. *For the Common Defense: A Military History of the United States of America*. New York: The Free Press, 1984.
Minardi, Lisa. *Pastors and Patriots: The Muhlenberg Family of Pennsylvania*. Kutztown, Pennsylvania: The Pennsylvania German Society. 2011
Moore, Charles. *The Family Life of George Washington*. New York: Houghton Mifflin, 1926.
Morgan, Robert. *Boone*. Chapel Hill, N.C.: Algonquin, 2009.
Nagel, Paul C.. *The Lees of Virginia: Seven Generations of an American Family*. Oxford: Oxford University Press, 1990.
O'Connell, Robert L. *Revolutionary: George Washington at War*. New York: Random House. 2019.
Racove, Jack N. *Revolutionaries: A New History of the Invention of America*. New York: Houghton Mifflin Harcourt, 2011.
Raphael, Ray. *Founding Myths: Stories That Hide Our Patriotic Past*. New York: MJF Books, 2004.
Rossiter, Clinton. *1787 The Grand Convention*. New York: The Macmillan Company, 1966.
Seymour, Joseph. *The Pennsylvania Associators, 1747-1777*. Yardley, Pennsylvania: Westholme Publishing, LLC. 2012.
Schweikart, Larry & Michael Allen. *A Patriot's History of the United States from Columbus's Great Discovery to the War on Terror*. New York: Penguin, 2004.
Sedgwick, John. *War of Two: Alexander Hamilton, Aaron Burr and the Duel That Stunned The Nation*. New York: Berkley Books, 2015.
Sharp, Arthur G. *Not Your Father's Founders*. Avon, Massachusetts: Adams Media, 2012.

Sources

Stahr, Walter. *John Jay: Founding Father*. New York: Diversion Books, 2017.

Taafee, Stephen R. *The Philadelphia Campaign, 1777-1778*. Lawrence, Kansas: University of Kansas Press, 2003.

Tinkcom, Harry Marlin, *The Republicans and the Federalists in Pennsylvania, 1790-1801*. Harrisburg, Pennsylvania: Pennsylvania Historical and Museum Commission. 1950.

Wagner, William Muhlenberg, Jr. *The Muhlenberg Family: Their Significance in Colonial America*. Morgantown, Pennsylvania: Masthof Press. 2006.

Wallace, Paul A.W. *The Muhlenbergs of Pennsylvania*. Philadelphia: University of Pennsylvania Press, 1950

Ward, Matthew C. *Breaking the Backcountry: The Seven Years' War in Virginia and Pennsylvania, 1754-1765*. Pittsburgh, Pennsylvania: University of Pittsburgh Press, 2003.

Weisberger, Bernard A. *America Afire: Jefferson, Adams, and the Revolutionary Election of 1800*. New York: HarperCollins, 2000.

Williams, Roger M. "Who's Got Button's Bones?" *American Heritage*. Volume 17, Issue 2 (February 1966).

Wood, Gordon S. *The Radicalism of the American Revolution*. New York: Vintage Books, 1993.

———. *Empire of Liberty: A History of the Early Republic, 1789-1815*. New York: Penguin Books, 2004.

———. *Revolutionary Characters: What Made the Founders Different*. New York: Penguin Books, 2006.

———. *The Americanization of Benjamin Franklin*. Oxford: Oxford University Press, 2009.

Wright, Benjamin F. *The Federalist: The Famous Papers on the Principles of American Government: Alexander Hamilton, James Madison, John Jay*. New York: Metro Books, 2002.

Young, Alfred F. *Masquerade: The Life and Times of Deborah Sampson, Continental Soldier*. New York: Alfred A. Knopf, 2004.

———. *The Shoemaker and the Tea Party: Memory and the American Revolution*. Boston: Beacon Press, 1999.

Zambone, Albert Louis. *Daniel Morgan: A Revolutionary Life*. Yardley, Pennsylvania: Westholme Publishing, LLC. 2019.

Zobel, Hiller B. *The Boston Massacre*. New York: W. W. Norton & Company, 1970.

Video Resources:

Guelzo, Allen C. *The Great Courses: America's Founding Fathers (Course N. 8525)*. Chantilly, Virginia: The Teaching Company, 2017.

Online Resources:

Archives.gov – for information on the Constitutional Convention.
CauseofLiberty.blogspot.com – for information on Daniel Carroll.

ColonialHall.com – for information about the signers of the Declaration of Independence.
DSDI1776.com – for information on many Founders.
FamousAmericans.net – for information on many Founders.
FindaGrave.com – for burial information, vital statistics and obituaries.
FirstLadies.org – for information on Abigail Adams.
Newspapers.com – Hundreds of newspaper articles were accessed—too numerous to mention here.
NPS.gov – for information on various park sites.
TeachingAmericanHistory.com – for information on Charles Pinckney and George Wythe.
TheHistoryJunkie.com – for information on multiple Founders.
USHistory.org – for information on multiple Founders.
Wikipedia.com – for general historical information.

Index

Adams Abigail, 17, 107, 297–298
Adam's, Andrew, 111
Adam's, James Truslow, 89
Adams, John, 13, 17, 51–52, 63, 87, 94–95, 107, 127–129, 133, 137, 145, 168, 176, 178, 217, 223, 287, 295, 297–298, 300, 309
Adam's, John Quincy, 158
Adams, Samuel, 17, 50–52, 86–89, 93, 121, 223
Adams, Thomas, 17–19
Albany Conference, 10
Albany Rural Cemetery, 246, 250
Alexander, Edward, 60
All Saints Parish Cemetery, 139
Alsop, John, 20–24, 155
Alsop, Mary, 21, 155
American Philosophical Society, 8
Amherst, Jeffrey, 198, 235, 261
Andre, John, 272
Annapolis, 136, 145, 174
Annapolis Convention, 27, 42, 46, 290
Anthony, Katherine, 298
Armstrong, John, 196
Arnold, Benedict, 97, 202, 204–205, 248
Articles of Association, 18
Articles of Confederation, 17–18, 28, 47, 55, 58, 60, 63, 74, 76–77, 79, 85, 88, 97, 109, 111, 114, 116, 119, 121, 130, 155, 164–165, 169, 181, 184, 209, 217, 223, 243, 292–293, 312, 314, 316

Barry, John, 145
Barlow, Joel, 113
Bassett, Elizabeth, 92
Bassett, Richard, 28
Battle at Guilford Courthouse, 192
Battle of Alamance, 102
Battle of Assunpink Creek, 200, 254
Battle of Brandywine, 41, 46, 254
Battle of Concord, 12, 142, 198, 224, 235
Battle of Cowpens, 202, 206
Battle of Drake's Farm, 254
Battle of Etchoe, 187
Battle of Eutaw Springs, 193
Battle of Fallen Timbers, 35258
Battle of Fort Frontenac, 248
Battle of Germantown, 46, 254, 314
Battle of Great Bridge, 254
Battle of Lake George, 72, 248

Battle of Lexington, 12, 64, 88, 142, 198, 224, 235
Battle of Monmouth, 46, 255, 272
Battle of Oswego River, 248
Battle of Point Pleasant, 33
Battle of Princeton, 46, 176–177, 195, 197, 200–201, 263, 267
Battle of Saratoga, 248
Battle of Sullivan's Island, 279
Battle of the Plains of Abraham, 262
Battle of Ticonderoga, 234
Battle of Trenton, 46, 68, 176–177, 199–200, 254, 263, 267
Battle of Trois-Rivieres, 263
Battle of the Wabash, 265
Bayard, James, 262
Bayard, Phoebe, 262
Beach, Anne, 141
Bedford Jr., Gunning, 26–29, 42
Bee, Thomas, 173
Bell, David, 252
Belle Isle Plantation Cemetery, 186
Berkeley Plantation, 91
Berks County, Pennsylvania, 30, 35
Bill of Rights, 295, 300
Bird, Rachel, 308
Blair, John, 176
Blake, Edward, 122
Blanchard, Joseph, 71
Bland, Richard, 94, 228
Bonhomme Richard, 149
Boone, Daniel, 30–39, 203
Boone, Rebecca, 33
Boone, Sarah Morgan, 30–32
Boone, Squire, 30–32
Borden, Ann, 106
Boston Evening Post, 51
Boston Latin School, 5, 49, 85, 100, 221
Boston Massacre, 51, 87, 89
Boston, Massachusetts, 5–6, 49–50, 54, 68, 73, 75, 78, 85, 87, 89, 100, 102, 126–127, 137, 150, 184, 204, 221–223, 236–237, 270, 290, 295, 298, 303
Boston Tea Party, 51, 67, 87, 94, 126, 137, 297, 303
Bowdoin, James, 52, 54, 89
Bowen, Catherine Drinker, 211
Braddock, Edward, 10, 32, 196, 203, 234, 252–253, 276

Bradstreet, John, 248
Brands, H. C., 5
Breed's Hill, 236
Broom, Jacob, 28, 40–43
Brown, John, 256
Brush, Edward Hale, 154
Bruton Parish Church Sanctuary, 226, 231
Bruton Parish Churchyard, 79, 84
Bryan, Rebecca, 32–33
Bunker Hill, 224, 232, 236
Burgoyne, John, 147, 161, 169, 205, 251
Burial Hill, 295, 300
Burr, Aaron, 84, 132, 240, 245, 249, 280
Byrd, William, 253
Byron, Lord, 38

Cadwalader, John, 68
Call, Rebecca, 75
Callendar, James T., 84
Cambridge University, 216
Canada, 235, 248, 263
Carleton, Guy, 205
Carlisle, 9, 56, 197, 202, 307, 310
Carr, Dabney, 94
Carroll, Charles, 288, 290
Carroll, Daniel, 69
Carter, Robert "King", 91, 215
Cary, Archibald, 94
Charleston, South Carolina, 119, 121–123, 172, 186–189, 191–193, 255, 276, 278–279, 282
Chase, Samuel, 137, 290
Chew, Benjamin, 105
Chief Blackfish, 34
Child, Anne, 5
Christ Church Burial Grounds, 5, 11, 16, 105, 108
Christ Episcopal Church, 60, 63
Christ Episcopal Church Cemetery, 140, 144
Christ Episcopal Churchyard, 40, 43, 307, 311
Christ's College, 215
Cicero, Marcus, 3
Circular Congregational Church Burying Ground, 119, 123
Clark, Abraham, 44–48
Clark, Anne, 101
Clark, George Rogers, 35, 97
Clay, Henry, 157
Clinton, George, 130, 132, 156
Clinton, Henry, 188, 191, 238
Clymer, George, 69
Cobb, Sally, 223
Coercive Acts, 51, 68, 303
College of New Jersey, 26
College of William and Mary, 91, 93, 99, 241, 277–278
Collins, Timothy L., 65

Colonial Cemetery, 114, 118
Columbia, Pennsylvania, 178
Committee of Five, 167–168
Common Burial Ground, 181, 185
Connecticut, 109–116, 140–144, 232–235, 238, 301, 303–304, 306
Conrad, Robert T., 116
Constitutional Convention, 14, 26–27, 40, 42, 47, 55, 59, 69, 77, 89, 97, 130, 140, 143, 153, 155, 159, 161, 211–212, 240, 242, 310, 314
Continental Association, 20, 22, 49, 52, 60, 62, 71, 73, 91, 95, 111, 124, 127, 135, 137, 226, 228, 288, 290
Continental Congress, 18, 22, 26–27, 44–46, 52–55, 57–58, 60, 62, 66, 68–69, 71, 73, 75–77, 79, 82–83, 85, 88, 91, 94, 100, 103, 108, 111, 114, 116, 121, 124, 126, 135, 137, 140, 142, 150, 153–154, 159, 164–165, 167–168, 172, 174, 181, 184, 188, 198, 204–205, 211, 217, 221, 224–225, 226, 236–237, 240, 242, 246, 248–250, 254, 261, 263, 283, 285, 287–288, 290, 292–293, 304, 308–309, 312, 314–315
Conway Cabal, 211
Cooke, Rebecca, 182, 185
Cooper James Fenimore, 34, 151
Crosby, David, 24
Curry, Abigail, 204
Cushing III, Thomas, 49–54

Dana, Francis, 121
Daniel Boone Burial Site And Monument, 30
Deane, Silas, 22, 95, 148, 303
Declaration of Independence, 3, 5, 13, 15, 22, 44–45, 49, 63, 85, 88, 91, 96, 100, 103, 105, 111, 114, 117–118, 128, 165, 167–168, 172, 174, 215, 221, 225–226, 229, 286, 290, 292–293, 301, 304–307, 309, 312, 314
Delancey, James, 62
DeLancey, James, 247
Delaware, 284
Devotion, Ebenezer, 115
Devotion, Martha, 115
Dickinson College, 56
Dickinson, John, 28, 42, 47, 55–59, 68, 285, 307
Digges, Dudley, 94
Dill, Ann, 316
Doyle. Welbore, 191–192
Drayton, Elias, 46
Drayton, Henry, 121
Duane, James, 22, 60–65, 95
Duane, John F., 65
Dumas, Alexander, 151

Elett, Elizabeth, 295
Ellery, William, 183–184

INDEX

Ellis, Joseph, 129, 134
Ellsworth, Oliver, 143
England, 5, 7, 11–13, 18–20, 30, 41, 49, 52, 56, 60, 62, 65, 81, 85, 100, 106, 109, 119, 124, 127–129, 132, 135, 137, 140, 142, 145, 148, 156, 160, 181, 183–184, 215, 217, 225, 228, 240, 245, 248, 278, 292, 309
Eton College, 172

Faneuil Hall, 295
Federalist Papers, 124, 130
Filson, John, 35, 37
Fitzsimons, Thomas, 66–70
Fletcher, Deborah, 49
Flint, Timothy, 38
Florida, 33
Folger, Abiah, 5
Folsom, Nathaniel, 71–74
Forbes, John, 197
Fort Clinton, 238
Fort Defiance, 258
Fort Duquesne, 196–197
Fort Gransby, 280
Fort Hamilton, 264
Fort Jefferson, 264–265
Fort Lee, 199
Fort Montgomery, 238
Fort Pitt, 197, 263
Fort Recovery, 257, 265
Fort Sumter, 276, 282
Fort Ticonderoga, 73, 261, 263
Fort Washington, 264–265
Fowler, William, 89
France, 13, 15, 82–83, 145, 147–149, 152, 161, 167, 169–170, 174, 212, 269, 314
Frankfort Cemetery, 30, 252, 260
Franklin and Marshall College, 16
Franklin, Benjamin, 5–16, 22, 28, 51, 69, 82, 96, 105, 129, 148–149, 168, 181–184, 243, 270, 284–285, 295, 309, 314
Franklin Field, 16
Franklin, James, 6
Franklin, Josiah, 5
Franklin, William, 7, 12
Fraser, Simon, 205
Frederick the Great, 269–270
French and Indian War, 32, 51, 72, 93, 142, 176–177, 187, 196, 204, 222, 232, 237, 247, 261, 301
Friends Meeting House Burial Grounds, 55, 59
Fulton, Robert, 170

Gadsden, Christopher, 121–122
Gage, Thomas, 52, 88, 142
Galloway, Joseph, 62
Galloway Plan Of Union, 62

Gates, Horatio, 32, 188–189, 191, 202, 205–206, 248
Georgia, 164–165, 188, 292–294
Germany, 268
Gerry, Elbridge, 52, 96, 121, 300
Gibson, Mel, 194, 202
Gilman, John Taylor, 71
Gilman, Joseph, 72
Gilman, Josiah, 72
Gilman, Nicholas, 162
Ginty, Simon, 264
Giuliani, Rudy, 65
Godcharles, Frederic A., 178
Goddard, William, 166
Goldsborough, Robert, 290
Gorham, Nathaniel, 264
Gotham, Nathaniel, 75–78
Goodrich, Charles A., 174
Grace Episcopal Churchyard, 215, 218
Granary Burial Ground, 49, 54, 85, 89, 221, 225
Gray, Hannah, 308
Greene, Nathanael, 191–192, 202, 206, 231, 236, 256, 271–272, 279–280
Griffin, Cyrus, 79–84
Grymes, Lucy, 216
Guilford Courthouse National Military Park, 100, 104
Gwinnett, Button, 165

Hall, David, 8
Hall, Timothy, 138
Hamilton, Alexander, 2, 47, 68, 130–131, 143, 156, 176, 179, 209, 246, 249–250, 271, 300
Hamilton, James, 106
Hancock, John, 13, 49–51, 53–54, 76, 85–90, 225
Hancock, Thomas, 85–86
Harmar, John, 256
Harmar, Josiah, 264
Harrisburg, Pennsylvania, 176, 178–180
Harris, John, 176
Harris, Mary McClure, 176–177
Harrison, Benjamin, 98
Harrison V, Benjamin, 91–99, 228, 240, 285
Harrison, Hannah, 285
Harrison, William Henry, 91–93, 98, 260
Hart, John, 45
Hartley, David, 129
Harvard, 9, 85, 100, 141, 154, 221, 301
Hastings, G. E., 108
Hatfield, Sarah, 44
Henderson, Richard, 33
Henry, Patrick, 33, 94, 217, 226, 228–229, 254
Herrick, Walter, 152
Hewes, Samuel, 51
Heyward Jr., Thomas, 121, 173–174

325

PENNSYLVANIA PATRIOTS

Hillsborough Old Town Cemetery, 100, 104
Hooper, William, 100–104
Hopkins, Stephen, 94
Hopkinson, Francis, 45, 105–108
Hopkinson, Joseph, 106
Hopkinson, Thomas, 105
Hosmer, Titus, 109–113
Howe, William, 46, 205, 236–237, 254
Hume, David, 183
Humphreys, David, 83
Huntington, Benjamin, 304
Huntington, Samuel, 111, 114–118
Huntington, Susan, 117
Hutchinson, Thomas, 51–52, 87–88, 297–298
Hutson, Richard, 119–123

Ingersoll, Jarad, 69
Innes, Harry, 256
Innes, James, 218
Intolerable Acts, 22, 62, 94
Ireland, 12, 66, 106, 127, 148, 283

Jameson, Mary Cantey, 278
Jay, John, 3, 22, 63, 116, 124–134, 156, 167–169, 209, 245
Jay Treaty, 124, 132–133
Jefferson, Thomas, 2, 13, 55, 57–59, 82–84, 93–94, 96, 103, 132, 147, 156, 162, 167, 169, 179, 212, 217, 226, 229, 240, 243–245, 265, 278, 287, 299–300, 309
Jennings, Anne, 136
John Jay Cemetery, 124, 134
Johnson, Thomas, 135–139, 290
Johnson, Sir William, 72
Johnson, William Samuel, 140–144
Johnston, George, 254
Jones, John Paul, 145–152, 161

Keith, William, 7
Kentucky, 30, 33–36, 207, 252, 256–258, 260
Ketchum, Richard, 237
Killen, William, 56
King George III, 22, 88, 93, 127, 225, 278
King, John Alsop, 24
King Louis XVI, 150
King, Rufus, 20, 23, 143, 153–158, 249
Kings College, 140, 167, 209
Klarman, Michael, 242–243, 310
Knokle, Burton Alva, 164
Knox, Henry, 46, 237, 264

Lafayette, Marquis de, 96, 198, 218, 255
Lancaster, 16, 97, 207
Lancaster County, 31
Langdon, John, 159–163

Langworthy, Edward, 164–166
Laurel Hill Cemetery, 195, 200, 283, 287
Laurens, Henry, 121, 129, 173
Lee, Arthur, 22, 148
Lee, Charles, 166, 255, 279
Lee, Francis, 217
Lee, Harry, 191, 207, 216
Lee, Richard Henry, 93–95, 147, 184, 228, 314
Lee, Thomas Ludwell, 229
Lewis, Ezekiel, 51
Lewis, Fielding, 198
Lewis, Meriwether, 207
Lincoln, Benjamin, 83
Livingston, Mary, 61
Livingston, Philip, 22
Livingston, Robert, 61, 125–126, 167–171, 309
Livingston, Sarah, 126, 134
Livingston, William, 126, 168
Lloyd, Anne, 290
Lloyd, Edward, 188
Locke, John, 314
Lockridge, Ross F., 99
Lofaro, Michael, 39
Logan, Benjamin, 35, 256–257
London, 7, 12, 17, 20, 51, 81, 140, 142, 166, 172, 183, 200, 215, 278, 289
Lord Cornwallis, 188, 190–191, 200, 206, 254–255, 263, 270
Lord Dunmore, 254, 263
Lord, Lydia, 109, 113
Lord Rawdon, 191–192
Lossing, Benson J., 233
Lothrop, Deborah, 235
Louisiana Purchase, 36, 167, 169
Lovejoy, David, 183
Low, Issac, 22
Lowndes, Rawlins, 173
Lynch, Thomas, 96, 172–175

Macaulay, Catherine, 183–184, 298, 300
Maclay, William, 176–180
Madison, James, 2, 26, 47, 68, 130, 132, 143, 156, 163, 179, 212, 230, 242, 260, 310, 314
Maier, Pauline, 308
Maine, 153, 270
Manwood, Charles, 200
Marchant, Henry, 83, 181–185
Marion, Francis, 2, 186–194, 280, 282
Marshall, John, 131, 134, 198, 242
Martin, Joseph, 278, 280
Maryland, 135–139, 145, 164, 166, 174, 205, 238, 288–291
Mason, George, 229–230
Massachusetts, 153–156, 181–182, 198, 221, 223–225, 232, 262, 295, 297–298, 300, 303

INDEX

Mather, Ruth, 285
Mathews, John, 121
McCormack, John, 277
McKean, Thomas, 58
McKee, Alexander, 264
Meade, Catherine, 66
Melville, Herman, 151
Mercer, Hugh, 195–201
Middleton, Arthur, 121, 173–174
Middleton, Henry, 173
Mifflin, Thomas, 69, 94
Milan, John, 56
Missouri Compromise, 157
Monroe, James, 157, 169, 198
Montgomery, Elizabeth, 312
Montgomery, Richard, 205, 248
Morgan, Daniel, 202–208
Morgan, John Hunt, 207
Morris, Gouverneur, 69, 121, 126, 143, 169, 209–214
Morris, Robert, 68–69, 211
Mortimer Cemetery, 109, 113
Moultrie, Alexander, 122
Moultrie, William, 174, 187–188
Mount Hebron Cemetery, 202, 207
Mount Olivet Cemetery, 135, 139
Moynihan, Daniel Patrick, 237
Muhlenberg, Frederick, 306
Muhlenberg, Peter, 256
Murray, John, 18
Mythbusters, 8

Nelson, Horatio, 215
Nelson, Thomas Jr., 215–220
New Hampshire, 71–72, 74, 159–163, 238
New Jersey, 44–48, 58, 68, 119, 137, 168, 199, 202, 205–206, 254–255, 273–274, 311, 312, 313, 317
New Jersey Plan, 28, 143
New York, 26–27, 60, 77, 95, 106–107, 121, 124–125, 130–134, 141, 153, 155, 158, 166–171, 188, 198–200, 204–205, 209–210, 212–213, 222, 234–235, 237–238, 246, 248, 250–251, 255, 263, 268, 272, 274, 298, 301
New York City, 20–24, 60, 62–63, 125–126, 129, 131, 143, 155–156, 167–171, 201, 209, 255, 273, 280
New York Daily News, 63
Nicholas, Elizabeth, 242
Nicholas, Robert Carter, 94, 242
Nielsen, Leslie, 194
Norris, Mary, 56
North Carolina, 100–101, 103–104, 189, 206, 222, 293, 311
North, William, 273

Oglethorpe, James, 164
Oglethorpe, Samuel, 290
Old Chapel Cemetery, 240, 245
Old Episcopal Church, 164, 166
Old Episcopal Churchyard, 153
Old Greensburg Cemetery, 266
Oldham, William, 257
Old North Cemetery, 159, 163
Old Norwichtown Cemetery, 114, 118
Olive Branch Petition, 91, 95, 137, 225, 228
Ostenaco, 277–278
Oswald, Richard, 129
Otis, James, 87, 101, 295–296
Oxford, 12, 142

Paca, William, 288
Paine, Robert Treat, 221–225
Paris, 22, 128–129, 145, 150–151, 270
Parker, Fess, 39
Parker, Jane Ballareau, 26
Parsons, Theophilus, 154–155
Paxton Presbyterian Churchyard, 176, 179
Peale, Charles Wilson, 200
Pendleton, Edmund, 94, 226–231
Pendleton, Nathanael, 226
Pennsylvania Gazette, 7
Penn, John, 226, 228
Penn, William, 11, 192
Phelps, Oliver, 78
Philadelphia, 5–8, 14–16, 22, 26, 28, 31, 40–41, 43, 45, 52, 56, 58, 62–63, 66–68, 73–74, 77, 81, 88, 94, 96–97, 105–106, 108, 111, 121, 126, 128, 130, 137, 143, 155, 161, 165, 172, 174, 183, 195–197, 200, 202, 205, 211, 217, 226, 228, 242, 254–255, 274, 284–285, 287, 293, 298, 304, 307, 309, 311, 313
Philbrick, Nathaniel, 239
Phipps Street Cemetery, 75, 78
Pickens, Andrew, 193, 282n
Pierce, Rachel, 40
Pierce, William, 42, 155
Pinckney, Charles, 156, 173, 280
Pinckney, Charles Cotesworth, 173
Pittsburgh, 196, 262, 266
Pollard, Sarah, 228
Pontiac's Rebellion, 235
Poor Richard's Almanac, 8–9, 295
Pope, Hannah, 233, 235
Porter, Horace, 152
Posey, Thomas, 198
Postell, John, 187
Prat, Benjamin, 222
Prescott, William, 236
Preston, Thomas, 223
Princeton Cemetery, 312, 316

Princeton University, 26, 119, 312
Putnam, Deborah, 238
Putnam, Israel, 232–239
Putnam Monument, 232

Quincy, Dorothy, 88

Rahway Cemetery, 44, 47
Randolph, Ann Cary, 212
Randolph, Edmund, 47, 138, 240–245
Randolph, Peyton, 94–96, 216, 228, 241
Randolph, Thomas Mann, 212
Read, George, 28, 42, 59
Read, Jacob, 122
Read, Joseph, 26, 309–310
Reed, Deborah, 7, 12, 14
Revere, Paul, 87–88, 127
Rich Neck Manor, 288, 289–290–291
Rindge, Daniel, 159
Rhode Island, 143, 181–185
Robinson, Benjamin, 227
Robinson. John, 228
Rodney, Caesar, 58
Rogers, Robert, 234
Roosevelt, Theodore, 24, 152
Ross, Betsy, 108
Rossiter, Clinton, 155, 242, 310
Roy, Elizabeth, 227
Rush, Benjamin, 96, 108, 200, 225, 311, 313
Russell, John, 296–297
Russell, William, 33
Rutherford, Robert, 207
Rutledge, Edward, 174
Rutledge, John, 173, 191, 309

Saint Ann's Episcopal Churchyard, 209, 212
Saint Clair Park Path, 261, 266
Saint Louis Cemetery, 151
Savannah Resolutions. 165
Schuyler, Elizabeth, 246, 249–250
Schuyler, Philip John, 246–251
Scotland, 80, 82, 145–146, 148, 183, 195, 261, 307, 312
Scott, Charles, 32, 252–260
Searle, James, 287
Second Continental Congress, 12–13, 62, 79, 88, 95, 103, 107, 121, 124, 127, 161, 224, 228, 288, 290, 301
Secretary of Foreign Affairs, 124, 129
Serapis, 149
Sharp, Arthur G., 129
Shay's Rebellion, 54, 76–77, 89, 264
Shelby, Issac, 256
Sherburne, Elizabeth, 161
Sherman, Roger, 111, 116, 121, 143, 168

Shubrick, Paige, 173
Smith, Dorothy, 71
Smith, Josiah, 122
Smith, Page, 309
Smith, Richard, 309
Smith, William, 209–210
Sons of Liberty, 87, 184, 235, 285, 303
South Carolina, 119, 121–122, 172–174, 186–189, 191–193, 202, 206, 208, 276, 278–282
South Cemetery, 238
Spain, 116, 124, 128–129, 222
Sprague, Mary, 71
Stahr, Walter, 126–127
Stamp Act, 86, 153, 217, 223, 227, 235, 285, 290
Stamp Act Congress, 135, 142
Stark, John, 161
St. Clair, Arthur, 256–257, 261–267
Stephen, Adam, 254, 276
Stevens, John, 168
Stevens, Mary, 168
Stiles, Ezra, 182–183
St. Mary's Catholic Church Cemetery, 66, 70
Stockton, Richard, 45, 313
St. Paul's Episcopal Church Cemetery, 167, 171
Strouppe, Peter, 247
Steuben, Baron von, 77, 268–275
Steuben State Memorial Site, 268, 273
Stuart, Charles, 80, 82
Stuart, Charles Edward, 195
Stuart, Christina, 80
Stuart, Nancy Rubin, 295, 298
Suffolk Resolves, 127
Sugar Act, 217
Sullivan's Island, 188
Sumter, Thomas, 191–192, 276–282
Sunbury, 177

Tarleton, Banastre, 35, 190, 206–207, 279–280
Taylor, John, 228
Tecumseh, 264
Thomas Sumter Memorial Park, 276, 281
Thompson, Channing Moon, 217
Thompson, Joseph J., 261
Thomson, Charles, 127, 283–287
Tilghman, Matthew, 288–291
Timberlake, Henry, 276
Townshend Acts, 56–57, 86, 93, 142, 303
Treaty of Paris, 13, 15, 124, 129, 132, 193
Trinity Church Cemetery, 20, 23
Trowbridge, Edmund, 182
Trumbull Cemetery, 301, 306
Trumbull, John, 48, 197, 200, 205, 251, 306
Trumbull, Johnathan, 111, 301, 303
Trumbull, Mary, 303
Tryon, William, 102

INDEX

United States Supreme Court, 124, 135, 138, 307, 310
University of Arkansas, 108
University of Edinburgh, 80, 100, 261, 307, 312
University of Pennsylvania, 70, 105, 108, 181, 285
University of Saint Andrews, 11, 307
U.S. Constitution, 5, 16, 23, 26, 28, 40, 54–55, 59, 66, 69, 75, 77–79, 82, 97, 104, 107, 117, 122, 124, 130–131, 138, 140, 153, 155, 159, 162, 176, 181, 184, 209, 229, 243, 246, 249, 300, 306–307, 310–312, 315
US Navel Academy Chapel, 145, 151–152

Valley Forge, 74, 211, 255, 270, 272, 274–275
Van Buren, Martin, 93
Van Dyke, Nickolas, 42
Videau, Mary Esther, 193
Virginia, 34–35, 79, 81–82, 84, 91, 93–94, 97, 99, 145, 147, 198, 198, 202, 204–205, 207, 215–218, 220, 226–227, 229–231, 238, 240–243, 245, 252–253, 255–256, 263, 272, 276, 278, 292
Virginia Plan, 242–243

Walcott, Oliver, 111, 116
Walker, Benjamin, 272–273
Wallace, David Duncan, 121
Wallace, Gustavus, 198
Walton, George, 292–294
Walton, John, 292–294
Ward, Artemas, 236
War of 1812, 156–157
Warren, James, 297–298
Warren, Joseph, 236
Warren, Mercy Otis, 295–300
Washington, D. C.,179, 274

Washington, George, 2, 13, 22, 28, 32, 38, 41–42, 46, 63, 65, 68, 79, 83–84, 95–96, 107, 117, 124, 128, 131–132, 137–139, 156, 162, 167, 169, 178–179, 184, 195, 197–202, 205–207, 211, 226, 228, 236–238, 240–242, 244–245, 248, 252–257, 263, 265, 267, 270–272, 280, 287, 289, 297, 307, 310
Watson, John, 191–192
Wayne, Anthony, 252, 257–258, 265
Weeden, George, 198
Weems, Parson, 38, 186
Weiser, Conrad, 9–11
West Birginia, 204
Whiskey Rebellion, 207
Wild, Philip,214
Willard, Samuel, 222
Williams, Ephraim, 302
Williams, Otho, 188
Williams, William, 301–306
Wilmington, Delaware, 26, 29, 40, 42–43, 55, 59
Wilmington – Brandywine Cemetery, 26, 29
Wilson, James, 15, 69, 307–311
Winter Street Cemetery, 71, 74
Witherspoon, James, 314
Witherspoon, John, 3, 45, 312–317
Wolfe, James, 262
Woodford, William, 198, 254
Wyatt, Jane, 25
Wyoming Massacre, 177
Wythe, George, 229

Yale, 9, 24, 109, 115, 141, 183, 301
York, Pennsylvania, 97, 111, 121, 165, 184, 270, 293
Yorktown, 35, 97, 207, 215, 218, 249, 255, 263, 272

Coming soon . . .
Graves of our Founders:
Volume 3
Volume 4

Also available from these authors:
The Keystone Tombstones series about famous graves found in Pennslvania:
Volume 1
Volume 2
Volume 3
Volume 4
Sports
Best of Keystone Tombstones
Civil War
Philadelphia Region
Anthracite Region
Susquehanna Valley
Pittsburgh Region
Battle of Gettysburg

The Gotham Graves series about famous graves found in New York City:
Volume 1
Volume 2

The Murders, Massacres, and Mayhem in the Mid-Atlantic series:
Volume 1

BY JOE FARRELL:
Jesus Runs Away ... and other stories of attending Catholic schools in the early 60s

BY JOE FARLEY:
Trumpet Call to Victory: The Final Years of Hazelton Saint Gabriel's Basketball
Song Poems in Search of Music

BY LAWRENCE KNORR:
Gettysburg Eddie: The Story of Eddie Plank
Wonder Boy: The Story of Carl Scheib

www.ingramcontent.com/pod-product-compliance
Lightning Source LLC
Chambersburg PA
CBHW032017230426
43671CB00005B/118